INDL

INDLISH

The Book for Every
English-Speaking Indian

Jyoti Sanyal

Edited by
Martin Cutts
Research Director
Plain Language Commission
England

Viva Books Private Limited
New Delhi • Mumbai • Chennai • Kolkata • Bangalore • Hyderabad

To Reshma, my daughter, who like most children, was born a prodigy – and has managed against all odds to stay that way

Contents

Contents

And I thank . . .

These articles were first published in the 'Language' column of 'Imprint', the Sunday supplement of *The Statesman*, Calcutta, between early August 1999 and mid-December 2000. I was in Bangalore, training would-be print journalists at Asian College of Journalism.

Mrs Shirley Kelly, then manager of Books for Change, the publishing unit of ActionAid India, proposed that I start a column in their newsletter. Her colleagues promptly vetoed what they saw as her sinister attempt to get them to learn plain English. Mr Ravindra Kumar, editor of *The Statesman*, then bolstered my plain English campaign with his offer of the column, kindly allowing my articles to be published unchanged.

I owe a debt to many correspondents, reporters, sub-editors and one edit writer in particular, who worked for Bangalore's self-styled 'leading English daily'. Their daily output invariably gave me more bad examples than I could use in my column.

Mr Martin Cutts, Research Director, Plain Language Commission, UK, felt the book 'deserved a large audience', and sounded out Oxford University Press, UK, who had published his *Oxford Guide to Plain English*.

It came to nothing after OUP, Delhi, let loose two venerable referees on a few sample articles. One of them found little time to read his portion, but plenty of time to offer much *gnan*. My work was worthless, he said, because like a shallow journalist, I had made the paragraphs too short; the mystique of worthwhile books lay in ponderous ones!

After reading the same pieces, though, Mr S Sreetilak, fresh out of college and assistant editor with Viva Books, told me to send him the whole thing. He vowed to shield my humble work from backwoodsmen. I owe him a big debt of gratitude for staying true to his word, and quietly steering this book to publication.

Martin Cutts agreed to scan all the articles and read the page proofs. I lack words that could adequately thank him for all the trouble he has taken.

To Ms C K Meena, and Mr S R Ramakrishna, my colleagues at Asian College of Journalism, my heartfelt thanks. Good writers both, they enriched my articles with their suggestions. Ms Sugandhi Ravindranathan punctiliously scanned them for punctuation.

I had all along wished Sarbajit Sen to handle what *The Statesman* printed as cartoons. I am thankful that my wish was granted at last for the book. Sarbajit insisted on autonomy; I merely handed over my articles.

Regrettably, Rita Singh, who helped me throughout – keying in examples and revising each article thoroughly – died in December 2005. I owe her a debt I see no way I can repay.

Jyoti Sanyal

Foreword

Enraged polemic though this book may be, it is also constructive, collected and funny. Where it is angry, it is righteous anger because the evils it condemns – if left unchecked – are likely to kill English as a truly expressive medium for journalistic and business writing in India. Indeed, the trend towards wallpaper English in all its clichéd drabness may already be unstoppable. This book may be the last hope for reform.

English should be clear, concise and fluent, and if it can also paint a picture, so much the better. Too often, though, it is obscure, verbose, muddled, and preachy. Indian English suffers from what Dr Johnson – one of Jyoti Sanyal's favourite punch-bags – might have called flatulent orotundity, a form of high-flown language that tries to impress but instead obscures. Busy readers do not want this. They want authors to have something to say and to say it in a clear, direct, vivid style – to engage them quickly with the gist of the story, to get on and tell it in an interesting way, and then to stop without adding a sermon.

I learn from this book that flatulent orotundity is partly a legacy of the Raj and the East India Company, but also stems from authors applying the structures of Indian languages to English, where they rarely fit well. This heightens the contrast between the English written in India and what we use in the West, which tends to favour the active voice, uses Latinate words sparingly, and shuns the noun-heavy style so common among English-language journalists in India today.

That is not to suggest that Westerners have any monopoly on good English. We can have difficulty expressing ourselves too, but our business websites, letters and emails tend to suffer from other problems, notably crass punctuation, meaningless jargon like 'pushing the envelope', and grammar so slovenly it would disgrace a schoolchild. Here are three modern examples, the first from a London hospital explaining why it had cancelled a patient's appointment:

> Unfortunately your appointment for 26 January had to be cancelled because there were no clinics running that day. It is normal practice for access to all clinics for this day being denied, however this was not possible on this occasion due to the outreach clinics still running.

– which is absurd, nonsensical . . . and personally signed by the chief executive.

The second is from BT, the UK's largest supplier of telephone lines, in a standard letter to householders:

> As part of BT's ongoing telegraph pole renewal programme, which ensures that all of BT's overhead apparatus meets the required safety regulation laid down in its operating licence, the telegraph pole serving your property requires renewal.

– which means, simply, 'We'll soon be renewing the telegraph pole that serves your property. This is part of a work programme that will help us meet new safety rules.' Twenty-six words instead of thirty-six. The busy reader doesn't need more.

And my third example, from a government report, supports the adage that the duller the notion, the more some writers want to cloak it in showy language:

> The physical condition of a property is a fundamental determinant of its quality.

– which probably just means 'The quality of a house depends mainly on its condition.'

There's a lot of shoddy writing about, so don't imagine that only Indian English needs maintenance, or that authors on the other side of the world are complying with some gold standard. Each of us who writes English, wherever we live, has plenty to learn about how to do it better.

'Plain' can sometimes be pejorative, yet in countries where English is most people's mother tongue 'plain language' or 'plain English' is generally regarded as a virtue in communications with the public. English that is clear for its intended audience has become the standard to which most well-run companies aspire. In European Union countries, many types of consumer contracts must by law be written in 'plain, intelligible language'. Regulators frown particularly on legalistic rhubarb such as *hereinafter, hereinbefore mentioned, therein, notwithstanding, foregoing provisions, condition precedent, lien* and *reversion*. In one case a major public company had to withdraw an entire 59-clause contract when the regulators decided it was not only unfair but would baffle typical readers.

The notion of plain language as a good thing is strong in other tongues, too. There has been a plain-Swedish movement for many years, influencing even the language of the law. No government bill, including proposed acts of parliament, can be printed without approval from the ministry of justice's 'division for legal and linguistic draft revision'. In 2000 the division revised more than 3,000 acts and ordinances in line with plain-language criteria.

To show how bad legal language can get, here is the first sentence of an Indian life insurance policy. It's meant for the ordinary person to read:

> The XYZ Corporation having received a proposal and Declaration and the first premium from the Proposer and the Life Assured named in the Schedule and the said Proposal and Declaration with the statements contained and referred to therein having been agreed to by the said Proposer and the Corporation as basis of this assurance do by this Policy agree, in consideration of and subject to the due receipt of the subsequent premiums as set out in the Schedule, to pay the Sum Assured (together with such further sum or sums as may be allocated by way of Bonus in the case of With Profits Policies) but without interest at the Branch Office of the Corporation where this policy is serviced to the person or persons to whom the same is payable in terms of the said Schedule, on proof to the satisfaction of the Corporation of the Sum Assured having become payable as set out in the Schedule, of the title of the said person or persons claiming payment and of the correctness of the age of the Life Assured stated in the Proposal if not previously admitted.

It should be a basic right in India that consumer contracts are written in a way that the likely readers will easily understand and that the type is large enough to be highly legible. Traditional small print, full of archaic and legalistic English, should be outlawed. In the United States – as a result of pressure from consumer groups – the laws of several states require plain language in consumer contracts, and this is backed by standards saying what will be clear to typical readers. National government has played a part. In 1978 President Carter signed an executive order requiring government regulations to be written in plain English. In 1998 President Clinton issued a memorandum, 'Plain Language in Government Writing' which began:

> The Federal Government's writing must be in plain language. By using plain language, we send a clear message about what the Government is doing, what it requires, and what services it offers. Plain language saves the Government and the private sector time, effort and money.
>
> Plain language requirements vary from one document to another, depending on the intended audience. Plain language documents have logical organization, easy-to-read design features, and use:
>
> - common, everyday words, except for necessary technical terms;
> - 'you' and other pronouns;
> - the active voice; and
> - short sentences.

The US Securities and Exchange Commission has instructed corporations to write key parts of stock and bond prospectuses – especially the cover page, summary and risk factors – in plain language. A leading exponent of this style is Warren Buffett, the second-richest man in the world and an investor with cult status in the United States, who says:

> When writing [my company's] annual report, I pretend that I'm talking to my sisters. I have no trouble picturing them: Though highly intelligent, they are not experts in accounting or finance. They will understand plain English, but jargon

may puzzle them. My goal is simply to give them the information I would wish them to supply me if our positions were reversed. To succeed, I don't need to be Shakespeare; I must, though, have a sincere desire to inform.

Buffett's sincere desire to inform is lacking in so much journalism and in so many business-to-consumer documents in India. It is only when authors genuinely seek to bridge the gap between themselves and the readers that they will begin to write well. Few authors would knowingly send incomprehensible rubbish to their own family members. So why do they do it when writing for the press, colleagues and customers? Whether the reason is one-upmanship, laziness, showing off, or the exercise of power, it is equally damaging and anti-social.

Jyoti Sanyal shows how to be concise, how to puncture pomposity and how to use a plainer, less pretentious style. He explains that this goes against the grain of Indian languages whose syntax gives primacy to the noun not the verb, so ears and minds attuned to Bengali and Hindi may lapse into 'nouniness' when modern English demands 'verbiness'. While showing how to avoid this and many other pitfalls, he explains how a keen ear for dialogue, a willingness to see things from a new angle and the ability to write in pictures will inject new life into the English-language press.

There are plenty of good examples to follow, and you don't have to scour great literature to find them. As I open the sports pages of London's *Daily Telegraph*, I see that the former England cricketer Geoffrey Boycott has applied himself to his writing as thoroughly as he once did to his batting. His is the bluff, no-nonsense style of the self-taught

Yorkshireman who calls a spade a bloody shovel, as in this
piece published before a crucial Ashes match:

> There can be no excuses this time. The players have been
> allowed to miss lots of county cricket and the board have
> granted them all kinds of helpers and hangers-on. Duncan
> Fletcher, their coach, has been operating with total authority.
> No expense has been spared on preparing the team properly,
> which is as it should be when money is pouring in from sell-
> out crowds. Now it's time to deliver otherwise all that public
> goodwill will evaporate . . . . Every batsman has to find a
> way to get runs. It doesn't matter whether they're ugly runs,
> lucky runs or edged runs. No one gives a stuff about how,
> it's how many.

Short sentences, vigorous expression, and a point of view:
these are three of the essentials of a good writer, whether
it's about sport or the price of fish. You don't need to be
interested in cricket to recognise that Boycott plies his new
trade better than many old-timers.

Indian journalists have a key role in improving the
use of English in India because newspaper and broadcast
English sets the standard for most of the population.
First, they should clear up their own act by dumping
the Victorian verbosity of which this book complains so
eloquently. (Memo to sub-editors and programme editors:
this is your job.) Second, they should regularly write about
the incoherent language of the law, government officials
and companies, and show how it damages the interests of
consumers and businesses – public derision is a powerful
weapon. Third, they should spend at least an hour a week
reading the quality dailies of the UK, imbibing their often
fresh phrasing and clarity of expression. Fourth, as Jyoti

Sanyal suggests, they should abandon their love of cliché and tap into those sources of vivid, precise description that exist in the creative writing of India's regional languages.

Some may say, 'There are more pressing worries in India than good English – what about our telephone services, what about our drinking water?' And of course they are right – good English can never be the top priority. But when a thing's worth writing, it's worth writing well whatever else is happening. During World War II when Winston Churchill, the prime minister, was grappling with the bombing of London, he found time to write a memo to the civil service headed 'Brevity'. Part of it says:

> To do our work, we all have to read a mass of papers. Nearly all of them are far too long. This wastes time, while energy has to be spent in looking for the essential points. I ask my colleagues and their staffs to see to it that their reports are shorter . . .
>
> Reports drawn up on the lines I propose may at first seem rough as compared with the flat surface of officialese jargon. But the saving in time will be great, while the discipline of setting out the real points concisely will prove an aid to clearer thinking.

Churchill may have been wrong about Indian independence, but he was surely correct about writing. To him, clarity and brevity were part of a life-and-death struggle for freedom.

At the request of the Federation of Consumer Organisations of Tamil Nadu, I visited India four times in the 1990s to give lectures and workshops for the British Council about clarity in business and official writing. Chennai,

Foreword

Delhi, Allahabad, Madurai, Bangalore, Hyderabad, Coimbatore – I came, I talked, I sowed a few seeds . . . but I fear I conquered not. There was no vigorous flowering of plain language in Indian education, journalism or business. Had the insights of this book been available then, there might have been.

Well, those insights are here now, and I hope they will lead to clear-writing skills being widely understood and practised in India. That day will also be hastened by the training courses and editing work that the author and his colleagues will be providing under the flag of Clear English India, a business venture that Plain Language Commission is proud to sponsor.

As the author of *The Statesman Style Book* – apparently the only style guide among 415 English-language news dailies and weeklies in India – Jyoti Sanyal is uniquely qualified to write this book, and I trust you will enjoy its riches as much as I have.

Martin Cutts
Research Director
Plain Language Commission, Whaley Bridge, UK
www.clearest.co.uk
Summer 2005

You must be armed!

Two groups of journalists whose job it is to use the English language abuse it frequently. They are print and TV journalists. Because of the durability of the printed word, the sins of the former remain with us longer than those of the latter. But the spread of television, and its acceptance as the primary source of news, ensures that the sins of the latter visit us more often.

People we meet every day, especially young people, see nothing wrong in saying 'I repeat again . . .' (used often by TV anchors attempting to overcome the handicap of a bad connection while conducting phone interviews), or in insisting that Tendulkar hit the ball 'all the way' to the boundary (a journey inflicted upon us by cricket commentators who see nothing wrong in cross-batting a language into oblivion).

Thus, while a lack of gentility is summed up by the phrase 'it's not cricket', similar courtesy is seldom extended to a language that finds, every day, fewer people around to complain, 'It's not English'.

It is bad enough that young TV and print journalists inflict abominations on us; worse is that their seniors appear to see nothing wrong with this, and often resist efforts at correction by explaining away errors of grammar and syntax as eccentricities imposed on them by style. No wonder bad English has become stylish.

It takes skill and perseverance to buck such 'stylish' trends. Jyoti Sanyal has them both. It takes an eccentric's passion for a language to fight what has increasingly become an uphill battle, but Mr Sanyal has soldiered on.

It was thus that he was asked a decade ago to compile *The Statesman Style Book*, a mammoth project that required anticipating every question that a young reporter or sub-editor might have and answering it. That it is in use, and frequent use, so many years later is because it is comprehensive and meticulous.

Mr Sanyal's other major contribution to the paper was a column on the language, its use and abuse. It was hugely popular and I hope he will one day revive it. But I am delighted to know that his articles are being compiled, and will thus be available to a wider audience.

As you read the pages that follow, you will discover how journalists pick up the *commercialese* of the East India Company, and the *officialese* of Kolkata's Writers' Buildings, transplanted like other bad habits to the Secretariat at New Delhi when the capital moved to north India. You will discover why journalists and writers must shun the language of obfuscation. While you may not overwhelm the enemy, at least you will identify him. And that is a battle won.

Ravindra Kumar
Editor, *The Statesman*
Kolkata
November 2005

I

Making a Botch of Writing

I

See-sawing to plain English

Should we write as we speak, or speak as we write? The write-as-you-speak/speak-as-you-write debate has been livelier in England than in any other European country. The Normans ruled England for about 200 years, and looked down on their subjects' Anglo-Saxon (the parent of English) as 'the language of peasants and barbarians'.

Creative writing in English began as a chauvinistic movement against the imposition of Latin and French by the Normans, and as an assertion of the plain language of peasants that Anglo-Saxon was. Geoffrey Chaucer (1343–1400) raised the East Midland dialect of England to the standard written form. His most famous work, *The Canterbury Tales*, is written in this dialect, and is close to speech of that time. Written English, therefore, *began* as a write-as-you-speak movement. But classical learning among those who aspired to identify with the ruling Normans meant Chaucer's movement must have been resisted too. Chaucer was a leading Latin scholar of his time, and his deviation to the coarse language of peasants must have dismayed his compatriots.

The Royal Society of London for the Promotion of Natural Knowledge was founded in 1660. Isaac Newton was its president from 1703 to 1727. The society achieved little, but took up Chaucer's crusade when it suggested that its members cultivate 'a *close, naked, natural way of speaking* ... a native easiness ... and prefer *the language of artisans, countrymen, and merchants before that of wits and scholars*'. The Society's message was: Englishmen should learn to write the language of plain speech.

Fifty years later, the tables were turned. Dr Samuel Johnson (1709–1784) and his group, called the Augustans, brought in a spirit of classical learning. Virtue for them lay in imitating Latin poets and writers. They felt that plain English was not ornate enough, not cultivated enough to express noble thoughts and sentiments! Dr Johnson's patron, Philip Dormer Stanhope, the Earl of Chesterfield, seemed to sum up the spirit of the Augustans in a letter to his son:

> We are refined, and plain manners, plain dress, and *plain diction*, would as little do in life, as acorns, herbage, and the water of the neighbouring well, would do at table.

That meant a reversal of the Royal Society's message: that educated Englishmen should learn to write as the Roman classicists did, and to speak as they learnt to write!

The revolt against stiff and formal writing came from the Romantic poets. William Wordsworth (1770–1850) took a stand diametrically opposed to the Augustans when he said, in his Advertisement to the *Lyrical Ballads* (1798) – a volume of poems he co-authored with Samuel Taylor Coleridge (1772–1834) – that poetry should use the *real language of men*:

> The majority of the following poems are to be considered as experiments. They were written chiefly with a view to ascertain how far the *language of conversation in the middle*

and lower classes of society is adapted to the purpose of poetic pleasure.

But if the Romantic movement succeeded in reinstating the write-as-you-speak rule, the Victorians brought back the pompous and grand style of the Augustans. Only, they imitated not the Augustans, but German philosophers who practised such writing. The Victorians reversed all that the Romantics had achieved, and the educated Victorian sought to speak as pompously as he wrote.

Charles Dickens lampooned this speak-as-you-write urge with his caricature of Mr Micawber in *David Copperfield*. So obsessed was Micawber with the fear that he might speak plain that he always read out as speech what he first wrote down in stilted prose!

The reason for this glance at the speech-vs-writing see-saw: we in India need to understand that

- the *mantra*-culture in our subconscious makes us prone to using 'automatic expressions' that cloud the message
- our East India Company legacy of *commercialese* fetters how we write English
- we remain bound to literary Victorian English, which the later Victorians rejected
- the industrial revolution, the two World Wars, and the modern-day need for quick communication have made stilted writing obsolete
- the most important criteria of good writing today are ease and clarity.

In *The King's English*, published five years after Queen Victoria's death in 1901, the Fowler brothers castigated all that was stilted in literary Victorian English. They told aspiring writers to be 'direct, simple, brief, vigorous and lucid'; and to

> Prefer the familiar word to the far-fetched.
> Prefer the concrete word to the abstract.
> Prefer the single word to the circumlocution.
> Prefer the short word to the long.
> Prefer the Saxon word to the Romance. [By Romance, they meant Latin-derived languages such as Italian, French and Spanish.]

If we must have a *mantra* for good writing, let those rules laid down by Henry and Frank Fowler serve.

Flesch's crusade

Forty-three years after *The King's English* was published in England, Rudolph Flesch began his write-as-you-speak crusade in the USA. In *The Art of Readable Writing* (New York: Harper & Row, 1949), Flesch reminded Americans of the position some philosophers had taken: 'Spoken language is the primary phenomenon, and writing is only a more or less imperfect reflection of it.'

Flesch pounded Americans with his vigorous campaign for writing in colloquial English. A few excerpts:

> If you want to learn how to write . . . forget the rules of grammar and usage you learned in school. Learn to write the way you talk. Go out of your way to re-learn informal, colloquial English and train yourself to put it on paper . . . you should learn to forget the false rules of prissy or overformal English implanted in your nervous system by your teachers and textbooks ever since you entered first grade.
>
> Why do we speak and write the way we do? Why aren't our books and letters and speeches full of racy, colloquial,

rhythmical, personal language? Why do we have to be told by books like this that we are stiff and formal and pompous and unnatural? Where does it all come from?

The answer goes far beyond grammar and usage; it even goes beyond psychology. Language is a social affair; we use it according to the social situation we are in.

We write stilted English because we unconsciously assume that this is expected of us in the position we happen to fill, or the organisation we belong to.

Typically, it [formal language] is the language of minor clerks, secondary officials, cogs in some social machine. It is their . . . psychological substitute for personal importance. The farther toward the bottom, the thicker the coat of assumed dignity.

But if we write English the way it is spoken in India, we could bring into our writing the very features of *Indlish* discussed in this book. What then do we do?

2

The familiar abuses . . . are now on hold

Senior journalists in India's English-language papers dote on the parenthetic clause. If it were banned, they'd probably stop writing. So they thrust parenthetic clauses between the subject and the verb in a sentence. That separates related words and ideas, and one must read back to retrieve the link. A sample from an editorial-page article on the Marxist–Congress tie-up against Trinamool:

> The familiar abuses, traditionally reserved for the Congress –
> 'a party of thoroughly corrupt, anti-socials, pimps, autocrats
> and communalists' – and hurled by the Marxists from Jyoti
> Basu downwards in every election until this one are now on
> hold.

Got the muddle? The subject ('the . . . *abuses*') is at the beginning and the related verb ('*are* . . . on hold') right at the end. Between them the author has strewn higgledy-piggledy four clauses 30 words long. The reader would have to back-pedal to the start to understand which ties up with what.

Had the writer kept related words and ideas together, and omitted words that only duplicate ideas stated in other words, this is how that might have read:

> On hold this time are the invectives the Marxists from Jyoti
> Basu downwards have hurled at the Congress before every

election – 'a party of thoroughly corrupt anti-socials, pimps, autocrats and communalists'.

That would have spared the reader the 'pick-and-assemble' effort he had to make with the original version. And no writer should expect that kind of effort from anyone scanning his morning paper for information.

Why then such foggy writing? Ah, but a senior writer's got to be a bit incomprehensible, don't you see? Or how would you know him from the run-of-the-mill reporter handing in his story after the routine beat? The senior writer is convinced he must write not so much to inform as to impress. He believes readers will be awed in proportion to their difficulty getting at his meaning.

But why do we use a string of parenthetic clauses in writing? Where does it come from?

If we search literature, we see that the parenthetic clause is rare even with Dr Johnson, who took delight in sounding incomprehensible. *Johnsonese*, as Macaulay dubbed his ponderous style, was replete with adjective-laden abstract Latinate nouns and independent (not parenthetic) clauses separated by semi-colons and commas, instead of full stops.

It is in samples of *commercialese* that we find the obfuscating parenthetic clause. As the British *baniya*s turned business English more and more unbusinesslike, they came up with devices that made language cumbrous and obfuscating. Unfortunately, *commercialese* was the only English Indians learnt from the British *baniya*s.

After the merchants turned administrators, Indians began to pick up *officialese*, the language of administration. And in *officialese*, too, we find a tendency to the parenthetic clause.

It made official announcements sonorous. A combination of *commercialese* and *officialese* made for the 'language of power' of the Raj days. Add to this the problem of tackling the rigid syntax of English, and we understand the disarray of parenthetic clauses in the newspaper sample. One often finds a string of ill-arranged parenthetic clauses in editorials in India's English-language newspapers. An example:

> In this day and age, it is unheard of that a civilized country should target a city with a population of 650,000 and little in the way of military installations, with three major sorties involving 800 planes which sent down hundreds of tons of incendiary bombs that killed 35,000 people, largely civilians, and caused Dresden, a most beautiful city, to burn for seven days and seven nights.

To give the reader relief from that plethora of loose clauses arranged higgledy-piggledy, we'd need to break that up into sentences that keep subject and verb together:

> It is barbaric that a country should seek to destroy a city with few military installations and 650,000 people. After three sorties by 800 planes had rained hundreds of tons of incendiary bombs, beautiful Dresden burnt for seven days and seven nights. The death toll was 35,000 – mostly civilians.

The parenthetic clause helps add information to a sentence. But it is more often used in officialdom to fog and obfuscate. The BBC's *Yes Minister* provides many examples of how the bureaucrat uses parenthetic clauses to obfuscate. Here is Jim Hacker, Minister for Administrative Affairs, trying to get a straight answer from Sir Humphrey Appleby, his department's permanent secretary:

> 'Humphrey, in your evidence to the Think-Tank, are you going to support my view that the Civil Service is overmanned

and feather-bedded or not? Yes or no! Straight answer!'

Could I have put this question more plainly? I don't think so.

This was the reply: 'Minister, if I am pressed for a straight answer I shall say that, as far as we can see, looking at it by and large, taking one thing with another, in terms of the average of departments, then in the last analysis it is probably true to say that, at the end of the day, you would find, in general terms that, not to put too fine a point on it, there really was not very much in it one way or the other.'

While I was still reeling from this, he added, no doubt for further clarification, 'As far as one can see, at this stage'.

3

The whirligig of circumlocution

Our *bhadralog* culture equates roundabout expressions with elegance. But this is not unique to India; it is bound to creep into any culture whenever misguided fashion decides that plain language won't do. Look what happened to writers like Dr Johnson. Convinced that plain English wasn't good enough, he ended up inventing such preposterous roundabouts as *repress the instantaneous motions of merriment* (read: 'stop laughing'). Didn't we play around with his *rotundity of leather* (read: football) till the 1920s? His patron, Philip Dormer Stanhope, Earl of Chesterfield, spelt out the fashion of the time in a letter to his son:

> We are refined, and plain manners, plain dress, and plain diction, would as little do in life, as acorns, herbage, and the water of the neighbouring well, would do at table.

The result of the search for an ornate language was the aberration Macaulay dubbed *Johnsonese*. Its distinguishing mark: circumlocution. A simple definition: putting things in a roundabout way. A sample:

> It is usual for those who are advised to the attainment of any new qualification, to look upon themselves as required to change the general course of their conduct, to dismiss their

business, and exclude pleasure, and to devote their days and nights to a peculiar attention.

The Victorians went at it again and made of the English language the mess that Dickens caricatured through Mr Micawber in *David Copperfield*. An excerpt from one of Micawber's letters:

> My dear young friend,
> The die is cast – all is over. Hiding the ravages of care with a sickly mask of mirth, I have not informed you this evening that there is no hope of the remittance! Under the circumstances, alike humiliating to endure, humiliating to contemplate, and humiliating to relate, I have discharged the pecuniary liability contracted at this establishment, by giving a note of hand made payable fourteen days after date, at my residence, Pentonville, London. When it becomes due, it will not be taken up. The result is destruction. The bolt is impending and the tree must fall.

Johnson wrote his piece in 1752; Dickens, around 1850. Common to their century-apart styles is what H W Fowler calls *abstractitis* (*A Dictionary of Modern English Usage*, OUP, 1926). This disease, says Fowler, makes the patient write 'with an abstract word always in command as the subject of the sentence. Persons and what they do, things and what is done to them, are put in the background.'

And when writers use abstract nouns, they invariably end up with what Fowler terms *periphrasis*, a more formal name for circumlocution. He says:

> The periphrastic style is hardly possible . . . without much use of abstract nouns such as *basis/case/character/ connection/dearth/description/duration/framework/lack/na- ture/reference/regard/respect*. . . . Strings of nouns depending

on one another and the use of compound prepositions are the most conspicuous symptoms of the periphrastic malady.

One has only to go through English-language papers in India to understand how deep this malady runs. An excerpt from what a reporter wrote as his newsletter from Arunachal:

> In the North East region's generally turbulent politics, a fresh storm is brewing. One that threatens to bring in a tremendous churn, which could see the emergence of an extremely volatile type of regionalism, total eclipse of all semblance of nationalism and complete marginalisation of the Congress in the region. . . . With a confrontation in the offing, observers in the North-east are prepared to write political epitaph of the Congress.

That was written in July 1996 – almost 150 years after the Micawber piece. This reporter emulated what Dickens invented as caricature.

Editorials in India's English-language papers are the breeding ground of *abstractitis*. And the inevitable result is circumlocution. The writers of editorials keep following obsolete models, and perpetuate fusty Victorian English. A typical excerpt from an abstract-noun-laden editorial in Bangalore's leading daily:

> The flip-flop by the government on the terms of the inquiry committee which has been appointed to go into the Kargil experience makes it uncertain whether the vital issues which have been raised by the controversy will be addressed effectively by it. The systemic response, whether it is of the forces or of the political leadership, to security-related warnings is a matter for public debate and enquiry. This does not compromise the need for confidentiality and for non-interference in the functioning of the forces.

What is alarming is that such drivel should try to pass for profundity. It would be no exaggeration to say that editorials in most English-language papers in India contain little but drivel; poverty of thought is concealed by a haze of abstract nouns. 'A writer uses abstract words', says Fowler, 'because his thoughts are cloudy; the habit of using them clouds his thoughts still further; he may end by concealing his meaning not only from his readers, but also from himself.' Proof that such writing does confuse the writer himself lies in the repetitions that sub-editors miss – as in this editorial from the same paper:

> Since the announcement of that result, East Timor has been in the grip of terror with rampaging gangs of militia killing those in favour of independence . . . collusion has reached dangerous proportions with Indonesian police and soldiers in East Timor actively participating in the violence against the East Timorese people. . . . The pogrom in East Timor over the last few days is enough evidence that Jakarta has failed to live up to its obligations.

Such writing shows up another feature of circumlocution: the use of absurd, automatic expressions such as *vital issues/address effectively/actively participate*.

Committed to grinding out so many editorials a week on topics they know little of, and feel nothing about, the hacks fall back on what George Orwell calls 'verbal false limbs'. Orwell says in his essay 'Politics and the English Language':

> These save the trouble of picking out appropriate verbs and nouns, and at the same time pad each sentence with extra syllables. The keynote is the elimination of simple verbs. Instead of being a single word . . . a verb becomes a phrase, made up of a noun or adjective tacked on to some general-purpose verb, such as *prove, serve, form, play, render*.

Such language, Orwell said, 'becomes ugly and inaccurate because our thoughts are foolish, but the slovenliness of our language makes it easier for us to have foolish thoughts.' This is the whirligig of circumlocution.

4

Bugs in our pens

The write-as-you-speak rule applied to English in India raises the question whose language do we use: the bureaucrat's, the lawyer's or the merchant office executive's? Obviously, none of these hideous models can serve for easy, human interaction. And yet, because English in India has been used more to serve commerce, trade and law than everyday human needs, most Indians serve a *khichri* of those models when they write in English – be it letters, textbooks or the news.

Automatic expressions

A book of model letters widely used in south India (the tenth edition of which has supposedly been reprinted thrice between 1971 and 1998) offers these formats 'for use in every home and office but mainly intended for use in Indian schools':

> **346. To a very dear friend who paid a flying visit to you:** It all seems like a dream! Your *dear visit* so *ardently wished* and *hoped for*, has *come and gone like lightning*! But not without having left much *comfort and gratitude*, especially in my heart! *Pray*, do come to us again *ere long* and stay longer.

347. Thanks for a gift: I *sit now* this *gay morning* to *convey my thanks* to you for the *loveliest* present, only wishing that my pen could set down at least a little of my *liveliest* feelings *with regard to* your *kind* choice! Oh! How can I *adequately* thank you!

Can we imagine writing such ludicrous stuff in our mother tongues? The expressions italicised are scraps of *baniya* English and *baboo* English. If such trash sells, doesn't it argue that something is wrong with the way Indians learn to write? The Indian child is forced to memorise model essays and regurgitate such *mantra* as 'The cow is a four-footed, herbivorous, domesticated animal'. No child perceives a cow in such hideous terms; they can occur only to some fossil-brained adult. Writing, like speech, is a faculty of self-expression and communication. Forcing a child to memorise and regurgitate hideous 'model essays' can only cripple his ability to ever express himself through writing. We can only wonder that the Indian child, tortured by unthinking teachers into memorising the equivalent in his/her language of the cow-*mantra* quoted, can ever write anything at all!

Such teaching methods instil an unthinking acceptance of 'automatic expressions'. The child grows up with a set of *mantras* or formulae to write on certain topics; he never learns to write what he might think, feel or wish to say about them. The result: if he has learnt models as ludicrous as the letter to 'a very dear friend who paid a flying visit', he will go on writing what will read equally ridiculous. The acceptance of automatic expressions is the greatest enemy of effective writing. The danger of using them is that they do the thinking and writing for us. We need to reject such expressions, and write what we see, touch, hear, smell, taste, feel and think.

We could divide our legacy of automatic English expressions into

1 *baniya* English/*commercialese* of the Company days
2 *officialese* that gained currency during the Raj days
3 mistranslations by Company clerks of our expressions
4 expressions manufactured by Company clerks (*baboo* English).

Elsewhere in the book I mention that our merchant offices and English-language newspapers still keep *baniya* English afloat (*apropos/as per/be in receipt of/beg to state/duly noted/esteemed favour/of even date/goodselves*, etc.)

In the second group are adjectives and adverbs that leech-like attach themselves to nouns and adjectives, and suck their vitality. Sir Ernest Gowers puts it across with quiet humour in *The Complete Plain Words*:

> It has been wisely said that the adjective is the enemy of the noun. If we make a habit of saying 'The *true* facts are these,' we shall come under suspicion when we profess to tell merely 'the facts'. If a *crisis* is always *acute* and an *emergency* always *grave*, what is left of those words to do by themselves? If *active* constantly accompanies *consideration*, we shall think we are being fobbed off when we are promised bare consideration. If a *decision* is always qualified by *definite*, a decision by itself becomes a poor filleted thing. If *conditions* are customarily described as *prerequisite* or *essential*, we shall doubt whether a condition without an adjective is really a condition at all. An *unfilled* vacancy may leave us wondering whether a mere vacancy is really vacant. If a *part* is always an *integral* or a *component* part, there is nothing left for a mere part except to be a spare part.

Cultivate the habit of reserving adjectives and adverbs to make your meaning *more precise*, and *suspect* those that you find yourself using to make it *more emphatic*.

Official writers have a curious shrinking from certain adjectives unless they are adorned by adverbs. It is as though they were naked and must hastily have an adverbial dressing gown thrown around them.

Readers will acknowledge that such automatic expressions as *true facts, acute crisis, grave emergency, active consideration, definite decision, prerequisite/essential condition, integral part*, etc. not only still adorn the English we use, but also that most Indians tend to drool over them, as though proof of knowing good English lies in their use.

Here is an excerpt from an editorial that appeared in a Karnataka daily:

> The *manner in which* the lives of six students and two others were *snuffed out* in a bus accident near . . . *is shocking* and once again underscores the *imperative* need for the authorities to *scrupulously* enforce the ban on roof-top travel. . . . Even though it is true that the *tragedy* would not have been so *severe* had there been no roof-top travelling by students, *what cannot be overlooked is the point that why did the bus conductor allow* the students to travel by roof-top in the first place.
>
> It is time the authorities took *appropriate* measures to enforce the ban on roof-top travelling. . . . If students have *genuine* difficulty in reaching their schools by 9.30 am [sic] every day, the authorities *concerned* should hold discussions with . . . to solve their *long-standing* problems.

So many formulae, so few original thoughts, stale adjectives and adverbs, used *mantra*-like supposedly for emphasis, serve only to make such synthetic indignation stale:

imperative need/*scrupulously* enforce/*appropriate* meas-
ures/*genuine* difficulty/authorities *concerned*/*long-standing*
problems.

They are the legacy of memorising stock phrases at school
and churning out model essays. The author may care to
ask himself whether authorities not concerned with such
things might *unscrupulously* enforce rules, take *inappropri-
ate* measures and act even though the students' difficulties
prove to be *less than genuine*, or their problems not so *long-
standing*. And then he might go on to improve his *Indlish*,
such as 'what cannot be overlooked *is the point that why
did* the bus conductor allow . . .'.

5

Tell, don't preach

The 'age-no-bar' group in a brief course on writing had been told about the importance of beginning with an anecdote, of focusing on a character, of story-telling. Each had the freedom to write on any subject. The assignments they handed in showed a near uniform pattern:

1   Mrs N S, 45, began with the relief that a young man and his family felt now that he had been cured of asthma. He had suffered for 18 years, and his family had suffered with him. The young man had been cured through the 'live fish treatment' administered by two brothers at Hyderabad. The patient was made to swallow a live fish that supposedly carried the medicine.

But the brothers wouldn't reveal their secret. This Mrs N S used as her launch pad for a string of *should*s: such secrets should be revealed, or such knowledge would die with the keeper; we should educate people who hold back such secrets to spill the beans for the greater good, etc.

2   Mrs J, 36, focused on a boy of nine, happily playing outside the operation theatre of a hospital. All eyes were on him, because he seemed unmindful of pus oozing from a wound below his right knee, where his leg 'bent'.

He had broken his leg and his parents had taken him to a quack bone-setter, who had promised wonders. A year had passed, but the 'bend' only became more pronounced, the pain worsened, and pus formed in his leg.

From that modicum of narration, Mrs J deviated to a sermon on how people should be educated about attending to such problems quickly, and not wait till they worsened; how this poor boy's suffering could have been avoided if only . . . etc.

3   Mr S M, 22, had joined the writing course soon after his graduation from college. He named an adolescent girl who had a passion for watches. She kept buying new watches. Not a word more about the girl or her passion. He deviated into a discussion of good watches with such banalities as 'Things have changed with the times. We used to have manual watches. Today we have electronic watches'.

4   Miss S N, 18, at her first year at college, spoke of her delight when the lineman called to repair her phone. She chatted with the man and was amazed at how much sense he talked about what and how she should write if she wished to be a journalist. From this, she deviated into the wisdom of ordinary people whom the 'educated' felt they had to 'enlighten' and 'uplift'.

Mrs N S went to a Kannada-medium school; Mrs J, Mr S M and Miss S N, to English-medium schools. Their ages may have varied from 45 to 18, but they all wrote the same way: they were incapable of sustaining an interesting narrative, and each used the narrative only to launch a sermon.

The same pattern emerged at a workshop for some bright schoolchildren: each began a story only to quickly deviate into preaching. None of them could tell a story in its entirety and leave it there. Isn't it strange that in spite of the wealth of stories that all of us have heard ever since we were children, we seem unable to sustain a narrative in writing? And yet, most schoolchildren tell stories to each other. So where does the preachy writing come from? A young teacher suggested it stemmed from the very stories that we hear as children: that the elders who tell stories to children are preachy, always bringing in *should*s between, and a moral at the end.

If we accept the simple definition that the narrative is a story, in prose or verse, of events, characters, and what the characters say and do, it has no place for a moral. Aesop may have started it all with his fables, but children hear umpteen fairy tales and horror stories without 'morals'. Most of these condition the young mind into faith in a benign world order: the wicked are ultimately punished, and the good live happily ever after. But that message is only implied; it isn't appended Aesop-like as the purpose of the story.

Can it be that the conditioning for preachy writing comes from the school essay format, of the Wren & Martin mould? Two teachers into their early middle age (both have been guiding students into writing) differed about the cause. Mrs H said most schools today had about 50 students to a class, and teachers could not possibly guide them into writing of any mould. She suggested that schoolchildren now hardly read good prose, and their ideas about writing had more to do with 'model' essays sold on the market.

Mrs J P agreed that the Wren & Martin model was as much to blame, as the expectation of examiners. Examiners reward the preachy model, and students learn to write it. Mrs J, who wrote the second piece cited, confirmed that Wren & Martin was the only guide-book teachers followed at her school. Wren & Martin is also the subconscious model for most editorial writers for India's English-language newspapers. Are Indian children (and adults) crippled by the Victorian model of didactic writing?

Teachers all over India emulated the Victorian model of crude didacticism – whether they taught through the English medium, or regional languages. And there lies the trouble. Such teachers obviously never thought of the wonderful narratives of the oral and written tradition that most Indians are exposed to.

I wish I could keep away the lump that distorts my voice each time I tell the story of the child Aswathama demanding that his mother let him taste what he heard other children call milk. His father, Dronacharya (later to become the king's general) could not afford to buy milk for his son. Aswathama's mother secretly stirs some powdered rice in water, sweetens it, and feeds her child. The child dances with joy, for he believes he has at last tasted milk; the mother weeps quietly over having to deceive her child this way.

The *Mahabharata* attaches no preachy moral to that story. It's a plain narration of what two characters say and do. How many narratives in world literature match that for a poignant portrayal of poverty? With models like that in our literature, who needs Victorian guidelines for writing narratives? That technique is what Tolstoy discovered, as discussed in 'Show, Don't Tell', pp. 325–30.

Buddhadev Bose compared Sailajananda Mukhopad-hyay's technique of *narration without comment* with Maupassant's. Many writers of short stories in all our regional languages have excelled in detached narration. Saadat Hasan Manto wrote the most powerful stories in Urdu on the partition of India; none of them preachy. Why is it teachers never think of such models? Why do they get their students to imitate crude Victorian didacticism?

And the moral of all that is this: teachers, please stop crippling children with crude didactic essays of the Victorian model; parents, never encourage your children to read those repulsive Victorian-vintage editorials in English-language newspapers.

6

The clatter of clutter

The stumbling blocks for writers in any language are the same:

- fuzzy thinking
- clutter
- vagueness
- faulty word arrangement.

Unless we are clear in our minds about what we wish to say, we cannot convey anything clearly. William Zinsser, much-quoted author of *On Writing Well* (New York: Harper Collins, 1976), puts it across in simple language:

> Writers must . . . constantly ask: what am I trying to say? Surprisingly often they don't know. Then they must look at what they have written and ask: have I said it? Is it clear to someone encountering the subject for the first time? If it's not, some fuzz has worked its way into the machinery. The clear writer is someone clearheaded enough to see this stuff for what it is: fuzz.

> Thinking clearly is a conscious act that writers must force on themselves, as if they were working on any other project that requires logic: making a shopping list or doing an algebra problem.

> Writing is hard work. A clear sentence is no accident. Very few sentences come out right the first time, or even the third

time. Remember this in moments of despair. If you find that
writing is hard, it's because it *is* hard.

The most frequent reason why our writing becomes fuzzy is
clutter. It may be caused by fuzzy thinking. It may also be
caused by faulty use of language. Clutter has on the reader's
mind the effect that static has on the radio audience, and
'snow' (horizontal dotted lines) on the TV viewer. Static and
snow mar reception. So does clutter.

We produce clutter when we use more words than is
needed to convey our message. So conditioned are we to
writing needless words that a reader lamented that the
brevity I advocated reduced a business letter to a telegram.
He would rather write a mini-*Mahabharata* each time he
makes an enquiry about the price of the latest underwear!

Here is an excerpt from a textbook recommended for
students seeking a bachelor's degree in business management
(BBM) from Bangalore University.

Chapter 2
Banker and Customer
This chapter deals with the relationship that exists between
the customer and banker. All the legal aspects associated
with these two vital organs of the banking operations are
discussed. Even before we go into the details of the relationship, let us understand the definitions of the terms 'Banker'
and 'Customer'.

Banker
Number of definitions of the term 'Banker' have been
put forward by different writers on the subject. We have
discussed here some of the important ones. But none of the
definitions give a precise meaning of the term 'Banker'.

There is nothing grossly wrong with the language; it is better than in many textbooks written in India. But let's see if a little more orderly thinking and economy of language can make the message a bit clearer:

> This chapter deals with banker–customer ties, and the laws that govern them. But before we go into them, we need to understand the terms 'banker' and 'customer'.
>
> **Banker**
> There are many definitions of 'banker', none of them clear. We have selected some important ones.

Or, let us take this excerpt from a newspaper report:

> The West Bengal Government has responded to the Centre's query on political clashes in the state by saying that the reported incidents had primarily been 'confined to certain pockets of three districts of Midnapur, Hooghly and Bankura and required steps were taken to contain the violence'.
>
> According to Union home ministry spokesman, Dr P D Shenoy, the response of the state government has come after the ministry urged 'serious remedial steps' and also sought a detailed feedback on the subject.
>
> The Government of West Bengal has reported that political clashes of this nature have primarily been confined to certain pockets of three districts – Midnapur, Hooghly and Bankura, where police officers have been repeatedly sensitised to remain extremely vigilant and to make all efforts for seizure of unlicensed arms and other illegal weapons.

Fuzzy thinking has led to repetition and clutter. An improvement:

> West Bengal has told the Centre that the recent political violence was confined to some pockets of Midnapur, Hooghly and Bankura, and that it had done what was needed to stop it.

The State Government said police in the three districts had been put on a drive against unlicensed arms, the Union Home Ministry spokesman told reporters today. Dr P D Shenoy said the ministry had asked for details and urged remedial action.

That removes much of the clutter and makes it easier for the reader to glean the facts.

Clutter has many faces. It can be the wasteful words with which we begin our sentences: 'It should be pointed out that . . ./We might add that . . ./It would be interesting to note that . . .'. If we are sure it should be added, we should add it without a preface. If what we feel is interesting does interest the reader, he will read it; if it doesn't, a preface won't help.

Clutter is caused by the vague and meaningless tail-ender that drags a sentence down: '[he] said in this context/. . . on the subject/. . . the authorities concerned'. The reader is not a fool and does not need reminding of the context or the subject. There is no point telling the reader that the writer got his facts on India's population from 'the authorities concerned'; he might read with interest the writer's conclusions from facts he got from the director of census operations of his State.

We bring in clutter each time we choose the long-winded phrase instead of the single word (*in view of the fact that* . . . instead of *because; pertaining to the fact that* . . . instead of *about*). Clutter is caused each time we use the stale euphemisms of the Victorians (*in an inebriated state* for *drunk; in an interesting state* or *in the family way* for *pregnant; succumbed to his injuries* for *died; relieved of his purse* for *robbed*).

Indians who write in English tend to clutter their sentences with preposterous bits of *officialese, commercialese* and *legalese* that have got into our system (*the subject referred to above; submissions given below; for your kind information and necessary action; for your kind comments thereon*).

Few writers have put across more forcefully than William Strunk the need to omit needless words in what we write:

> Vigorous writing is concise. A sentence should contain no unnecessary words, a paragraph no unnecessary sentences, for the same reason that a drawing should have no unnecessary lines, and a machine no unnecessary parts. This requires not that the writer make all his sentences short, or that he avoid all detail and treat his subject only in outline, but that [he makes] every word tell.
>
> (*The Elements of Style*, New York: Macmillan, 1959 and 1972; London: Collier Macmillan, 1979)

7

Clutter bugs

From the foreword to a book on Indian wood:

> If in our country, we are to undertake programmes *designed for the protection* of forests and thus improve our wood resources, the basic need *is to make available* to scientists, industrialists, educationists and environmentalists *involved in activities related to* wood and wood-products, information on scientific techniques for *rational and economic utilisation of timber resource.* . . . *It is hoped* that this publication will meet the *long-felt need* toward *achieving this objective.* (70 words)

The clauses italicised show how we clutter our writing. Let's remove the clutter:

> If we wish to protect our forests, and add to our wealth of wood, we must provide information on the economic use of timber to scientists, industrialists, teachers and environmentalists interested in wood and wood-products. . . . This publication, I hope, will meet that need. (43 words)

That now gets the meaning across more easily.

Needless words clutter writing. We need to recognise these four patterns of wordiness:

- circumlocution
- pleonasm
- redundancy

- tautology

These defects overlap.

Circumlocution

Its Greek name, *periphrasis*, means *talking around*. We do this when we choose an indirect way of saying things. This is what brought about Victorian euphemisms such as *in an inebriated condition* for *drunk*. It didn't end with the Victorians. American officials use this device to mislead or be evasive. Hospital officials would rather say a patient *underwent negative patient care outcome* than *the patient died*. During their misadventure in Vietnam, American officials fell back on circumlocution to inject vagueness into their statements to the press. Pentagon officials coined such periphrastic euphemisms as *reinforced protective reaction strike* for *invasion*. General Alexander Haig, President Reagan's Secretary of State, invented *at this juncture of maturization* to mean *now*. That beats Dr Johnson's *rotundity of leather* (football), or *repress the instantaneous motions of merriment* (stop laughing).

The commonest cause for our roundabout expressions lies in our use of the noun instead of the verb (discussed in 'Jest *Choop* and *Chel*', pp. 264–9). A close second is our love of the pompous. Editorial writers use circumlocution to camouflage their drivel (discussed in 'The Whirligig of Circumlocution', pp. 14–19). For business writers, prices don't go up; they *undergo an upward revision*. Nor do prices fall; they *undergo a downward revision*.

Our English-language papers keep circulating roundabout

Victorian expressions, for each of which a single word (here in brackets) suffices:

a large proportion/percentage of (many)
during the time that (while)
give rise to (cause)
in a hasty manner (hastily)
in view of the fact that (because)
owing to the fact that (since/because)
take action on the issue (act)
the question as to whether (whether)
was of the opinion that (said/believed/thought), and so on.

Pleonasm

This word from the Greek *pleonasmos* (which translates into 'more-ness') means the unnecessary word or phrase that merely repeats an idea conveyed by another. The test: a pleonasm can be deleted without any difference to sense. Most 'siamese twins' lawyers use are pleonasms: *aid and abet*; *null and void*; *save and except* (discussed in 'Words without Meaning', pp. 167–72).

Our English-language newspapers serve pleonasms by the dozen each day. They tell us of 'new innovations', without pondering whether anything *not* new could ever qualify as an *innovation* (its Latin root, *novus*, means *new*). Each word italicised in these familiar newspaper terms only duplicates the idea in the word next to it:

active accomplice
advance planning
appear *on the scene*
consensus *of opinion*
end product
final outcome

general public
joint collaboration
merge *together*
original source
past history
proposed plan
prototype model
root cause
rise *up*
still continue/persist
temporary respite
total destruction

Redundancy

Derived from the Latin *redundantia* (excess) and *redundare* (to overflow), *redundancy* is often used in industry for retrenching labour. It also describes a common defect of writing – the repetition of information, or the use of more words than are necessary to put across a piece of information.

All the defects discussed here lead to redundancy or verbosity. The difference: redundancy is a general term for the use of excess words; verbosity describes an excess especially of Latinate words, aimed to impress. Dr Johnson's prose was verbose. Our English-language papers keep serving redundancies by tagging needless words such as *condition, issue, position, problem, purpose, question, situation*. They tell us of the crime *situation*, instead of crime; of the weather *condition*, instead of the weather.

Tautology

Coming from the Greek *tauto* (the same), *tautology* is the error of repeating what we have already said. Its difference from pleonasm: tautology repeats an idea anywhere in a sentence or a passage; pleonasm duplicates an idea in the preceding or the very next word – usually, in an adverb or adjective that repeats an idea contained in the verb or the noun it qualifies. We can (to quote William Strunk) make every word tell, if we omit these defects of language and logic. How do we do this? William Zinsser tells us:

> The secret of good writing is to strip every sentence to its cleanest components. Every word that serves no function, every long word that could be a short word, every adverb that carries the *same* meaning that's already in the verb, every passive construction that leaves the reader unsure of who is doing what – those are the thousand and one adulterants that weaken *the strength of* a sentence. And they usually occur in proportion to education and rank.
>
> (*On Writing Well*, New York: Harper Collins, 1976)

Zinsser's words hold true for writing in any language. But such discipline does not come easily: even Zinsser failed to strip four redundant words (*same* and *the strength of*) from his first sentence.

Indians who wish to write good English need to first study writing in our regional languages. Bengalis have in short stories by Parashuram (Rajshekhar Basu) and Rabindranath Tagore perhaps the world's best models for precision and economy of language. In his first three collections (*Kawjjoli, Gawddolikaa, Hanumaaner Swapna Ityadi Gawlpo*), Parashuram's prose defies editing. Not a word is excess; every sentence is stripped to its cleanest component.

And yet, the East India Company's Bengali clerks spawned *Baboo* English, characterised by a ludicrously flowery, deferential and indirect style. Many of them were semi-literate; nor did they have much Bengali prose to fall back on.

Today's Bengali has a wealth of excellent prose in his or her mother tongue to emulate, just as today's Malayalee, Tamilavan, Kannadiga, Teluguvaaru, or readers of Hindi and Urdu have. We need to upgrade the English we write to the level of our excellent regional-language prose. That calls for a little humility and some labour among our *Indlish*-wallahs, who must identify and reject Company clerks' pidgin.

8

Shrink or sink

'I just don't agree with this hoo-ha about short sentences and simple words,' said PM. 'If I can write long sentences well, why shouldn't I?' Nor does PM agree with advice on the use of everyday words. 'But if I know how to use the long and difficult word, why shouldn't I use it?'

PM, a journalist with one of Calcutta's leading English-language dailies, isn't alone in viewing writing solely from his end of the communication channel. Too many writers forget the other end: the reader. Engrossed in their narcissistic exercise, they never ask themselves a simple question: 'Who am I writing for?'

Such writers should spend some time finding out about readability tests by individuals and press associations. They might then realise that their readers could ask these legitimate questions: 'Why does a writer use the difficult word, if it has an everyday synonym that readers can understand more quickly and easily? And why does a writer serve long sentences when short sentences are easier to read?'

A muddle-headed writer may, of course, create just as much confusion with a short sentence as with a long one. But usually, sentence length is closely related to clarity – or its absence. Harold Evans, guru of British journalists, explained this relationship:

A sentence is more likely to be clear if it is a short sentence communicating one thought, or a closely connected range of ideas. . . .

The length of sentences with too many ideas is not the cause of the disease; but it is often a clear symptom. It is the reason why some writers advise a limit on length . . . where the ideas in a sentence are complex, they cannot intelligibly be presented in subsidiary clauses separated by a mere comma. The full-stop is a great help to sanity.

Evans stressed the load of ideas a sentence is made to carry:

The real seduction of the simple sentence is that taken by itself, it is short and it is confined to one idea. The real trouble with so many compound-complex sentences is that they have to carry too many ideas.

(*Newsman's English*, London: William Heineman, 1972)

Every day, our English-language newspapers serve examples of what Evans called the overloaded sentence. Here is the first sentence of the lead item a Karnataka paper printed:

The delicate negotiations that the Karnataka and Tamil Nadu governments have been holding with forest brigand Veerappan through an emissary for the release of Kannada film star Rajkumar and three others being held hostage by him for the past 12 days have reached a dead-end with the bandit raising four new demands, including reference of the Cauvery water dispute to the International Court of Justice, in addition to the 10 already conceded in principle and the two governments politely but firmly rejecting most of them. (85 words)

One wonders how long it took readers to find a nugget of fresh information in that dung-heap of subsidiary clauses.

The long sentence stuffed with several ideas violates an elementary rule of communication stated by George Polya,

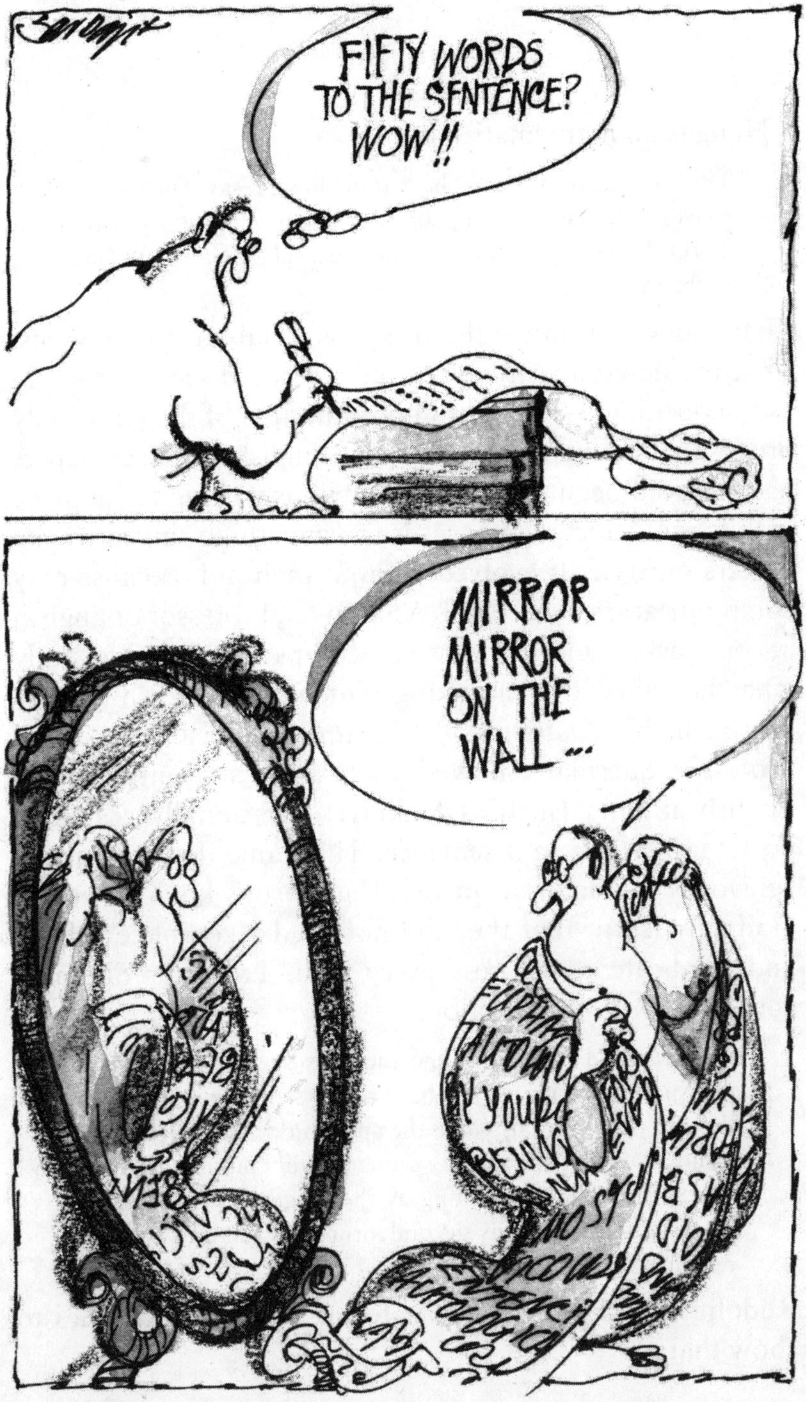
FIFTY WORDS TO THE SENTENCE? WOW!!
MIRROR MIRROR ON THE WALL...

a Hungarian mathematician:

> The first rule of style is to have something to say. The second rule of style is to control yourself when, by chance, you have TWO things to say; say first one, then the other, not BOTH at the same time.

That sounds so simple that it seems to labour the obvious. That the newspaper sentence quoted could see print – and as the opening of the most important item of the day – only proves that many journalists in our English-language papers haven't even begun thinking of obvious writing techniques.

But the short sentence isn't something invented by writers on style. It evolved without their aid, because easy communication needed it. L A Sherman, Professor of English at Nebraska University, was perhaps the first to study what he called the 'shrinking sentence in English literary prose'. In his *Analytics of Literature*, published in 1893, Professor Sherman showed that some sixteenth-century English authors (such as Hakluyt) occasionally crammed 60 to 118 words in a sentence. This came down to about 30 words in Victorian prose. The reason: English writers gradually learnt that they did not need a complete subject and predicate to express every idea. Professor Sherman concluded with a prediction:

> The standard English of the future is sure to be close to the spoken norm. . . . The written sentence is growing shorter year by year, while the spoken does not alter. This means, not that the literary sentence will continue to grow shorter and shorter as long as the language lasts, but on reaching approximately the oral form and structure will there remain . . . .

Rudolph Flesch borrowed Professor Sherman's samples to show that:

the average Elizabethan written sentence ran to about 45 words; the Victorian sentence to 29; ours to 20 and less. . . . When we try to imitate dialogue or conversation on paper, we naturally stick to short sentences and our average may turn to 15 or even 10 words per sentence. But as soon as we get the itch to appear more serious and dignified, up it goes and we get more and more Victorian; and when we yield to the temptation of pomposity, we get downright monstrous and write sentences no man has ever said aloud.

(*The Art of Readable Writing*, New York: Harper & Row, 1948)

Flesch quoted excerpts from his contemporary academics and political pundits, who had written sentences more than 100 words long, and said: 'The cure for this type of sentence elephantiasis is very simple. All you need is to stop being stuffy and talk like a human being, and that's that.'

Based on several studies, press associations in the USA have laid down a readability table. Their survey shows readers find sentences of 8 words or less very easy to read; 11 words, easy; 14 words fairly easy; 17 words standard; 21 words fairly difficult; 25 words difficult and 29 words or more, very difficult. Flesch drew up an elaborate and complicated test to assess 'reading ease' and 'human interest', taking into account both sentence and word length. That has been simplified into one that is designed to assess clarity:

The Fog Factor
Take a sample of your writing (about 200 words).
Count the number of sentences.
Count all words with three or more syllables (e.g. cla-ri-ty has three), excluding personal pronouns (names).
Then apply the Fog Factor:

Divide the number of long words by the number of sentences.

Clear writing has a fog factor of between 2 and 3.

Below 2 may be childishly simple.

Above 3 may be rather FOGGY!

Those who still believe that the insistence on short sentences in English is a modern fad might be surprised to learn that no Englishman spoke of it before a Frenchman put it across forcefully more than 125 years ago. Gustav Flaubert (1821–1880), who wrote *Madame Bovary*, and whom Europe acknowledged as the master of prose style, said: 'Whenever you can shorten a sentence, do. And one always can. The best sentence? The shortest.'

9

The logic of it

'But if I wrote all my sentences short, and removed redundancy, would that guarantee clarity?' SM asked. The trainee journalist sounded frustrated over the way his copy had been marked in red ink. No, of course it wouldn't. Other components of clarity are logic and grammar. Most grammatical errors are errors of logic. These are the errors of logic we commit most frequently:

- misplacing words, phrases or clauses
- leaving a participle dangling
- confusing number of verb and subject
- using a pronoun without an antecedent.

Misplacing words

Because we are used to a flexible syntax, we forget to check for the logical error or distortion of sense that, given the rigid syntax of English, a wrong arrangement of words often causes. A newspaper report on a film director's offer to Saurav Ganguly and his wife ended with this sentence:

> Dona, who runs an Odissi Centre in Calcutta, has left its operations to a teacher hired from Orissa *to spend time with her husband.*

That arrangement of words can only mean the teacher has been hired to spend time with Saurav! Obviously, the reporter arranged the words as he would have done in Bengali. But Bengali, like all written Indian languages, has an extremely flexible syntax. The rigid syntax of English demanded the last six words (italicised) at the beginning. There would have been no ambiguity in

> To spend time with her husband, Dona has left her Odissi centre in the care of a teacher she hired from Orissa.

Our flexible syntax makes us prone to such errors. But we do not have a monopoly over them. Fuzzy thinking causes errors of logic, and people whose mother tongue is English are just as likely to commit them. Here is an excerpt from an AP report:

> Russian President Vladimir Putin was to fly on Tuesday to the navy's main base in northern Russia, his press service said, and Russian news reports said that he might go on a warship to the area where *the* Kursk *sank on August 12 to honour the crew.*

That arrangement of words suggests the preposterous: that the Russian submarine sank in order to honour its crew! The easiest way to avoid such errors of logic is never to separate related words (discussed also in 'The Lady with Mahogany Legs', pp. 259–63). Such absurdity could have been avoided had Putin not been separated from his intention to honour the crew, nor the *Kursk* from the day it sank:

> . . . and Russian news reports said that to honour the crew, he might go on a warship to the area where the *Kursk* sank on August 12.

We become prone to similar errors of logic each time we separate qualifiers from the words they qualify.

The dangling participle

This creates absurdities similar to errors of syntax, and we commit this most often when:

1. we forget that the reader needs to be told which word the participle beginning a sentence refers to, or
2. because of a faulty arrangement, the participle beginning a sentence refers to the wrong word.

1. In 'Lying idly, watching TV, the clock rang out the alarm set for 3.30' the reader has not been told that the participle 'lying' as also 'watching' refers not to the clock, but to the narrator. The reader therefore connects those participles dangling in mid-air to the clock. The resulting nonsense can be avoided if the writer makes clear *he* lay idle, watching TV:

> I lay idle, watching TV, and was startled when the clock rang out the alarm.

Our English-language newspapers often serve such illogical sentences as 'Convicted of the rape charge, the judge reserved sentence till Monday'. At first glance, the reader gets the message that it was the judge who was convicted of the rape charge, because the reporter forgets to mention the accused, to whom 'convicted' refers. Let's make things clear:

> The accused was convicted of the rape charge, and the judge reserved sentence till Monday.

2. In 'Walking through the forest, Veerappan's men shadowed Gopal along a parallel track', the reader is not

told whether 'walking' refers to Gopal, or Veerappan's men. The reporter could have avoided this ambiguity with

> As Gopal walked through the forest, Veerappan's men shadowed him along a parallel track.

3. A third pattern of logical error creeps in when the dangling participle seems to relate two sets of facts that have no logical connection. Such *non sequiturs* (i.e. conclusions that do not logically follow) often creep into obituaries: 'Born in Serampore, Hooghly, he stood first class first in Chemistry and obtained a research scholarship from . . . .' That would seem to imply that his performance had something to do with his place of birth!

Confusing number of verb and subject

Haste makes all of us prone to this error, when we forget that the number of the verb must match the number of the subject. We tend all too often to be guided by the number of the word closest to the verb. The most common confusion occurs over the number of the verb in clauses that follow 'one of . . .' or collectives, such as *team of/group of/herd of*, etc. In 'Veerappan's men shot at the group of policemen that was following Gopal', a writer is likely to be guided by 'policemen' which is closest to the verb, and use a plural verb (*were*), forgetting that the verb must agree instead with 'the group' and therefore be singular. On the other hand, clauses that follow 'one of . . .' most often require a plural verb. Correct example:

> He was one of the policemen who *were* following Gopal at
> a distance.

Using a pronoun without an antecedent

In 'Mr Subhas Chakraborty offered to resign, but *it* was refused', the reader isn't told which noun *it* stands for. The pronoun would have been justified had the noun (*resignation*) been used instead of the verb: in 'Mr Subhas Chakraborty offered his resignation, but it was refused' *it* stands for *resignation*, and there is no confusion.

Ambiguity of another kind is caused when we use a pronoun without making clear which of several nouns in a sentence it stands for. The writer of 'If the baby does not thrive on raw milk, boil it' seems to advise readers to boil the baby, who is the subject of the sentence. That absurdity can be removed only if the sentence makes clear that *it* refers to the other noun, *milk*. 'Boil the milk if baby does not thrive on it raw' is one way of making it clear.

Mixing tenses, or mismatching the number of the pronoun and its antecedent, cause errors of logic too. But these mistakes are obvious, and few writers commit them often. To serve clarity, we need to remember only two criteria for the sentences we write:

1   Communication slows if the reader must make an effort to understand sentences we write. (Clutter is the chief cause.)

2 Communication breaks down if a sentence we write can mean something other than what we intended to say. (An error of logic causes this.)

10

The secret of bad writing

Where shall we hunt for techniques of writing well? Aren't we swamped with tips and advice? Would it be a little more stimulating instead to explore how to write badly?

An American writer once thought along those lines. He wrote an essay, 'The Principles of Poor Writing', in which he complained that too much attention was given to good writing, thus making it difficult to learn about poor writing.

Paul W Merrill's essay was published in *The Scientific Monthly* 64, January 1974. Even though advice on good writing was blowing in the wind, Merrill said, 'The average student finds it surprisingly easy to acquire the usual tricks of poor writing.' His tongue way inside his cheek, he went on to suggest that those who wished to consistently make a botch of their writing 'must grasp a few essential principles'. Merrill's principles:

1 Ignore the reader.
2 Be verbose, vague and pompous.
3 Do not revise.

Facetious though that may sound, Merrill accurately named the three most common defects we see in our newspapers and books. An excerpt from a Bangalore newspaper report:

> Minister for Primary and Secondary education H Vishwa-
> nath today said the Government would allow a public

debate on the interim report of the Education Task Force which has made *a host of suggestions* to improve the primary education system in the State.

Speaking to reporters who met him at Vidhana Soudha, the Minister said the interim report submitted to the Government recently by Dr Rajaramanna, who headed the Task Force, was in English language and the same was being translated to Kannada.

'Once the report is ready in Kannada, a wide public debate would be allowed before taking any decision to implement the same,' he added.

He also said the report was only experts' opinion. In a democratic system like ours, public opinion should be sought.

That is typical of the fare our English-language papers serve each day. What information does the reader gather from those 127 words? Why isn't the reader told of even *one* of the 'host of suggestions'?

What is the significance of a lengthy report that tells a reader only that a task force on primary education had made 'a host of suggestions'? Perhaps the reporter had secret information that the task force was set up to keep mum on the subject. Instead, it had made 'a host of suggestions'. And a minister had said so. That made it earth-shaking news!

Reports in our English-language papers show that even though none of them may have heard of Merrill, their reporters work by Merrill's principles:

1 Their reporters are concerned only with sucking up to officials and ministers for their 'he said/she said' staple. They can't be bothered with reader interest, so they ignore the reader.
2 English-language paper reporters are sworn to a cult of vagueness. They never deviate to specific information

on anything. Hence generalities such as 'a host of suggestions/many suggestions', without specifying any of the many. Their cult has them sworn to verbosity and pomposity.

3 East India Company clerks' lingo ('*the same* was being translated/decision to implement *the same*'); the omission of the definite article ('was in English language') and drab language throughout only prove that those who write for our English-language papers religiously follow Merrill's third principle ('Do not revise').

Contrast that with this excerpt from a report in *The Independent*, London:

> **Warning: Homework Can Harm**
> Homework is not always a good thing. Much of the evidence about its benefits is inconclusive and the case for it in the primary schools is weak, a paper published today says.
>
> As the Government prepares the first national guidelines on how much homework pupils should do and pours money into homework clubs, academics from London University's Institute of Education attack the view that homework necessarily raises standards.
>
> In a review of nearly half a century's research on homework, Dr Susan Hallam and Dr Richard Cowan also warn parents who help their children with homework that their efforts may be counter-productive.

The reader is uppermost in this reporter's mind. He serves specific information the reader wants: what it's all about; how authoritative the paper is; who the researchers are; what span of time the research samples cover; what challenging conclusions follow from the study; how relevant the study is to parents of children in primary schools, and to all who are

connected with primary education. That is a lot of specific detail to serve in 101 words. Nowhere is there the slightest vagueness. The language throughout is clear and concise, and shows that the report has been well edited and revised.

Vagueness in writing corresponds to babble. No one listens to babble. And no one reads vague writing. If one had to pinpoint one defect common to all bad writing in India, it would be vagueness. A new genre of bad writing is being promoted in India through foreign funds. This is the world of NGO literature. Here is an excerpt from a book written by a 'gender activist':

> The *thrust* of this book is to take the gender debate forward to include a wider *spectrum* of issues in the *field of gender* and development. Planners and practitioners are keen on gaining the know-how of *integrating gender* in their *interventions*. Many *tool kits* have been brought out on the best *practices in gender*. In this book, we have kept away from giving *specific* tools and *techniques*. Our belief is that a large part of *gender interventions*/equality falls in the area of *values and orientation*. It is only a *humanistic* approach that can reveal the connections between *subjective perceptions* of reality and the *objective social world*.

That babble shows the author is a firm believer in Merrill's principles:

1 She ignores the reader, to whom her mumbo-jumbo can imply only lewd connotations.
2 She is verbose, vague to the point of obscurity, and pompous.
3 She will not revise her writing.

What makes for good writing? Let's listen to William Zinsser:

The secret of bad writing

Unlike medicine or the other sciences, writing has no new discoveries to spring on us. We are in no danger of reading in our morning newspaper that a breakthrough has been made in how to write a clear English sentence – that information has been around since the King James Bible. We know that verbs have more vigour than nouns, that active verbs are better than passive verbs, that short words and sentences are easier to read than long ones, that concrete details are easier to process than vague abstractions.

Where then is the edge? Ninety per cent of the answer lies in the hard work of mastering the tools discussed.

If you would like to write better than everybody else, you have to *want* to write better than everybody else. You must take an obsessive pride in the smallest details of your craft.

(*On Writing Well*, New York: Harper Collins, 1976)

II

The cult of vagueness

What makes writing vague? Does a writer go out to be vague? The first question turns us to the writer's technique; the second, to the writer's intent. In his much-quoted essay, 'Politics and the English Language', George Orwell suggested that politics encouraged a cult of vagueness, and this had married technique with intent:

> In our time, political speech and writing are largely the defence of the indefensible . . . Millions of peasants are robbed of their farms and sent trudging along the roads with no more than they can carry: this is called *transfer of population* or *rectification of frontiers*. People are imprisoned for years without trial, or shot in the back of the neck or sent to die of scurvy in Arctic lumber camps: this is called *elimination of unreliable elements*.
>
> Such phraseology is needed if one wants to *name things without calling up mental pictures of them*.

Orwell accurately identifies vague writing: the kind that calls up no mental pictures. In asking writers to avoid vagueness, William Strunk said:

> If those who have studied the art of writing are in accord on any one point, it is on this: the surest way to arouse and hold the attention of the reader is by being specific, definite and concrete. The greatest writers – Homer, Dante, Shakespeare – are effective largely because they deal in particulars and

report the details that matter. *Their words call up pictures.*
(*The Elements of Style*, New York: Macmillan, 1959)

Strunk advised the writer to reject the vagueness in 'A period of unfavourable weather set in' and fill in specific detail: 'It rained every day for a week'. The effeteness in 'He showed satisfaction as he took possession of his well-earned reward' could change into a lively picture in 'He grinned as he pocketed the coin'.

What about writing we see every day – the newspaper report that tells us nothing specific; the editorial that is a fog of abstractions; the dissertation wrapped in vague profundity; books by NGOs that spew unintelligible jargon; the supposedly profound *academese* that university professors plagiarise from books? The truth is we in India are so swamped by vague speech and writing that we've long ceased to bother about these things. Vagueness is always a convenient refuge of the fraud. And such fraud succeeds because our cultural values long ago made incomprehensibility and vagueness respectable.

Such cultural values are rooted in medieval times, when the pundit was revered by the common folk who knew no Sanskrit. The incomprehensibility of the pundit's utterances was the reason he was held in awe and esteem. This equation of incomprehensibility with greatness goes back to a universal primeval culture that invested the *shaman* or witch-doctor with mystical powers precisely because his supposedly magical incantations were incomprehensible to others.

In using language not for communication, but for fraud, the *shaman*, or the cult guru, sought the same ends as their modern-day *avatars* do – the politician who rants *bafflegab*;

the trade union leader who delivers speeches laden with jargon workers do not understand; the NGOs that blab incomprehensible fad coinages; the editorial writer who garbs drivel in what passes for 'high-flown' language; the fraud academic who spews abstractions twenty to the dozen. All these pollute speech and writing with their vagueness.

What we should worry about is the effect such models of speech and writing have on each generation. The average schoolboy is forced to emulate model essays that nosedive into generalities and abstractions. Here is a model from as venerable a source as Wren & Martin's *Grammar and Composition*:

> Happy is the man who acquires the habit of reading when he is young. He has *secured* a life-long source of *pleasure, instruction and inspiration.* So long as he has his *beloved* books, he need never feel lonely. He always has a *pleasant occupation of leisure moments*, so that he need never feel bored. He is the *possessor of wealth* more precious than gold. . . .

The model essay goes on extolling abstract virtues of reading. There is no mention of anything specific; nothing that calls up a picture to the mind. That model is guaranteed to instil the habit of pontificating on all subjects under the sun. And that is precisely what the schoolboy learns: to heap hackneyed phrases into boring sermons. That habit he carries into adulthood. Whence our English-language newspaper editorials.

Bengali children have the best model of writing that can convey pictures – *Booro Anglaa*, Abanindranath Tagore's adaptation of *Tom Thumb*. The Bengali Tom Thumb ties himself to the foot of a duck, one of a migratory flock on

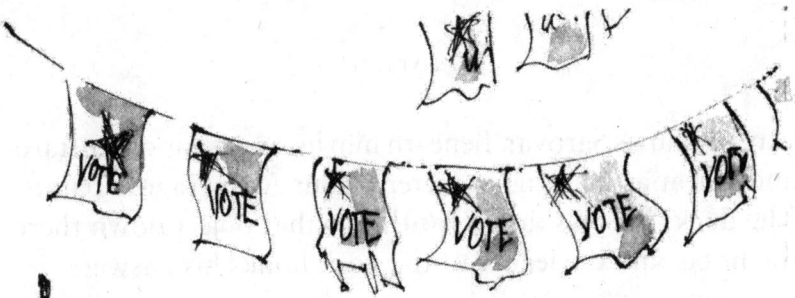

way to Manas Sarovar. Beneath him he sees fields of mustard and wheat as patterns in water colour Aban Tagore paints. The ducks keep asking what this or that object down there might be, and the leader of the flock honks his answer:

'Whose house?'
'Tagore house.'
'Which Tagore?'
'Obin Tagore; (he) *writes pictures*.'

Abanindranath Tagore, guru of a new generation of painters he trained at Santiniketan, gifted to Bengali children perhaps the world's best work in 'word painting'. But few adults got the message. They instead taught their children what they thought was a 'romantic vagueness'.

To this day, Bengali schoolchildren begin their essays on nature with the call of some *naam-naa-jaanaa paakhee* (name-not-known bird), and a breeze wafting the scent of a *naam-naa-jaanaa phool* (name-not-known flower). To this day, no teacher has told them that it's not romantic, and downright moronic, for a Bengali not to know the names of flowers and birds in his region, and that he should find those out before he writes about them.

Nor do teachers tell them never to use such ready-made phrases – the bane of much of the writing one sees in India.

Orwell considered the use of ready-made expressions the worst defect of writing, because these thwart fresh thinking:

> Writing at its worst does not consist in picking out words for the sake of their meaning and inventing images in order to make the meaning clearer. It consists in gumming together long strips of words that have already been set in order by someone else, and making the results presentable by sheer humbug. The attraction of this way of writing is that it is

easy. It is easier – even quicker, once you have the habit – to say *In my opinion it is a not unjustifiable assumption that . . .* than to say *I think.*

What then should the writer do to avoid such defects? Orwell set down six simple rules for all writers:

1 Never use a metaphor, simile, or other figure of speech that you are *used to seeing* in print.
2 Never use a long word where a short one will do.
3 If it is possible to cut a word out, always cut it out.
4 Never use the passive [voice] where you can use the active.
5 Never use a foreign phrase, a scientific word, or a jargon word, if you can think of an everyday English equivalent.
6 Break any of these rules sooner than say anything outright barbarous.

II

THE LETTERS WE WRITE

12

Cancel forthwith under intimation . . .

Some readers might dismiss as 'old hat' advice that in all our letters we should 'be clear, be brief, and be human'. They would be correct: that's as old as 1948, when Sir Ernest Gowers laid it down for British civil servants (in *Plain Words*, revised in 1951 as *The ABC of Plain Words* and published in 1954 as a single volume, *The Complete Plain Words*).

Churchill saw to it that British civil servants followed Gowers's people-friendly style in their official correspondence. When Sir Bruce Fraser revised Gowers's work in 1973, he acknowledged the change the book had brought about in official writing. Over the 25 years since the first version was published, he remarked:

> *Officialese*, in the sense of a species of bad writing peculiarly characteristic of public officials, is not nearly as serious an offender as it was. One sees plenty of bad official writing, but nowadays its faults are not usually of a kind peculiar to officials: they are to be found in even greater profusion elsewhere, and the official is to be blamed more often for following a bad example than for setting one.

Fraser upheld a senior bureaucrat's comment on the familiar criticism of official writing. A Permanent Secretary wrote to Fraser:

Our impression is that the worst offenders against the Queen's English nowadays are academics, businessmen and journalists. We ourselves have no cause for complacency, but we have gained some ground in the battle for plain words and we believe that much of the credit must go to Gowers. What troubles us now is not the pompous circumlocution which was once the mark of official writing, but the threat of 'expert' writing which characteristically tends towards abstraction and jargon. The battle must be continued on a different front.

India's administrative juggernaut replicates the British pattern. Have our mandarins too moved away from *officialese*? Consider this letter from a senior IAS officer, who served as the Registrar of Bangalore University, to the Chairman of the university's Sociology Department:

> Sir,
> Sub: Cancellation of admission to I year MA Sociology in respect of Sri KCM . . . regarding . . . .
>
> With reference to the above, I am directed to inform you that the admission of Mr KCM . . ., student of I year MA Sociology, be cancelled forthwith under intimation to this office, as it is found that he is not eligible to seek admission to I MA Sociology as per the records available from the examination branch. The matter may kindly be treated as *most urgent*.
> Yours faithfully
> REGISTRAR

Some questions that letter raises:

1 The 'subject' announces that the letter deals with the cancellation of admission 'in respect of' (read: *of*) the student. What then does 'regarding' after that announcement relate to?

2 The 'subject' above the text makes the theme clear. Why then must the text begin with 'with reference to the above' when there is nothing else above the text to refer to?

3 The Registrar controls admission to a university. Why does he say he has 'been directed to inform' the academic of his decision? Who directed the Registrar to take a decision only the Registrar can take?

4 The letter was meant to ask the academic to carry out the Registrar's directive, not to merely inform him of the decision. Why then 'inform you . . . be cancelled forthwith' instead of 'Please cancel . . .'?

5 How was the academic to cancel the admission *under* (or, for that matter, *over/atop/alongside*) an intimation? Was it an underhand action he was being asked to take?

6 What was the academic to gather from 'as per the records . . . examination branch'? That the student had failed, or been reported against? What exactly did those records show? If those records proved that the student was not eligible for admission, why the impersonal 'it is found'? Who found what?

7 Was the student not eligible for admission, or not eligible even to 'seek' admission? How then did he get admitted?

8 Why the last line asking the academic to 'kindly treat the matter'? The letter gave a directive. Did the academic have a choice in treating the matter 'kindly' or less than kindly?

9 Since this went from the Registrar to a senior academic in the campus, why was a formal letter necessary? Wouldn't an official memo have sufficed?

If the Registrar agreed to answer those questions, he would only repeat 'It is the form . . .' for each. This, then, is the trouble with letters our mandarins write. Meaningless ritual and form matter more than meaningful message. And no one calculates the cost.

Official correspondence implies the cost of employing stenos, typists, filing clerks and dispatch clerks, plus the cost of paper, typewriters or computers, ribbons or cartridges and envelopes. All this is paid for with taxpayers' money. So are the officers who dictate such inane letters. How much does the nation pay for letters without sense? What does meaningless ritual cost the nation? How much would the nation save by training officers to write sense?

The text of the Registrar's letter is about 70 words, about 30 of which are meaningless. A memo worded in not much more than 30 might have been clearer and more human:

> Mr . . .
> Please cancel the inadvertent admission of Mr KCM . . . to MA Sociology. Records with the Controller of Examinations show that this student is not eligible because . . . (the exact reason stated).
> Regards
> REGISTRAR

13

As per your esteemed order of the 26th ult . . .

How should we begin our letters? Consider these three samples

1 Dear Madam – Your letter of the 23rd inst. is at hand.
2 Dear Sir – We have your letter of July 21 and note that it is your intention to include – in your book on modern English prose style, to be published by . . . under the title . . . a few brief passages from our . . . .
3 Dear Sir – We beg to acknowledge receipt of your letter of the 16th instant regarding the price charged for the lubricating oil which we supplied to you sometime back.

The first is from a letter an American publishing firm wrote in May 1882; the second, from one an American textbook company wrote in 1946, and the third, from one in a widely used letter-writing guide book, the Madras-based publishers of which reprinted their tenth edition in 1998.

Business letters, we are told, are meant to be brief and to the point. And yet, over the 117 years between the first and the third letter, no one seems to have wondered why one should begin one's reply to a business query with such acknowledgment, when the addressee knows even before he opens the envelope that it contains a reply to his letter. How would one be replying to a letter unless one had received it?

Ditto with what follows that bit of useless information. The second and the third samples merely summarise what information the writer sought. Surely, the writer hardly needs the responder to tell him that?

What does the entire first paragraph of the second sample tell the recipient that he didn't already know? And yet, that useless summary of a business enquiry takes 40 words, not counting those omitted. The 27 words in the first paragraph of the third sample tell the recipient no more than what he had written in his letter. Is that the most important function of a reply?

At a recent workshop on effective communication, participants found it difficult to accept that a reply would be more meaningful if it began with the information its writer sought, than with a reminder of the date on which he wrote it. They took a long time to agree that such an opening served no purpose, but wondered how they could dismiss what they had always been told was essential form.

Form. Convention. Ritual. The first conditions us to uphold the second, and the second to perpetuate the third. This whirligig of our culture of thinking keeps out the need to think. Or to question what we've been conditioned to accept. A proposal for a fresh look meets the same resistance: 'But that is form.'

The third sample from the letter-writing guide begins 'We beg to acknowledge . . .'. If such acknowledgment is the form we must observe (even though we may agree it's in no way so important that we must begin with it), then what purpose is served by assuming a beggary we'd normally feel humiliated to accept? Why must we *beg* to state anything?

And yet to this day, applications for anything from a ration card (which is one's right) to a job (which should be) begin with the inevitable *I beg to state/I humbly beg to state that* ....

Over 70 years ago, Fowler traced two origins of the beggary one found in Victorian usage (*A Dictionary of Modern English Usage*, OUP 1926). Such expressions as *beg to state/beg to remain*, Fowler said, originated in the abbreviation of a polite *I beg leave to state* .... Also, what was considered a polite way of contradicting another required such expressions as *beg pardon/beg leave to doubt*, etc. 'But,' said Fowler, 'the beg-phrases of *commercialese* now serve merely to introduce a flavour of stiffness and artificiality into what should be spontaneous and friendly.'

Since *commercialese* was the only form of English we Indians picked up from the East India Company, that distinction was never made clear, and beggary in all its forms became the norm for letters here.

If we traced the origins of the many expressions that mean little, but are used much in our business letters, we'd see how hopelessly mired in outdated *commercialese* letter-writing in India remains.

Here is advice Sir Ernest Gowers gave British civil servants on keeping *commercialese* out of their letters (in *Plain Words*, 1948, later revised and published as *The Complete Plain Words*, 1954):

> Do not use what have been called the 'dry meaningless formulae' of *commercialese*. Against some of these a warning is not needed: officials do not write your *esteemed favour to hand*, or address their correspondents as *your good self*.

THAT TAKES CARE OF THE ULTIMOS & PROXIMOS!

But if they are not careful they may find themselves using *same* as a pronoun [Gowers condemned as 'reprehensible because it gives an air of artificiality and pretentiousness' the pronominal use of *same* and *the same*, instead of *he/she/him/ her/they/them/it*] or *enclosed please find* instead of *I enclose*.

Per should not be permitted to get too free with the English language. Such convenient abbreviations as *mph* and *rpm* are no doubt with us for good. But generally it is well to confine *per* to its own language – e.g. *per cent*, *per capita*, *per stirpes*, *per contra*, and not to prefer *per day* to *a day*, or *per passenger train* to *by passenger train*, or *as per my letter* to *as I said in my letter*.

Even for phrases in which *per* is linked to a Latin word, there are often English equivalents which serve as well, if not better. A letter can be signed AB *for* CD, as CD *per pro* AB. *A hundred pounds a year* is more natural than *a hundred pounds per annum*. *Per se* does not ordinarily mean anything more than *by itself* or *in itself*.

Another Latin word better left alone is *re*. This is the ablative case of the Latin word *res*. It means *in the matter of* . . . . It has passed into *commercialese* as an equivalent of the English preposition *about*. It has no business there, or anywhere else outside a lawyer's office. It is not needed either to introduce a heading (*re: your application for a grant*), which can stand without its support, or in the body of a letter, where an honest *about* will serve your purpose better. . . .

Finally, there is no reason for preferring the Latin abbreviations *inst.*, *ult.* and *prox.* to the name of the month, which is also capable of abbreviation and has the advantage over them of conveying an immediate and certain meaning.

All that was laid down a long time ago. But are our bureaucrats and 'covenanted officers' of private firms listening?

14

Of false starts

How best to begin a message? Rudolph Flesch, author of *The Art of Readable Writing*, did a somersault – 25 years after he spoke of messages starting on the wrong foot. What he initially wrote in the chapter 'From False Starts to Wrong Conclusions':

> Almost all reading matter in this country [i.e. the USA] gets off to a false start. . . . What is a false start? It's a beginning that doesn't do what a beginning ought to do. . . . Take the three most common pieces of writing in American life: the business letter, the newspaper report, and the magazine short story. Each of them has a standardized opening; each of these openings is wrong.
>
> Ninety-nine out of a hundred business letters start with an acknowledgment of the addressee's last letter. Have you ever asked yourself why? The only plausible answer I found is that it's always been done that way. It's an old, old custom. . . .
>
> Of course, people who have the souls of file clerks always say this stock opening is needed for filing. But that's no argument: there's always room for a reference somewhere in a corner of the letter; and quite often it doesn't make a bit of difference to anybody who wrote what on what date. . . .
>
> Now let's look at newspaper reports . . . war correspondents invented a writing technique that made the story look

complete even if the wire service broke down. . . . This is the famous 5-W lead: it tells *Who, What, When, Where,* and *Why* in the opening paragraph, then starts all over again. . . .

Obviously this is an upside-down method of telling a story; newspapermen call it aptly the inverted-pyramid formula. . . . The standard letter opening is dull, the standard news lead spills the beans.

Somersault

When Flesch revised his book for its '25th anniversary edition' in 1973, he added this about-face to that chapter:

> This is the chapter where I made a mistake. I underrated the value of spill-the-beans newspaper opening.
>
> Let's look once more at business letters and news reports. Sure enough, the old-style business letter – with its standard 'your letter of . . .' opening – is hopelessly old-fashioned. That much is clear. But how should it be changed? Answer: by using the example of the spill-the-beans, inverted-pyramid news reports. Start your letter with the main item of information and you can't go wrong. . . .
>
> The inverted-pyramid newspaper story can and should be used as a model for any kind of writing – business letters, memos, reports, factual material of any kind. Start with a brief spill-the-beans lead and follow it up with more and more details, in descending order of importance. When you've said what you wanted to say, stop.

The newspaper story serves the latest and best news first, then follows up with paragraphs of gradually diminishing news value, and ends with background information. Let's apply that technique to this letter the Karnataka Government's Department of Information and Publicity sent to heads of schools, colleges, and research institutes in the State:

Dear Sir
Sub: Publication of 'Pioneering Educational and Research Institutions of Karnataka'

The Department of Information and Publicity desires to bring out a Publication, which intends to introduce the premier educational institutions in Karnataka to the public at large. The proposed publication aims to explain the educational opportunities and avenues available in Karnataka. The publication is designed to incorporate all the relevant information on each of the premier institutions for the benefit of the students in particular. Therefore, I request you to provide all the information available about your institution right from its inception, courses offered, facilities available and the present status of the institutions. As the publication has to be brought out very early, your cooperation is highly solicitated [sic].

Thanking you,
Yours sincerely,
Senior Assistant Director (Publication's) [sic]

That text (not counting the 'subject' and ending) runs to 108 words. But not even after an addressee reads the first 65 of them does he understand how he relates to the 'proposed publication'. The reason: the letter first talks about a 'proposed publication' and only after three sentences 65 words long begins to tell the addressee that he must contribute to it.

Inversion of that order would place what is relevant to the addressee first, and details about the 'proposed publication' second. That would make the letter read something like this:

Of false starts

Dear Sir

Would you send me as soon as possible such details about your institute as potential students need to know.

We wish to include this in a directory our department will soon publish of Karnataka's premier educational institutes. Readers should find all relevant information below each entry.

Yours faithfully
Senior Assistant Director (Publications)

That 51-word text now places the project's relevance to the addressee first (that's most important to him). Only then does it detail the scope of the book. The head of an institute surely does not need the official to spell out what information he should send; the words 'details . . . students need to know' suffice.

15

Of breech-delivery formats

Now that fax and email have sped communication, have we changed over to more efficient formats for our messages? Here is a letter the Delhi headquarters of a well-known Chamber of Commerce sent in June 1999 to business houses in all metros:

Subject: Provide E-Mail address for Priority and Quick Mailing

Dear Sir

You will most certainly agree that, in this age what matters most is the E-Factor – Efficiency – Economy and – E-mail!

Needless to say, the onslaught of Internet has made communication globally much easier, faster and on the whole more efficient and definitely economical. Postal Services no matter how efficient, do certainly take time to deliver. One cannot overlook delays due to strikes, at times indefinite, climatic conditions and delay due to postal overload during peak seasons etc.

Nevertheless, there is respite from these and the good news is that logging on to the Internet does provide an excellent solution.

Therefore, you are requested to kindly fill up the following form, clearly indicating your e-mail address along with your telephone numbers and the postal address so that we can include the name and the details of your company on our priority mailing list.

Please send this reply form back to us either per fax [number cited] or post at the above address. You may also send the same information via E-Mail [address cited] at the very earliest.
Thanking you,
Yours truly,

The way the sender printed the entire fourth paragraph in bold shows he knew the preceding 88 words had nothing to do with his message. He chose this device because he was afraid an addressee might stop before he came to the only relevant bit in that 160-word text.

One can only wonder at the first three paragraphs – a cross between 'model letters' one sees in books meant to train typists and clerks, and the drivel one sees in English-language newspaper editorials. One wonders all the more because in the second paragraph, the sender agrees that it's 'needless to say . . .' the 79 words that follow.

The fourth paragraph goes back to the impersonal passive of East India Company days (Therefore you are requested to . . .) and the last paragraph, to eighteenth-century *commercialese* ('*per* fax or post/at the above address'). Surely, that letter would have been more business-like had it begun with the message described as its 'subject':

Dear Sir
We wish to place your company on our priority mailing list, and would be happy if you could fill in the form below and post it to us, or send the information sought by e-mail or fax.
Yours faithfully,

That 37-word text would have told the addressee all that was relevant to him, and not wasted his time with three paragraphs of gibberish.

Breech delivery always poses problems for the midwife. The baby on its way out feet or buttocks foremost is a threat to the mother, and must be turned about, so that it can be delivered in the normal head-first position.

Bottom-first messages cannot deliver. They need to be turned about, to be effective. Why are letters and messages worded in this 'bottom-first, head later' format? Its origin in India surely goes back to the East India Company *baniya*s, with whom form mattered more than message. Their letters had to begin with either an elaborate 'salutation', or a meaninglessly elaborate acknowledgment of a letter. That pushed the message down into an afterthought.

One can only wonder that we Indians should carry into the Internet models that belong to the age of the quill pen and dry sand (before blotting paper was invented). Here is another sample. The only meaningful message in this circular from an Institute of Chartered Accountants branch is tucked away in two sentences in the second last and last paragraphs. Each begins 'May we . . .'. All else only elaborates on, or repeats what was served in an earlier newsletter. The wording of the 'subject' shows the sender at least knew what his message was:

> Dear Member
> Sub: Request for Delegates to the GOLDEN JUBILEE CONFERENCE and Sponsorship
>
> You would have already received the information that Bangalore Branch of the Institute of Chartered Accountants

of India is organising a three-day Conference to mark the Golden Jubilee of the Institute on July 1st, 2nd and 3rd. The newsletter of June giving the details of the conference is again enclosed.

Ten seminars/workshops will be held *parallely* across various halls in this Conference and the delegates can attend any seminar at any time. These are seminars on . . . [the topics and who will address the delegates follow, in about 85 words].

For only Rs. 2,500/- the delegates will have the benefit of listening to eminent speakers at Bangalore. For delegates from out of Bangalore the fee is only Rs. 2,000. . . . May we request you to take this opportunity and depute your personnel to the Conference.

As already informed in the Newsletter this Conference is also a means of raising finance to complete our Building Project. May we also request you to support this effort through sponsorships. The brochure in this regard is also enclosed.

Thanking you
Yours faithfully,
CHAIRMAN

III

JOHN COMPANY *BABOO* AS HACK

16

Case for the defence

Nothing so well illustrates the failings of Indian English as our English-language papers. Every day, these papers prove that we haven't yet begun using English the way all languages are meant to be used: for exchange of ideas and thoughts, for everyday give and take. English for us remains a language that serves commerce, law, official dealings and administration. To understand where we go wrong, we have only to contrast the clarity, ease and flair in our regional-language dailies with the fuddy-duddy ways of our English-language papers.

The components of *Indlish* are *commercialese, officialese, legalese*, archaisms, and unidiomatic expressions. Anyone who wishes to write good, clear English needs to avoid them. But surely, this demands that he must first be able to *identify* them.

Thanks to the East India Company, we absorbed *commercialese* and *officialese* first, *legalese* later and fuddy-duddy literary Victorian English thereafter. The gross defects of English, therefore, became the essence of Indian English, and most of us accept without question precisely what is an aberration. Our English-language papers demonstrate this unquestioning acceptance every day.

India's English-language papers do not have a monopoly of *officialese*. It tends to get into papers in English-speaking countries too. But it is what journalists are trained to spot and keep away from. Here's what the guru of British journalists has to say:

> English has no greater enemy than *officialese*. Daily the stream of language is polluted by viscous verbiage. Meaning is clouded by vague abstraction, euphemism conceals identity, and words, words, words weigh the mind down.
> (Harold Evans, *Newsman's English*, London: Heinemann, 1972)

This is why it is important to identify *commercialese* and *officialese* that plague the use of English in India.

Indian English abounds in archaisms. This is especially evident in the Victorian euphemisms one finds in English-language papers, such as 'Police said he was *in an inebriated condition*' instead of 'He was drunk'. A prominent daily of Karnataka goes several steps further in its crime reports:

> A three-member gang waylaid two persons travelling on a scooter . . . and *relieved them* of their wrist watches and cash together worth Rs 5,500.

> A 50-year-old woman was *relieved of* her gold chain worth over Rs . . . in . . . on . . . .

> Six women were *relieved of* their gold chains in different chain snatching and cheating incidents reported in the city during the last 48 hours. A woman walking near the . . . bus stop in . . . was accosted by three motorcycle-borne miscreants and *relieved of* her gold chain . . . .

> Four women were *relieved of* their gold chains in a similar fashion . . . in a span of two and a half hours today evening.

> An elderly lady was *relieved of* her gold chain while she was walking . . . .

Those six examples from daily crime reports show the absurdity of archaic euphemisms. Money or gold chains aren't snatched, and no one is robbed. Each is *relieved* of a burden. Reporters in our English-language papers believe snatchers and 'miscreants' do a favour each time!

One would have to search pre-Victorian literature to find some words and expressions that appear with distressing regularity in English-language papers every day:

> A four-member dacoit gang struck again at . . . and *decamped* with seven tolas of gold items.
>
> The dacoits attacked the inmates of the house *in the wee hours* of the morning before they escaped into the darkness with the loot.
>
> BJP MP, Uma Bharati . . . had gone underground after the police visited her protest venue at the Secretariat complex here *in the wee hours* of May 5 to arrest her.
>
> In another case a person who had rented a car to reach Bangalore from Hyderabad reportedly *made away with* the car after throwing chilly powder at the driver . . . in the *wee hours* of the morning.
>
> According to Christian community leaders, four unidentified persons came in a car *in the wee hours* of today to St Peter's Church . . . with the intention of damaging it.
>
> The baby hippopotamus which was born at the Banerghatta National Park recently died *in the wee hours* of Saturday.

The Middle English word *wee* lives only in nursery rhymes such as *This little pig said wee, wee, wee, I can't find my way home/Wee Willie Winky runs through the town*. But our English-language papers keep this ludicrous archaism circulating, just as they do *decamped* in the first example. The latter comes from the East India Company's survey teams that pitched camp each evening and then *decamped* (demolished and left it) the next morning, when they moved on. Why a gang of dacoits should pitch camp anywhere near their target and leave clues when they *decamp* defies logic.

Archaic *commercialese* unknown outside business correspondence appears in almost all reports in our English-language papers:

> According to them, working of *the same in regard to* spice exports had not been encouraging.

> The police have booked several motorists for drunken driving and added that stern measures have been *initiated* to check *the same*.

> Mr Gowda said . . . that it was impossible to absorb the workers of government secretariat canteen as government employees. . . . The issue was also pending before the High Court and hence it was wise not to discuss *the same*, he added.

> Chief Minister . . . was extremely disgusted with the worthless expenditure and said: 'What can we do with this worn out equipment. The only option left with us is to dispose off [sic] *the same*.'

> The minister said the BMP alone owed the Social Welfare Department Rs Six crores which had been collected as beggar cess. But, the BMP had expressed helplessness to remit the fund on the grounds that *the same* had been diverted for other activities.

All these were printed in July 2000. Here is what Fowler said about such use over 75 years ago:

> *Same*, or *the same*, in the sense 'the aforesaid thing(s)/ person(s)', as a substitute for a pronoun (*it, him, her, them,*

they) was once good English, abundant in the Bible and the Prayer Book, but is now an *archaism*, surviving mainly in legal documents and *commercialese*.

(*A Dictionary of Modern English Usage*, Great Britain:
OUP, 1926)

Why do our English-language papers keep circulating all that is fuddy-duddy? Obviously, because the reporters and sub-editors who work for them absorbed all that is fuddy-duddy from the papers and books they read. And because no one taught them to identify *commercialese, officialese* and archaisms.

17

He noted, and said and added

A trainee journalist, who briefly interned with a newspaper, submitted her copy to a 'senior' reporter. He assumed a solemn look and, robot-like, inserted 'he noted', 'he added' and 'he said and added' at the end of several sentences. Having thus butchered a well-written piece, the 'senior' reporter told her patronisingly: 'Don't worry, you'll learn . . .'.

What the intern quickly learnt: India's English-language papers have reduced reporting to 'he said/she said'. Going by our English-language press, nothing ever *happens* in this country of 1,000 million; some of its people (usually semi-literate politicians) only *say* things that reporters tell us they 'noted', or 'said and added'. At least 80 per cent of the day's local news items in any English-language paper are 'he said/she said' pieces based on either press conferences, or briefing by officials. It's a wonder such newspapers employ reporters at all. A few stenographers would do the work better: at least they'd be more accurate. These 'stenos-alias-reporters' have little to do except tag on such phrases as *he said and added* to sentences they regurgitate after a briefing or copy from the handout that goes by the sanctimo-nious name of a 'Press Note'. After years of such mindless work, they come to believe (like the 'senior' reporter who 'corrected' the intern) that the craft of journalism lies in sprinkling some *mantra*s that convert gibberish to news.

Clerks of the East India Company were taught a rigid format for letters they copied. They had to begin with the day and the date, but only after they had penned *Dated:* with a flourish. The Company clerk learnt to so revere such *mantra* that he became convinced that if one were to omit the florid *Dated:*, the entry would convey no date at all!

When V S Naipaul said that journalism in India was a clerical pursuit, he did not specify whether he had the mindlessness of Indian journalists in mind. The language of reports in this daily shows the reverence that these clerks-turned-reporters have for their *mantras*:

> *Noting* that the position of women in Indian society has changed over the years, the Governor *opined* that . . . .
>
> Ms Rama Devi *noted* that women advocates have a persuasive approach. . . . The condition of women advocates has markedly improved . . . she *noted*.

What is one to make of such use of 'noted'? Dictionaries will not help us, for they make clear that the verb *note* is a formal way of saying 'to take notice of/give attention to/make a record of'. But then, a dictionary usually records contemporary meaning and usage. Some, like the *Concise Oxford Dictionary*, do carry notes on archaic usage. But not even the *COD* mentions an archaic use of 'noted' as a synonym for 'said'. Most dictionaries would describe *opine* as an archaic expression, in vogue around the seventeenth century. Reporters working for English-language papers, on the other hand, are convinced that *note* is a synonym for 'said'. Where do they get this conviction from?

Just as our clerks to this day cling to the orientation the East India Company gave their forebears, so India's English-language press reporters fall back on *journalese* of the pre-Victorian days. And in those days, English-language papers did indulge in such preposterous use of the word. No paper published in English-speaking countries would use *noted* in this absurd fashion today. But then, no reporter in India's English-language press would know that, for his reading is limited solely to what is churned out as 'Press Notes' by people whose orientation goes back to the East India Company!

Some reporters even opt for double attribution in their 'he said/she said' fare, as in the first sentence of the excerpt above. Each variant of this *mantra* can only confuse the reader:

> *Speaking* at a function organised by the India–China Friendship Society . . . he *said* . . . . The bilateral trade had been rapidly growing . . . he *noted.*

That absurd construction could have been rewritten to say 'Trade between India and China was growing rapidly, Mr . . . said today. He was speaking at a function organised by . . .'.

More variants:

> Chief Minister S M Krishna on Saturday categorically *denied* any mega project coming up in Uttara Kannada *stating* that he did not visualise any such big project in the district.

Better: 'No major project is coming up in Uttara Kannada. The Chief Minister scotched such rumours on Saturday.'

> *Stating* that corporate support for this project was encouraging, he *said* . . . .

Better: 'Corporate support for this project was encouraging, he said.'

> Minister for Kannada and Culture Rani Satish, who *spoke, called on* the pourakarmikas to take a pledge against alcohol consumption. She *pointed out* . . . BMP Commissioner . . . also *spoke*.

Better: 'Rani Satish, Minister for . . . asked pourakarmikas to . . .'

Other *mantra*s of the English-language paper's reporter are *said and added/he further said/further added/further noted*.

> Mr Gowda said the Congress had attempted to review the Constitution during Indira Gandhi's regime and the BJP had strongly opposed it. Now the roles have reversed, *he said and added* that both parties did not have a moral right to raise the issue.
>
> Mr Gowda *further said* the Janata Dal (Secular) was the only party . . . .

Since few journalists in India's English-language papers have a better acquaintance with English than the average lower-division clerk, it would be too much to expect them to understand the absurdity in '*both* parties *did not* have' (discussed in 'No Parking *Both* Sides', pp. 228–34).

The sub-editor could have improved that with: 'Mr Gowda said that when Congress tried to review the Constitution during Indira Gandhi's regime the BJP opposed the move tooth and nail. They had now reversed roles. *Neither* had the moral right to . . . .' Did the reporter import the two verbs (*said* and *added*) because he perceived the first five words ('Now the roles have reversed') to be the bit

that Mr Gowda *said* and the next twelve ('both parties . . . the issue') as the bit that he *added*? On what basis does a reporter divide a strand of thought into such bits? If the reader examines these bits, he will discover at least two patterns:

1 Some reporters obviously believe one should begin with *he said*, and alternate with *he added/he said and added/he also said*, regardless of whether what they report as having been *added* was an afterthought or no.

2 Others see *he added* as 'reporters' adhesive' with which to glue any part of their *he said/she said* hotchpotch to any other part, regardless of unity of thought.

18

Meanwhile, he pointed out

Mr Justice . . . of the Karnataka High Court has exhorted young advocates to utilise the *ensuing* summer vacation to *enrich* their legal knowledge. . . . Young advocates should particularly concentrate more on pleading and drafting, he *pointed out.*

That excerpt from a report in a Karnataka daily keeps the reader guessing:

1 The dictionary says *ensue* means *happen afterwards/ occur as a result.* How does that fit in with the court's annual summer vacation?

2 One *points out,* the dictionary tells us, what one wishes to *indicate/show/draw attention to.* The veteran judge, to go by the report, offered his advice to young lawyers at the annual day celebrations of the Advocates' Association at Bangalore. He neither indicated, nor showed them, nor drew their attention to, anything. But the English-language newspaper reporter will have him *pointing* his advice *out.*

Day after day, these reporters tell us of politicians and officials *pointing out* banalities to us, and to each other. Often, we have no means of knowing who pointed out what to whom, as in this editorial:

The recent attacks on missionary schools and convents in the Mathura and Agra region . . . are a throwback to similar harassment of Christians in Gujarat's Dangs district in December 1998. . . .

The UP Government and the district administration have taken the position that the attacks were localised events. . . . It has been *pointed out* that the incidents took place in the month of Easter, while the Dangs atrocities *also* took place in the Christmas week.

The reader can only wonder who did the pointing out here, and why the edit writer must hide behind the impersonal passive, the style of East India Company officials (discussed in 'Two Miscreants Aborted . . . and Escaped', pp. 113–18). Nor can the reader find an explanation for *also* in the last sentence, when the writer makes clear the two incidents did *not* occur at the same time.

With their *as per, decamped, further stated and added, ensuing, miscreants,* and such abracadabra, journalists stay rooted in obsolete expressions and remain a grotesque parody of the communicators they imagine they are. What, for example, does the reporter communicate here?

Mr Fernandes said that during his visit last month US President Bill Clinton had referred to the issue [India's claim to a permanent seat in the Security Council]. . . . But when *it was pointed out* that the US President had not really backed India's claim . . . .

Who pointed this out? The reporter who wrote this? What did whoever did the pointing out *show* Mr Fernandes? And why the impersonal passive?

Meanwhile

Because the English-language press reporter is caught in a time warp (between now and the East India Company days), he leaves his readers baffled each time he uses words that denote time past and present. One such word is *meanwhile*. The dictionary tells us that when used as a noun (*in the meanwhile*), it means *in the intervening period of time* ('I've sent my TV for repair; can I hire a set in the meanwhile?') The word may also be used as an adverb to mean *at the same time as something else happens* ('I'll pick up your laundry; could you check the household accounts meanwhile?') But reporters in English-language papers are convinced *meanwhile* is all-purpose glue with which to join unrelated facts in their *he said/she said* gibberish:

> KERC [Karnataka Electricity Regulatory Commission] Chairman . . . *notes* that . . . T & D [transmission and distribution] losses are fundamental to all other issues and it is not possible to tackle other things unless this is settled, he *states*.
>
> *Meanwhile*, the chief ministers themselves held the power portfolio in both J H Patel and S M Krishna Governments (ministers of state were also appointed).

If one were to go by the meaning of *meanwhile*, that gibberish would imply that it took the KERC chairman all of two chief ministers' tenures to *note* and *state* this!

> AICC President Sonia Gandhi will formally launch the . . . special package for development of Bellary district here on April 22. . . . This would be Ms Gandhi's first visit to Bellary after she won the seat. . . . *Meanwhile*, Superintendent of Police . . . said police had made elaborate security arrangements for Ms Gandhi's visit.

What may have been happening *during the period* police arrangements were being made to justify that *meanwhile*? The reader will never know.

Trying to make sense of the *Indlish* (often, Company

clerks' *pidgin*) in English-language newspapers takes expertise most readers cannot muster. A few examples of mystifying reports:

> The move was obviously *the sanctioned* by Mr Pawar . . . Mr Pawar, *though warned of 'ruthless action'* against the dissidents, *it is quite clear* that given the numbers game, the Maharashtra strongman *just* cannot afford to expel the dissident MLAs.

> It is also *to be recalled* that the BJP leader, Mr Gopinath Munde, *though withdrew the cases* against the Sena chief, Mr Bal Thackeray, when he was heading the home department *he did not withdrew* one case against Mr Thackeray pertaining to *the inflammatory* speech.

> When cornered by the Opposition on the suicides [by 16 farmers in Mahbubnagar], Civil Supplies Minister . . . attributed them to a psychological disorder and even offered to send a *team of doctors to examine the doctors.*

> The Hubli police have solved the mysterious murder of . . . by arresting his son. . . .
> After finishing last rites of his father, the accused . . . *admitted of committing the offence*, because of *financial crunch* . . . .
> The Commissioner said that accused along with a partner were running . . . after borrowing huge sum from a private finance company. . . . On occasions he *borrowed loan* to repay another loan. . . .
> The *motto behind* was to kill his father so that he did not have to *see the difficulties* in the family.
> The accused reportedly attempted three times to kill his father in last week, but *developed nervousness*.
> Finally, he got up at 3 am on Thursday to *commit the offence*. However, the other family members got up after hearing the dog bark continuously.

Again he got up at 4 am, *strangulated* . . . with the iron box wire and then hit him with the rod killing him on the spot.

Later, he poured kerosene in the *entire house* so as to *prevent* finger prints.

The commissioner said that when the wife of the accused got up . . . told her that somebody had killed his father. . . .

The other family members were asked to *inform the neighbours about the incident to the police and also to relatives.*

Replying to a question . . . [the commissioner] said the accused was a *dropped* engineering student.

Words fail me, as they clearly failed the author.

19

Two miscreants aborted . . .
and escaped

'Six Felicitated for Helping Nab Miscreants'. So screams the headline across three columns in a newspaper. The dictionary tells us that *miscreant* is an archaic word that meant *heretic*. In the Middle Ages, people branded as working against the Church were labelled *miscreants* (its Latin root *credere* means *faith/belief*) and were punished brutally, or were banished from their villages. The closest idea we'd be familiar with is *kafir*, the Arabic word for an infidel, or non-believer. The first paragraph of the news item said:

> Six persons who . . . rescued a car driver from the *clutches of* two *miscreants* recently were *felicitated* at a function organised in . . . .

What exactly had the *miscreants* done? How sinister were their *clutches*? Had they forced the car driver away from his faith, and did the six who rescued him manage to restore his creed? Another item about these *miscreants* did suggest a connection with the Church:

> *Miscreants* broke into a *church* in . . . on Sunday night and took away cash amounting to . . . . According to police . . . *miscreants gained entry into* the *church* by breaking window grills.

Only, their connection with the church had little to do with faith, and more to do with burglary.

To go by English-language newspapers in India, *people* turn into *miscreants* when a police officer briefs reporters. And it is the police officer who decides when one is to be described as which, as this report makes clear:

> Two motor-bike borne *miscreants* stabbed a petrol bunk worker in . . . . According to police, two *persons* on a motorbike came to a bunk located in . . . for refuelling . . . and picked a quarrel. . . . The two *miscreants* returned around 8 pm and stabbed . . . with a knife and escaped.

In the Middle Ages, a committee decided if someone accused of working against the Church was a *miscreant*. Reporters in English-language papers wait for a police verdict. A police inspector decided that as long as those two were on the motorbike, or off it and quarrelling, they were *persons*. They became *miscreants* only when they returned to the place after 8 pm (are then *miscreants* close cousins of vampires?)

The real problem is: the reader often has no clue what exactly a *miscreant* is supposed to be up to. To go by reports in English-language papers, he may be endowed with dangerous 'clutches' from which people need to be rescued (and the rescuers *felicitated*!) And again, he might be no more than an ordinary burglar. What, for instance, is the reader to understand from this account of what a senior police officer told reporters?

> He cited *an* example *of robbery incident* in HAL police stations where *miscreants* robbed 10 persons within half an hour.

To go by the emphasis on the singular number, there was either only one *robbery* or one *incident*, but for some strange reason, several police stations got into the melee. An undisclosed number of *miscreants* did their thing with 10 *persons* in (of all places) HAL police stations! And it all took half an hour!

Now and again, reporters do leave some clues for the reader:

> *Miscreants* broke into a video coverage shop in . . . and made away with electronic gadgets worth . . . .
>
> The *miscreants* had entered the house by breaking open the rear door, police said.
>
> Two *miscreants* who were attempting to *burgle* a house in . . . *aborted* their plan and escaped after assaulting two persons on . . . .

The reader is able to guess that as with those who got into the church, the *miscreants* in these three reports were *burglars*. What he cannot figure out is why then they aren't said to be *burglars*. Nor can he figure out why HAL police decided that those who 'robbed 10 persons within half an hour' were not *robbers*, but *miscreants*. To understand why, the reader needs a clue about how the English-language press reporter works.

The reporter on the 'crime beat' of a newspaper works as a stenographer of the police department; only, the paper that recruited him pays his salary. Similarly, the reporter assigned to corridors of administration functions as a steno of all the bureaucrats he calls upon, and so on. All they do is jot down what is no more than a dictation of whatever the officer has decided to feed the press.

This 'steno culture' preserves language handed down since the East India Company days. One can only suppose that during those days, some police officer somewhere used *miscreants* to describe some law-breaker he considered a greater scoundrel than others. Other officers may have liked the ring of the word, so that it then gained wider currency. Only research can show whether it ever indicated a specific crime.

The Company-day officers handed down a legacy for those who succeeded them, so that police officers to this day keep using this meaningless term, rather than a word that conveys any specific crime. Being faithful stenos of the police department, so do reporters – even when they have specific words that tell the reader the nature of the crime, e.g., *pickpocket, thief, burglar, robber, dacoit, murderer*, and so on. The reason: the English-language press reporter believes his work has nothing to do with informing his readers, and everything to do with playing stenos to officials.

The pity is reporters in the regional-language press often imitate what the English-language press does. And instead of shunning Raj-day gobbledygook, they force Sanskrit 'transliterations' of such meaningless terms on their readers. The Bengali press has invented *dushkritakari*; the Kannada press, *dushkarmi* (which too the Bengali press uses) as equivalents of the mystifying *miscreants*. Kannada tabloids, however, use more colourful words to describe wrongdoers: *kalla* (thief), *khadeema* (crook), *mosagaara* (cheat), 420, and so on.

Thus goes the whirligig that corrupts language all round. The language circulated by newspapers gets into the consciousness of all readers. The English-language newspapers keep circulating East India Company clerks' pidgin. As this gains circulation, readers believe pidgin is *journalese* and stop questioning whether the language they read is English. When the regional-language press reporter discovers wide acceptance of pidgin, he feels he would be left behind if he did not invent an equivalent. Because he does not delve deeper, he does not know that the pidgin was an invention of Company-day clerks and officials. His 'translation' imports an absurd expression the language could have done without. Regional-language papers bristle with present-day 'Sanskritisation' of Company-day pidgin.

The harm done by India's English-language newspapers does not stop at circulating pidgin (often accepted as *Indlish*). The contagion fouls our regional languages. The harm goes deeper than the use of absurd language: the absurdity seeps into our thinking. George Orwell spoke of another abuse, but his words apply so aptly to this process of thrusting respectability on pidgin: 'Such language becomes ugly and inaccurate because our thoughts are foolish, but the slovenliness of our language makes it easier for us to have foolish thoughts.'

20

Criminals with calling cards

Do criminals wear identity armbands? Are they supposed to leave calling cards behind after burgling houses? Do murderers leave whodunit notes on the bodies they leave behind them? To go by India's English-language press, that was always the rule; only, we ignorant readers never knew it.

Our English-language papers tell us we have three kinds of criminals: the 'unidentified' or 'unknown' criminal; the 'identified *as*' criminal; and 'miscreants'. The third is the more privileged sort. His identity is not to be questioned. Nor may readers know why. Reporters always take 'serious note' of the unprivileged criminal *not* identifying himself. This he promptly reports. Consider these recent reports:

> A youth, aged between 25 and 30 years, was found bludgeoned to death at . . . this morning. According to police, *unidentified* person [sic] murdered the youth, who's [sic] *identity* is yet to be ascertained, at some other place and later dumped the body at . . . .

To go by English-language papers, the 'unidentified' tag carries a significance the reporter understands, and the reader doesn't. Perhaps the reporter knows that the 'identified *as*' tag can mean that police imposed an identity on the criminal; not that it was his. The criminal with an identity therefore gets only the reporter's scorn: 'Police arrested one Kallu, resident of . . .'. Such a criminal can at most be the *object* of the police action (the arrest). The unidentified criminal is always the *subject* of the reporter's sentence:

> *Unidentified* men looted a convent in Jhansi in UP and desecrated the prayer room of the nuns.

The lack of identity so enthuses the reporter that he forgets, for instance, that vehicles carry number plates:

> A 70-year-old woman was fatally knocked down by an *unidentified* vehicle in . . . last night . . . .
>
> A 35-year-old cyclist died after some *unknown* vehicle knocked him down at . . . last night.

The mystery of the missing identity thickens when *miscreants* get into their act. Because of some unidentified understanding between police officers and reporters, nobody ever mentions that criminals fail to leave calling cards:

> Some *miscreants* broke into a building housing the . . . Cooperative Society in . . . and made away with Rs . . . on Thursday night.

Once a police officer tags *miscreant* to a criminal, the English-language press reporter asks no questions. Perhaps the very word implies an identity that police and reporters keep secret from the reader:

> *Miscreants* on . . . attacked a jeep being used for publicity [by a missionary]. . . . The police chief said that three persons came in the jeep from . . . . On the way, some youths, *who were not identified* by the police, suddenly stopped the jeep. They began to *smash the windows* of the jeep with stones.

The youths stoned the jeep *in which the panes of the vehicle* were damaged. The tape recorder inside the jeep was also destroyed.

Reporters keep mum about the *miscreant*'s identity even when he is up to something more dastardly:

Three *miscreants*, posing as cops, intercepted a . . . truck near . . . and robbed the truck driver of . . . after assaulting him with a knife. . . . The truck driver succumbed to injuries he had sustained while being shifted to hospital.

Nothing more is said about the identity of the *miscreants*, and the report goes on to identify the victim:

The deceased has been identified as . . . a native of Trichy.

In a month-long search, I found only one mention of the lack of a *miscreant*'s identity:

A 50-year-old woman was *relieved of* her gold chain worth over Rs 21,000 by some *unidentified miscreant* in . . . . Police said . . . a resident of . . . was walking on . . . when the *miscreant* came from behind and snatched the gold chain.

Perhaps this reporter was a greenhorn, so the sub-editor decided to compensate the *miscreant* by presenting the snatching as a favour: she was *relieved* of the burden of her chain!

Now and then, reporters are prompted (perhaps by police officers) to show more concern for the identity of hapless human beings:

A 65-year-old beggar died on the spot after a truck ran over him in . . . . The *identity* of the deceased is yet to be ascertained.

A 30-year-old woman was found murdered in . . . . The *identity* of the deceased is yet to be established.

Reporters apparently have to follow a complicated set of
rules on the identity of offenders. To go by what is published,
questions about identity must not be raised when large
groups go on the rampage:

> The trouble began . . . when about 40–50 people pulled down
> the idol of Shivaji at . . . and later damaged some tempos.

The reader may not be told anything about the identity of the
40 or 50 people. But if the offenders are a more manageable
number, their identities become important, whether the
reader can recognise them or not:

> In a major breakthrough . . . police busted a fake currency
> racket. . . . Six persons . . . have been arrested. . . . A police
> team rushed to . . . and picked up four persons for question-
> ing. The four, *identified as* . . . [the name and age of each
> follows].

As already discussed in 'Two Miscreants Aborted . . . and
Escaped', pp. 113–18, the regional language press falls back
on Sanskrit to convey such *mantras* as have been handed
down from the East India Company days. The Bengali press
has come up with the *agyataparichay* criminal; the Kannada
press is close with *aparichita aparadhi*.

Our colonial hangover accords an undeserved importance
to English-language newspapers that care about neither
quality nor content: getting their advertisement revenue is all
that matters. Their reporters' only function is to mindlessly
regurgitate whatever they are fed by officials who brief them.
Language is the first casualty in this process, and meaning the
second. The language that English-language papers circulate
is *officialese* – mostly automatic expressions that convey no
meaning.

Served such meaningless language day after day, readers stop questioning the relevance of the information in English-language papers. What relevant information, for instance, does the reader gather from being told that a vehicle that knocked down an old woman at night was not identified? How is the reader any the wiser when he is told that some *unidentified* person murdered an *unidentified* youth?

The English-language press cultivates the bureaucracy and police. And its reporters' jobs end at picking up a daily dose of fossil administrative jargon. The meaningless language in their reports shows the harm done to their minds. The circulation of such language can only harm young readers.

21

The member charged . . . and the minister assured

The reporter in India's English-language paper is in his element when he covers a press conference, speech or seminar. Such assignments are tailor-made for the *he said/she said* format that is the staple of his trade: all he need do is regurgitate some scraps, and punctuate these with *he noted/he stated/he said and added/and he further stated*. These '(in)elegant variations' for the plain 'he said' are the *mantra*s the novice reporter memorises first. Imagine therefore the glee of the reporter assigned to the State Assembly or Parliament. These assignments are the high point of his career, a-bristle with *he said/she said* situations. Little wonder he runs amok, throws off any journalistic skills he ever acquired, and foxes his readers.

His method is simple: he keeps using some transitive verbs intransitively. Since the transitive verb requires an object, and the intransitive one doesn't, the latter lightens the reporter's burden: he can do away with the need to remember its object and the related details. Thus, he memorises another set of *mantra*s to chant: *assured, charged,* and *informed*. By using these as intransitives, he eliminates the need to remember their objects. Consider these excerpts:

> Chief Minister S M Krishna today assured in the Legislative
> Assembly that he will ensure due recognition to the
> Opposition party members in functions organised by the
> government.

That leaves the reader wondering who in the Assembly
the Chief Minister picked out to extend this assurance to.
Readers know that *assured* is a transitive verb – so named
because the action in such a verb passes over (transits) to its
object. To omit the object leaves the message incomplete.
But to use it correctly, the reporter needs to learn a bit
of grammar, and remember the object of the verb. Since
meaning and message rarely matter in India's English-
language newspapers, the reporter can (and always does)
scoff at the idea of having to learn or remember anything.

The text of the report says an Opposition member had
alleged that a minister had asked a senior bureaucrat to
exclude Opposition members from government functions.
Here is one way that could have been made clear: 'The Chief
Minister today assured members of the Opposition that they
would never be excluded from government functions.'

> Speaker M V Venkatappa assured that he would ensure that
> the minister would immediately send an officer to Hassan
> today itself.

Who did the Speaker give this assurance to? What does *itself*
add to *today*? It would be clearer as: 'The Speaker assured
the House that the minister would send an officer to Hassan
today.'

> BJP member . . . wanted the government to take effective
> measures to curb fake raids and trappings. The Chief
> Minister assured to look into specific instances.

Was this assurance given to the BJP member? What language is this? Clearer: 'The Chief Minister assured the member that he would look into . . . .'

Charge

The meaning of *charge* as a transitive verb varies according to the preposition that follows it. Your bank may charge the cost of some service *to* your account; police may charge you *with* rash driving, and a magistrate could *charge* you a penalty for the traffic offence. But the intransitive *charge* usually implies making a rushing attack ('into the valley of death charged the six hundred'). In the English-language paper, the word is almost always used intransitively, and the reader can only wonder who charged through the news report like a bull in a china shop – the reporter, or the sub-editor?

> (Lok Shakti) today charged that the State Government has not initiated any action against some civil servants, though the Lokayukta had booked cases against them.

What was probably meant: '. . . today charged the State Government with refusal to act against some civil servants the Lokayukta had booked.'

> Tabling a question in this regard, Mr Vakil charged that despite bringing the irregularities to the notice of the government, no action had been taken.

Who brought the irregularities to the government's notice – Mr Vakil, or others? If he tabled a question, in what other 'regard' could he have done it? Clearer: 'Mr Vakil, who had tabled a question, alleged that the government refused to act even after being told of the irregularities.'

> Raising the matter during zero hour . . . said that . . . the
> Governor was made to sit slightly lower than the Swamijis
> on the dais. And, this was done at the behest of . . . he charged.

Indian legislators often do charge at each other, and hurl
microphones and chairs. Whom did this man charge –
the Speaker, or the man at whose 'behest' this was done?
Clearer: 'The Governor was made to sit at a level lower
than . . . dais. This, he alleged, was done at the behest
of . . . .'

Informed

Well may the *Concise Oxford Dictionary* tell us that inform
is a transitive verb that is followed by its object (*informed
them of their rights/informed us that the train was late*).
India's English-language pressmen dispense with the object
and thrust the infinitive (*to*) after the word:

> This was informed to Congress Member of Parliament . . . by
> Minister of State for Water Resources . . . in a written answer
> in Lok Sabha.

Better: 'The Minister of State . . . told the Congress MP in a
written answer.'

> The amount . . . to be sanctioned . . . for conducting the
> census 2001 was about . . . . Informing this to . . . Minister
> of State for Home . . . said . . . .

Better: 'The amount . . . was about . . . the Minister of State
for Home told . . . .'

> The chief executive officer, Zila panchayat, Bijapur,
> has informed that there are several complaints against
> these NGOs in respect of implementation of watershed
> programmes.

Better: 'There were complaints about the way these NGOs had built watersheds, the . . . officer . . . Bijapur, said.'

Going by the number of Indians who use English, ours is the third largest English-speaking country in the world. That, if nothing else, makes correct use of English important to us all. To quote Harold Evans, guru of British journalists, 'No professor of linguistics has as much influence on the language as the deskman who edits the day's news.' That holds true for India's English-language papers too. Because these papers do nothing to train their reporters and sub-editors into exacting standards, the gibberish they circulate seeps into the reader's subconscious. India's English-language press thrives because the English language is still used in India. Yet it does the greatest harm to its use.

22

With regard to the matter regarding . . .

India's English-language papers are much possessed by *regards*, yet show scant regard for their readers. News reports and editorials bristle with quaint *regard* phrases. To go by English-language papers, officials, politicians or people whom reporters consider important never utter anything *about* or *on* something; they always say things either *regarding* the 'issue' or add some banality *in this regard*. The second expression is a riddle. Fowler does not mention such an expression in his *Dictionary of Modern English Usage* (OUP, 1926). Frederick T Wood (in *Current English Usage*, Macmillan, 1962) tells us that the constructions are:

> to *have regard to* (no *-s*)
> *with regard to* (no *-s*)
> *as regards* (verb)
> *to have regard for*
> *give one's regards to* (= pay one's respects)
> *with kind regards* (the formal ending of a letter to friends or acquaintances)

But day after day, some dailies insist on using the little-known and less-used expression *in this regard*:

> Minister for . . . today declined to write off . . . dues owed by cashew traders in the State. However, he said the traders may pay the dues in instalments.

> Replying to *a matter* raised *in this regard* during zero hour in the legislative assembly, the Minister said . . . .

That leaves the reader nonplussed on at least three counts:

1 To go by the sense intended, the Minister replied to a question *on* the cashew traders' dues. What do the ten words (*matter . . . assembly*) tell the reader that isn't conveyed by 'Replying to a question during zero hour, the Minister said . . .'?

2 The Minister was replying to a question on the traders' dues (how does one *reply* to *a matter*?); in what 'other' *regard* might he have said what he did?

3 Does *in this regard* mean *on*, as it seems to do here?

We might look at more examples for an answer to the third question:

> Transport Minister . . . today informed the Legislative Council that an enquiry officer had been appointed to probe into the affairs of the Death cum Retirement Benefit Fund of the . . . employees.
> The final claims are now being settled by taking permission of the High Court *as per* its order *in this regard*.

The reader must spend some time clearing that jungle to get at the message:

> The High Court had passed an order *on* settling claims.
> The Minister said claims were being settled according to the court's directive.

That leaves a few things unclear: Why had permission to be sought to act as the court had ordered? If the court had passed an order on settlement of the claims, in what *regard* other than the claims could that order apply to? What extra information is the reader supposed to gather from *in this regard*? If the minister meant the 11 words 'The claims are

being settled according to the High Court's order', why did
the reporter/sub-editor create a fog with 21?

In that second example too, *in this regard* means no more
than *on*. More examples:

> Chief Minister . . . today said that he will take up with
> Union Information Minister . . . the reduction in duration of
> Kannada programmes on the main channel of Doordarshan.
> Intervening during question hour, he said he had already
> drawn the attention of the Centre *in this regard*.

The reader must first translate that mumbo-jumbo into
sense:

> Chief Minister . . . today said he would take up with the
> Union Information Minister . . . the pruning of Kannada
> programmes on Doordarshan's main channel. . . . He said he
> had already sounded the Centre on this.

Here, *on this* makes things clearer than *in this regard*.

> Fire services will not be available free of cost for industries
> in future if the suggestion made by the Department of Fire
> Services is accepted by the state government.
> Home Minister . . . assured the Fire Services Department of
> considering the suggestion *in this regard* which was made by
> the DGP and Director of Fire Services at a function organised
> here today to present the Chief Minister's Medals to fire
> personnel.

Did the reporter mean:

> At a function where he presented the Chief Minister's medals
> to firemen today, Home Minister . . . said he would consider
> the suggestion the DGP and Director of Fire Services had
> made on getting industries to pay for firemen's services.

The report later makes clear those officials suggested that a
portion of the insurance money industries collected for fire

damage should be paid to the department for putting fires out. In this example, *on* does the work that *in this regard* botches.

What then does *in this regard* mean? The *Concise Oxford Dictionary* says it means *a respect, a point attended to*. The *Cambridge International Dictionary of English* shows how the phrase is used:

> The union is the largest in the country and *in this/that regard* is best placed to serve its members.

But that is nowhere near the sense in which the phrase is used in our dailies. To go by the Cambridge dictionary, the meaning comes closer to *on this/that count*, or *in this/that respect/thus*.

Other *regard* phrases are used where a single preposition would suffice. Of such Victorian long-windedness that India's English-language press refuses to be weaned from, Fowler said as long ago as 1926 that sentences in which *about* can serve for *with regard to* and *in* for *in regard to* 'are near everyday expressions of a practice . . . [that] cumulatively spoils a writer's style and injures the language.'

Fifty years ago, Ernest Gowers laid down this advice in *The Complete Plain Words* (first published as *Plain Words*, 1948): 'If two words convey your meaning equally well, choose the common one rather than the less common. Do not prefer *regarding, respecting* or *concerning* to *about*, or say *advert* for *refer*, or *state, inform, acquaint*, or *advise* when you might use the word *say* or *tell*.' But English-language press reporters in India *will* cling to their Company-day orientation:

> Primary and Secondary Education Minister . . . announced that the State government is considering a proposal to involve

parents while framing curriculum for primary schools. . . .

Regarding the new education policy, the minister said that it would be announced only after holding extensive deliberations with the public, educationists, students and parents *regarding* its content.

The opinion of the public *regarding* the ... have already started pouring in.

This, then, is the situation *in regard to* our English-language newspapers:

- Each is up with the latest, but each competes with the other *in regard to* use of pre-Mutiny, Company-day language.
- Reporters and sub-editors in each specialise in gibberish, and shun books *with regard to* usage and grammar.
- Reporters and sub-editors in each will fall back on expressions used by their forebears, *regardless of* distortion or absence of sense.
- Since ad revenue is all that their owners *have regard for*, they cannot *have regard to* non-revenue matters such as need for training and quality.

23

In their respective dhotis and saris, respectively

The use of legal and official jargon in everyday dealing is a feature of *Indlish*, and in this, our English-language newspapers take the cake. Reports and editorials bristle with words that are dragged in to affect thoroughness, but achieve stiffness or obscurity. One bit of *officialese* favoured by editorial writers and reporters is *respective/respectively*. 'Delight in these words', Fowler said 75 years ago, 'is a widespread but depraved taste . . . of ten sentences in which they occur, nine would be improved by their removal' (*A Dictionary of Modern English Usage*, OUP, 1926).

Fowler sorted examples he had collected into six groups:

1   in which the words (*respective/respectively*) give information needed by sensible readers
2   in which they give information that may be needed by fools
3   in which they say again what is said elsewhere
4   in which they say nothing intelligible
5   in which they are used wrongly for some other word
6   in which they give a positively wrong sense.

Examples like the following could serve well to illustrate some of Fowler's conclusions:

The Commissioner for Public Instruction has requested all

teachers of the Department of Public Education to register
their names for election duty during the Zilla Panchayat and
Taluk Panchayat elections which have been scheduled for
June 2 and June 6, *respectively*.

The *respectively* is supposed to make clear that the first
would be held on June 2 and the second, on June 6. But
greater clarity and ease can be got with '. . . during the
zilla panchayat poll on June 2, and taluk panchayat poll on
June 6'. The word injects stiffness into a sentence:

> Twins Divya and Dinesh of Pavan English Medium School,
> who scored 90 and 92 per cent, *respectively*, also want to
> pursue engineering.

Although that ties up the two subjects with the single verb
scored, the stiffness can be smoothened with 'Divya scored
90 per cent, and her twin Dinesh, 92, from Pavan English
Medium School; both wish to pursue engineering.'

Sir Ernest Gowers said 50 years ago: '*Respective* and
respectively are used wrongly or unnecessarily far more
often than they are used rightly, and I advise you to
leave them alone. You can nearly always get on without
them' (*The Complete Plain Words*, first published as *Plain
Words*, 1948).

These four excerpts from a single news item show the
truth of Fowler's and Gowers' words:

> As many as two medical colleges and thirteen dental colleges
> have not been permitted by the Medical Council of India and
> the Dental Council of India *respectively* to admit students this
> year.

The meaning would have been clearer, and the sentence rid
of *officialese*, with either 'Permission to admit students has
been denied to two medical colleges by the MCI, and to

13 dental colleges by the DCI' or 'The MCI has barred two medical colleges, and the DCI, 13 dental colleges, from admitting students.'

> In the provisional medical and dental matrix for admissions to first year MBBS and BDS *respectively* was [sic] notified here on Tuesday, the government has fixed the total number of medical seats this year at 2,370.

The *respectively* here can only serve the fool who could possibly confuse MBBS with BDS even after *medical* and *dental* had been specified. The omission of *respectively* and *was* helps sense, but leaves unclear whether the 'total number of medical seats' includes those for dentistry.

In the next two, *respectively* (to quote Fowler) says nothing intelligible:

> As many as 89 and 33 seats have been allotted to religious and linguistic minority colleges under the management quota and NRI quota *respectively*.

> As many as 112 and 44 seats have been allotted to religious and linguistic minority colleges under the management quota and NRI quota *respectively*.

Nor does *respectively* say anything intelligible in this excerpt from an editorial:

> The present gap between operational cost per kilometer [sic] and revenue is Rs 14.50 and Rs 13.75 *respectively*.

The *gap* between the two can only be a single sum. The hack must have meant not the *gap* between cost and revenue, but the *figures* for them (read: 'For each kilometre, the operational cost is Rs 14.50 and the earning, Rs 13.75'). Editorial writers in English-language papers cannot resist the lure of meaningless *officialese*. They are convinced it persuades readers of their thoroughness.

T. P. SECTION
For Photocopying

I am sending_____Sheet(s).

Please make_____Copy/Copies

Total Copy/Copies_____

This is for official purposes.

*Date*_____   *Signature*

Fowler said *respective* and *respectively* are used wrongly for some other word. Often, the first is used where *each* would be appropriate, as here:

> The delimitation and reservation of the constituencies have been made according to the norms of the election commission, *in* proportionate [sic] to the population of the *respective* constituency, he said.

Omit *in* and read: '. . . proportionate to *each* constituency's population'.

The use of meaningless words becomes a habit with our pressmen, and they cease to examine what they write:

> 'The zilla and taluk panchayat elections are a real challenge to the party and the ministers in charge of their *respective* districts will have to be accountable,' he said.

The *respective* here can only serve the fool to whom its omission would imply that ministers would be accountable for districts *other* than those they were in charge of.

In each of these four excerpts from a single report on the recent election to the legislative council, *respective/respectively* needs to be deleted for euphony:

> While the Congress bagged eight seats, the BJP and the JD(U) won two and one seat *respectively*.

Better: 'While the Congress bagged eight seats, the BJP won two, and the JD(U) one.'

> Mr P and Mr Y had been members of the Assembly for three and four terms *respectively* before they lost the 1999 Assembly elections.

Better: 'Before they lost the 1999 elections, Mr P had been a member of the Assembly for three terms, and Mr Y, for four.'

Among the first-time legislators, Ms J N, Mr K, and Ms V G have been active in their *respective* parties for a long time.

They could hardly have been active in parties other than theirs; omit *respective*.

Mr K who is from Bangalore and Mr M of Gulbarga, are not known names in politics and they made it to the council because of their proximity to Chief Minister . . . and Home Minister . . . *respectively*.

Better: 'Neither is well known in politics, but made it to the council because of their connections: Mr K of Bangalore is close to the Chief Minister, and Mr M of Gulbarga, to the Home Minister.'

Fowler said: '. . . *respective(ly)* are words seldom needed, but . . . pretentious or meticulous writers drag them in at every opportunity for the air of thoroughness and precision they are supposed to give to a sentence – a fault to which lawyers and officials are specially prone.' Fowler couldn't have known that India's English-language press would vow to foster the lingo of lawyers and officials, and shun the language of everyday human dealing.

24

A facility for *facilities*

Because a newspaper is supposed to inform readers, one would imagine that reporters would choose words that convey concrete information. Reporters in India's English-language papers, however, prefer words that can mean all things in general and nothing in particular. These they acquire from the official handouts they are given. Such words serve officials well, because they are more often concerned with keeping back information. When reporters, supposed to be concerned with serving it, adopt the vocabulary of stuffy officials, readers are left groping for meaning and message.

Among the *officialese* used by English-language press reporters and editorial writers is *facility/facilities*. The dictionary tells the reader:

1 The singular form means *ease/fluency/skill/ability* (as in *facility of expression*).
2 The plural form means the *building(s)/equipment/services/resources* for doing something.

Going by those meanings, he is often left clueless over the spatter of *facilities* he finds in news reports. A few typical examples:

> The controversy over the free phone *facility*, promised for
> telecom employees took a new turn today with the Finance

Ministry distancing itself from the Telecom Ministry's decision.

What ability or fluency can *facility* imply here? The intended sense would become clearer if the word were deleted: 'The controversy over free phones for telecom employees took a new turn today . . . .'

The reporters fall back on the plural form of the word when they are unsure of their facts and can say nothing concrete:

> [In rural hospitals] Although there are some *facilities* for blood examination and emergency treatment for malaria, *facilities* for treatment of jaundice and viral fever are lacking.

What are *some facilities* for blood examination? Does the reporter mean a rural hospital has equipment to carry out only some simple tests such as blood count? What are *facilities for . . . emergency treatment* as opposed to routine treatment of malaria? What are *facilities* for treating jaundice? Jaundice of which kind? Medical science hasn't yet come up with cures for viral attacks. What instruments/appliances/procedures (*facilities*) for treating viral fever has the reporter seen in urban hospitals?

The way editorials are strewn with the word leaves one wondering whether *facilities*-wallahs aren't specially recruited to write them:

> The Centre has now embarked on a comprehensive action plan (2000–03) to popularise rainwater harvesting. This includes among other things . . . provision of one lakh rural drinking water wells with recharge *facilities*. . . .
>
> Government organisations should act as *facilitators* and provide all technical and financial support for creating the *facilities* for the success of the programme.

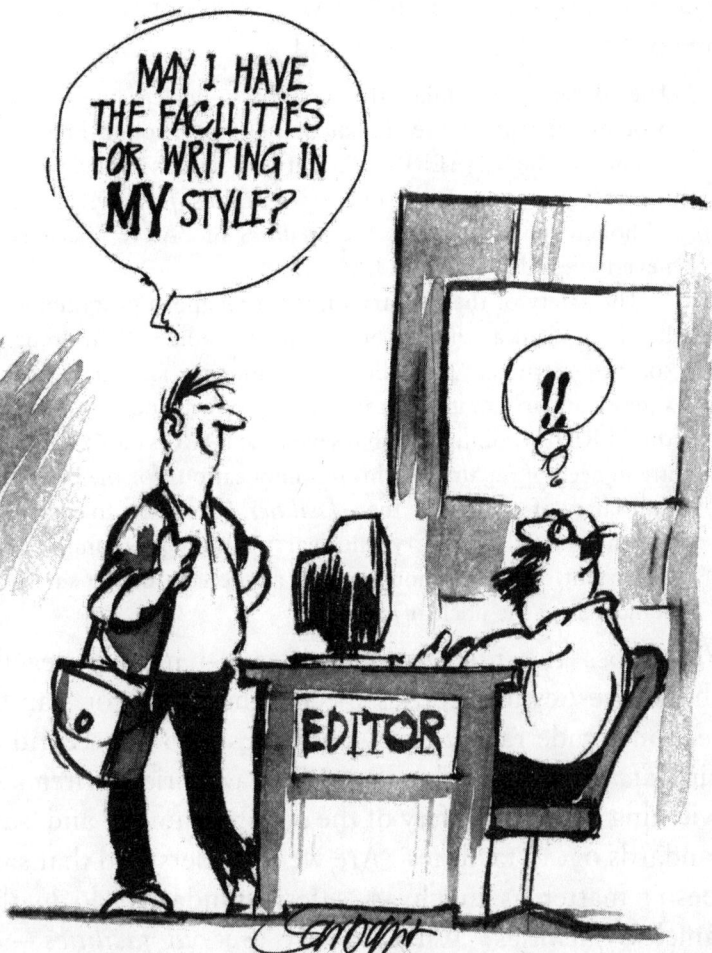

Does the first bit mean that these wells will be equipped with some special device that collects and so fills them with rain water? What *facilities* (building/equipment) would technical and financial support *create* – the rechargeable wells? But that's what the Centre's action plan will provide. The last sentence is a vacuous refrain almost all edits carry: no matter what the subject, the editorial writer will affect a know-all tone of banal advice to the world.

> The decision to take the country's nuclear weapons programme out of the jurisdiction of the Atomic Energy Regulatory Board (AERB) ... could have serious implications for safety standards of nuclear weapons *facilities*. . . . Although the AERB uses the *facilities* of BARC . . . it is nevertheless distinct from BARC. . . .
>
> The safety of the country's nuclear weapons programme has been cited as the reason for the decision. . . . In doing so, the government is sidelining the more crucial issue of the safety standards of its nuclear *facilities*. A former chairman of the AERB has pointed out that several of BARC's old *facilities* are in need of repair, and this has implications for the health and safety of workers in these *facilities*. . . . Action to ensure the safety of the country's nuclear weapons programme is important. But it cannot be done at the cost of the safety standards of the nuclear *facilities*.

What does the first *facilities* mean – nuclear reactors/laboratories/testing houses/special chambers for handling weapons-grade radioactive substances? Do the second and third *facilities* mean the same? The editorial writer keeps switching between 'safety of the . . . programme' and 'safety standards of . . . facilities'. Are we to understand that safety doesn't matter as much as 'safety standards' do in these nameless *facilities*? What exactly are *old facilities* – old buildings, reactors and labs? Does this dump of *facilities* mean anything to anyone? What did it mean to the author? Obviously, he didn't have a clue about the subject, and so he created a fog with a plethora of *facilities*.

> The Union Human Resource Development Ministry's proposal . . . to increase the tuition fee for students of all universities and colleges . . . does not come as a surprise. . . . Some of the colleges in States such as Orissa, Andhra Pradesh . . . are ill-equipped and do not have proper infrastructural *facilities*. Higher tuition fee would help them mobilise resources which could be utilised on improving buildings, furniture and library and laboratory *facilities*. . . . Those belonging to the lower middle income groups . . . would certainly face problems because of higher tuition fee. To help them, the Government could extend *facilities* such as book banks, lending libraries and liberalise norms for providing easy loans. . . .
>
> The proposal for curtailment of subsidies on account of hostel, electricity . . . is pragmatic. . . . But this should in no way affect those belonging to the poorer and weaker sections of society. For instance, it is only because of subsidised hostel *facilities* that . . . tribals and other downtrodden classes are able to send their children for education.

What are the '*proper* infrastructural facilities' that these colleges lack, and which *improper* facilities do they possess? Higher tuition fees would bring them more money, and they could then afford better buildings and furniture, etc. What 'resources' would the higher tuition fees 'help them mobilise?' Obviously, this *mantra* comes from the official handouts. Authors chant it whenever they talk about getting and spending. Most news writers use *facilities* when they can think of nothing concrete; this editorial writer tags it to concrete notions: buildings, furniture, library and laboratory, book banks, lending libraries, easy loans, subsidised hostels. He is convinced he need only sprinkle this fail-safe *mantra* among words he strings together and readers will be impressed.

25

This involves the involvement of . . .

Among the all-purpose words that turn news vague in English-language dailies are *involve/involvement*. Of *involve*, Fowler said 75 years ago: 'This word is overworked as a general-purpose verb that saves the trouble of precise thought. . . . The proper meaning of *involve* is wrap up, and so entangle, embarrass . . .' (*A Dictionary of Modern English Usage*, OUP, 1926). Reporters in our English-language dailies to this day grab *involve/involvement* rather than search for a more precise word whenever they write about road accidents, crime, shady deals, and people's participation in some activity.

Some typical examples:

> The driver of the Rajasthan State Road Transport Corporation bus *involved* in the collision with the jeep driven by Congress leader Rajesh Pilot has been booked . . . for negligent driving.

If the bus *hit* the jeep, it might explain why its driver was booked; 'involved in the collision' means that the bus was as involved in it as the jeep was. Why then book its driver?

> One more person succumbed to the injuries he had suffered in the accident *involving* three vehicles on . . . .

Better: 'One more person died of the injuries he suffered *in* the three-vehicle collision on . . . .'

> The minister said a study conducted by the NIMHANS showed that deaths *involving* two-wheeler accidents were on the rise since 1997. . . . According to a study conducted by NIMHANS the death *involving* two wheelers in Bangalore is as follows . . . .

Just how does death 'wrap up, and so entangle/embarrass' two-wheeler accidents/two-wheelers? The first bit would be clearer as 'NIMHANS showed that deaths *in* two-wheeler accidents have been increasing since 1997' and the second, as 'A NIMHANS study cites these figures for fatal two-wheeler accidents in Bangalore.'

Reporters seldom bother about a more apt word for *involvement* in wrongdoing or crime:

> Kallis said he was amazed to hear that Cronje was involved in wrongdoing. . . . 'I was absolutely shattered . . . I thought he was the last person in the world who would do such a thing,' he said.

More precise: 'Kallis said he was amazed to hear that Cronje had *stooped* to this . . . .'

> Cronje, Williams and Gibbs have been offered immunity . . .
> if they come clean on their *involvement* in match-fixing.

More precise: '. . . if they come clean on their *role* in fixing matches.'

> Pakistani cricket umpire Javed Akhtar has rejected as 'a load of rubbish' the statement by South African cricket chief Ali Bacher that he was *involved* in match-fixing.

Clearer: '. . . the statement . . . that he *fixed/helped fix* matches . . . .'

> Sources did not rule out the *involvement* of officials of the BMP, politicians and other government officials in the scam.

Better: '. . . did not rule out connivance/collusion *of* BMP officials, politicians . . . .'

> As the political scenario gets murkier, several ministers, senior party leaders and their kins [sic] are getting more and more *involved* in the cable war and other shady deals. Mr Patel's son's *involvement* in several land deals in Saurashtra is well known. . . . Mr S, a known underworld don and an independent municipal councillor then, was indicted by the Srikrishna Commission for his *involvement* in the 1992–93 Mumbai riots.

Better: '. . . are getting *deeper into* the cable war . . ./Most people know of the shady land deals Mr Patel's son *clinched in* Saurashtra/. . . was indicted . . . for his *role in* the 1992–93 Mumbai riots.'

> The Corps of Detectives (CoD) today arrested a person for his alleged *involvement* in a multi-crore land scam in which properties worth . . . was sold by fabricating documents.

Better: '. . . arrested a man who allegedly *forged* documents and sold property worth . . . .'

Reporters become entangled in such lingo when police officers brief them on crime:

> Twelve members of a dacoit gang which was *involved* in nine dacoities and a murder for gain has been arrested by . . . . According to the police . . . M H, main accused, who was on the run for the last four years, was *involved* in the sensational Bombay Hamid murder case . . . and was *involved* in a kidnap case in . . . a dacoity in . . . and extortion in . . . . R was *involved* in a kidnap case in . . . . Another accused, S, was *involved* in theft cases in . . . . Apart from stealing goods-laden trucks, the gang was also *involved* in vehicle-lifting.

That, in everyday human language, means: 'Twelve of a gang

wanted for nine dacoities and a murder were arrested/Police said M H, who had been on the run for the past four years, was wanted also in connection with the Bombay Hamid murder, a kidnapping in . . . a dacoity in . . . and extortion in . . ./R was wanted for kidnapping in . . . and S for thefts in . . ./The gang had hijacked goods-laden trucks and other vehicles.'

Reporters seem to believe no other word can serve when they must convey the sense of participation in some activity or a movement:

> The All India Muslim Law Board will *involve* Imams of mosques to accelerate its drive for social reforms.

More precise: 'The . . . Board will urge/plead with/ask Imams to help speed its drive for social reforms.'

> Delivering a lecture on 'controlling corruption through information technology' . . . he said that he was also thinking of *involving* college students in fighting corruption. . . . He said that he was also thinking of *involving* voluntary organisation [sic] and retired officials as honorary vigilance officers to help in trapping corrupt officials.

Less vague: '. . . he was thinking of getting college students and voluntary organisations to fight corruption. . . . He wondered if retired officials might act as honorary vigilance officers and help trap corrupt officials.'

> Tamil Manila Congress leader G K Moopanar today welcomed Foreign Minister Jaswant Singh's offer . . . to the Sri Lankan Government and said . . . the LTTE and other Tamil parties should be *involved* in the negotiations.

More precise: '. . . and said . . . the LTTE and other Tamil parties should *participate in/join* the negotiations.'

Fifty years ago, Sir Ernest Gowers found *involvement*

'a vague word which is . . . being reached for too often as a cosy substitute for exact meaning, and there are signs that it may before long become not merely tiresome but menacing to the language' (*The Complete Plain Words*, first published as *Plain Words*, 1948).

26

Making an issue of it

Reporters in India's English-language papers dread words that stand alone. They will maim them, and give each a crutch. They will then use the word leaning on its crutch; never independently. Manufactured in merchant and government offices during the colonial days, some such crutches are *condition, issue, position, problem, purpose(s), question* and *situation*. Of them, *issue* is the crutch most favoured by reporters and edit writers.

Not that reporters are averse to the other crutches. Don't they tell us always of the power supply *situation*, rather than a better/poor/erratic power supply? These crutches have so become the English-language newspaper's fare that we no longer get cloudy or rainy days; only cloudy/rainy *condition*. Calcutta streets aren't waterlogged, but are in a waterlogged *condition*. Bricks aren't made for building, but for construction *purposes*.

Eric Partridge said more than 50 years ago: '*Issue* (noun) is misused in a dozen contradictory and confusing senses, especially by politicians and leader writers' (*Usage and Abusage*, Great Britain: Hamish Hamilton, 1947). Partridge didn't foresee that reporters in India's English-language papers would beat leader writers of his day at the game. These excerpts are typical daily fare:

Jammu and Kashmir Chief Minister Farooq Abdullah tonight met the Prime Minister. . . .

He told reporters after the meeting . . . that the autonomy *issue* would be discussed with the Centre and his government had no plans to get a resolution first in the State Assembly on the *issue*.

He said he wanted the prime minister to initiate a discussion. . . . 'The *issue* of autonomy is 50-years-old [sic] and it cannot be solved in a day or year. . . .'

. . . Mr Abdullah said the Prime Minister gave a patient hearing to the *issue* of state's autonomy. However, Mr Vajpayee gave no word about forming a ministerial team to discuss the *issue* with the State Government, he added.

Reacting to the apprehension of imposition of president's rule if this *issue* was taken too far, he said 'the days are gone when Centre could arbitrarily dismiss state governments. . . .'

This reporter will not have *autonomy* without its *issue* crutch and will force *issue* to fill in for *subject/topic/dispute*.

[Hurriyat Conference leader Abdul Gani Lone] added that *talks issue* is the creation of the Union government to mislead the international community and to cover up . . . custodial killings in Kashmir.

This reporter believes that unless he gets the *talks* to lean on *issue*, they can't be worth talking about!

In headlines, *issue* is tagged to everything. The headline for a recent editorial in a daily read 'Issue in Question'. It pretended to comment on the Centre's 'second set of measures to liberalise *conditions for* foreign direct investment'. It left one wondering why he hadn't written *Question at issue*.

LDF Talks on RS Seat *Issue* Fail
The crisis over the Rajya Sabha seat *issue* continued to dog

the ruling coalition in Kerala, with the meeting of the LDF
state committee here today failing to bring up any viable
solution. The leaders of the coalition would meet again on
Friday to discuss the *issue* once more.

The state committee had met this morning in an attempt
to bring in some fresh perspective on the *issue*. . . . LDF
convener V S A – said that the *issue* was seriously discussed
by the Front partners. . . .

The convener expressed the hope that the *issue* would be
resolved in Friday's meeting.

The *talks* in that headline, and the *crisis* if there was one,
related to a Rajya Sabha seat, not a *seat issue*. The leaders
of the coalition may have discussed the *dispute/controversy*,
but only the reporter can explain how and from where the
committee members brought *fresh perspective on* an *issue*.

Avoiding any move to go against a Cabinet decision, the
prime minister's task force on infrastructure today dropped
the controversial *issue* to [sic] allow foreign airlines to pick
up equity participation in the domestic sector.

The task force, which also discussed the *issue* of creation
of a Railway Regulatory Board postponed the decision until
the next meeting. . . .

The task force also discussed the *issue* of augmenting the
revenue of airports from non-aeronautical services such as
shops and hotels. . . .

This was the lead item in a daily recently. One must throw
away the *issue* crutch at each place to understand that the
task force skirted the controversy over allowing foreign
airlines to pick up shares; put off a decision on setting up a
railway regulatory board, and discussed how airports might
increase their earnings from shops and hotels in their area.

In a conciliatory approach, the Congress today announced to
send [sic] a team of observers, in place of a probe committee,

to look into the *issue* of cross-voting in the recent Rajya Sabha polls.

The observers couldn't possibly look into the *issue*, only into *allegations* of cross-voting.

> The Lok Sabha will hold a special discussion on the price *issue*, including the hike in the administered price of essential items such as kerosene, food and sugar on April 27.

If that discussion were held, it would have centred on *rising/soaring prices*, not *the price issue*.

> Former state planning board deputy chairman and economist D M N – today called for a national debate on the *issue* of privatisation of Public Sector Banks.

He must have called for a debate on *privatisation* of such banks, not on its *issue*.

> Asked to comment on . . . Deve Gowda's statement that the NDA government was trying to hoodwink the people by claiming that the Cauvery *issue* had been solved when the *issue* was still before the tribunal, Mr Karunanidhi quipped: 'When he himself was the prime minister, he could have solved the Cauvery *issue*.'

Why must *issue* be forced to fill in for *dispute*?

Editorial writers have always believed *issue* turns everything into grist for their mill:

> The prolonged and habitual absence of some ministers in both Houses of the Karnataka legislature *when the session is on* is a matter of serious concern . . . [chief minister] Mr K is upset about the *issue* to such an extent that he is reported to be ready to drop from the ministry the ministers who continue to be irregular in their attendance of the House.

Surely, the chief minister was upset over their *habitual absence*, not *about the issue*, and he wouldn't want them

to be sitting in those Houses when the session *wasn't* on.
    After he examined official correspondence in Britain 50
years ago, Sir Ernest Gowers said this about *issue*:

> This word has a very wide range of proper meanings as
> a noun, and should not be made to do any more work –
> the work, for instance, of *subject, topic, consideration* and
> *dispute.*'
>
> (*The Complete Plain Words*, first published as *Plain
> Words*, 1948)

27

Indulging in fraudulent activities

Among the crutches imposed on words by reporters in India's English-language papers, none is more ludicrous than *activities*. It is appended to verbs and participles, as in this headline:

> Prevent Illegal Dynamiting *Activities* in Cauvery

Such use is peculiar to India's English-language papers. Quaint words such as *miscreants* have inspired the ridiculous *karya-kalaap/kriya-kalaap* (as in *asaamaajik karya-kalaap*, intended to correspond to *anti-social activities* – which police jargon covers everything that *miscreants* are supposed to do). Kannada papers have adopted *chatuvatike* as the equivalent of *activities*.

As these examples show, *activities* used as a noun that stands alone implies nothing sinister; the reporter uses the plural form when the precise word eludes him:

> Bangalore University . . . has set up 'Bangalore University Cell for Alumni internet interaction'. . . . Explaining the *activities*, Dr S said the cell would organise seminars, placement *activities* and bring out a newsletter twice in a year.

The first noun shows the reporter couldn't think of the appropriate word; the second, that he is given to woolly thinking: the precise word is rendered into an adjective and made to qualify (and therefore, lean on) the meaningless *activities*. In most instances, removal of the crutch or the phrase containing it makes the meaning clearer: 'Dr S said the cell would organise seminars, placement of graduates and bring out . . . .'

> Many of the migrants are landless people and non-agricultural labourers who have not benefited much from the increasing agricultural *activities*.

Delete the last three words and read: '. . . the growth in farming'.

> If the quarrying *activity* is not stopped, he would resort to hunger strike, the seer [the pontiff of Udupi Sri Krishna Pejawar Math] said.

The verb *quarrying* needs to be freed of its ludicrous crutch, so that it might read: 'The *Guru/Swamy* said he would go on a fast unless the quarrying is stopped.'

> The small industries development organization under the ministry of small scale, agro and rural industries has been assigned the responsibility of registering the units engaged in the *activities* of 1) aerosol products 2) foam products 3) air-conditioners and refrigerators.

Delete *engaged in the activities of*, so that it reads: '. . . registering units making . . .'.

> A division bench . . . passed the interim order when the Karnataka State Pollution Control Board (KSPCB) submitted that it has not permitted the Trust to carry on construction *activities*.

Removal of the crutch is all that is needed for sense.

Reporters feel they cannot do without this ludicrous appendage when they wish to imply wrongdoing, or something vaguely shady:

Mr Mahapatra however, made it clear that his party [BJP] was not involved in these conversion or reconversion *activities*, neither the party had any links with the organizations involved in these *activities*. 'The BJP is not involved in any kind of religious *activities*,' he insisted.

The nouns *conversion/reconversion* have been converted to adjectives only to accommodate the ludicrous crutch; their 'reconversion' into nouns helps sense:

Mr Mahapatra made it clear his party had nothing to do with conversion or reconversion, or with organisations that might be arranging them. 'The BJP does not have anything to do with religion,' he said.

Reporters in India's English-language papers share the comical belief that *activities* adds seriousness to anything that is sinister, or blameworthy:

Even though the Jammu and Kashmir government were trying to 'clear the hurdles' for the proposed talks with the Hurriyat Conference, the latter was still indulging in anti-national and anti-people *activities*, official sources said in New Delhi today.

That needs to be recast to read something like this: 'The . . . government was trying to get the talks going, but the Hurriyat was bent on working against the nation.'

Mr Krishna said that several cross-border *activities* were also set to destroy the secular credentials of India.

What is the reader supposed to understand from '*several* cross-border *activities*'? Assuming he meant terrorism and infiltration, how would such acts be '*set* to destroy' our *secular* credentials? Reporters in our English-language papers practise the same fraud as politicians: both string meaningless words that are supposed to be sonorous, but amount to nonsense.

Among the automatic expressions that this word has spawned, the most ridiculous is *illegal activities*. Reporters fall back on this expression to mean so many things that it has ceased to convey anything at all:

> The Mizoram police have launched a massive crackdown on . . . militants following reports that the outfit was indulging in extortion and other *illegal activities* official sources said here today.

What the *other* activities are the 'official sources' never name; the reporter never finds out, and the reader can never figure out. One can only assume that the three words together form an automatic expression that serves to pad drivel.

> S S, a 33-year-old divorced mother of a son, killed herself. . . . In her suicide note she charged two senior advocates with sexually harassing her . . . . [One of the two advocates] . . . reportedly wanted her to lend her apartment which she had rented out, for the weekend and also participate in the '*illegal activities*' there.

Here the expression is placed within quote marks. There is a vague hint of some sexual orgy. The reader can only assume that some quaint printing convention known only to English-language papers in India requires quote marks for anything that implies sexual misdemeanour.

The word is often inserted at random for sonorousness, and achieves the ridiculous:

> Earlier, former chief minister and MP, S B . . . said that religious fanatics were set to disturb the secular fabric of the nation. Every religion had its own fanatics and fundamentalists and their *threatening activities* needed to be curbed if the secular image of India had to be saved, he said.

More often, its use only betrays that the writer has a grasp of neither the language nor basic grammar. The noun is tagged on to nouns that cannot be used as adjectives:

> Lashing out on Pakistan for indulging in terrorist and insurgency *activities*, the [BJP] party supreme [sic] said that Kargil has shown their incapability.

Obviously, the writer does not know that the nouns *terrorism* and *insurgency* would better convey his idea, and cannot be used as adjectives. And Pakistan may *engage in* or *promote* insurgency, not *indulge* in it.

Reporters and sub-editors in English-language papers need to find out the meaning and use of words. They must buy good dictionaries – preferably one each.

28

Words without meaning

In *A Dictionary of Modern English Usage*, H W Fowler described as 'meaningless' words and phrases used more as props in conversation than as conveying any specific message. Among them he listed *actually/definitely/incidentally/sort of thing/well/you know*. That was in 1926. If we took stock today, we'd find additions to that list. We'd also find a difference in origin. Fowler said:

> One would suppose that they originated in a subconscious feeling that there was a need in the one case to emphasize a right word and in the other to apologize for a possibly wrong one. But any meaning they ever had was soon rubbed off them, and they became *noises automatically produced*.

Among *Indlish*-mouthing Indians, the new meaningless words exist alongside the old. The old ones are used for the needless emphasis we keep feeling the need for: the flexible syntax of Indian languages creates such need. The new ones are used by way not of apology, but herd identity, and a kind of snobbery. But old or new, they remain 'noises automatically produced'.

First the old ones. What better place than editorials in English-language papers for all that is fuddy-duddy! Excerpt from a recent editorial:

> While an inquiry would help ascertain the actual reasons
> for the violence and whether or not firing was ordered by
> the police, there is no denying that the people *took resort to*
> violence because of erratic power supply in Badavanahalli....
> *In this context,* what is *particularly* disturbing is that the
> police authorities did not seem to have prepared themselves
> to tackle the situation.

All the italicised words there (except the bad English
in 'took resort to') are meaningless. Like a minor clerk
in a government office, the edit writer uses automatic
expressions such as *in this context* after he has made his
context clear. In this group we may fit all the meaningless
'tail-enders' one finds in editorials and newspaper reports,
such as *in this respect/in this regard/persons concerned,*
etc. Such edit writers as are overpromoted clerks cannot
do without the circumlocutory phrases which Raj-day pen-
pushers used to add sound to trivia. Among such phrases is *a
section of/sections of* which is *officialese* for *some.* A recent
editorial in the same Karnataka paper had this:

> Russian authorities have blamed Islamic militants who
> are fighting Russian security forces in Dagestan for the
> bomb blasts. *Sections of* the Russian government, including
> Prime Minister Vladimir Putin, have accused the Chechen
> leadership, for backing the fighters.... But they are indicative
> of the kind of nationalist feeling that is being nurtured by
> *sections of* the political elite. . . . But the fact that Russia
> lacks a law on procedures for declaring a state of emergency
> would raise fears among liberal *sections.*

Clerks in government offices cannot do without meaningless
words such as *facilities/adversely affect/inadequate.* Nor
can the clerk-turned-journalist, who relies on these to add
decibels to his drivel – as this excerpt from an editorial in
the same paper shows:

> The death of a tigress in the Bannerghata National Park should *draw attention to* the need to improve *facilities* for animals there. . . . While some officials attribute the attack to unpredictable animal behaviour, it is believed that the *inadequate facilities* in the park played a role. Around 14 tigers can be accommodated in the *existing facilities* at the Bannerghata Park.

The day before that editorial was printed, the paper carried a report on the subject. It had this sentence:

> Though, the forest authorities described the tigers' *attack on the feline* as unpredictable animal behaviour, doubts have been expressed that *inadequate facilities* in the park might have led to the aggressive behaviour of tigers.

Siamese twins

Fowler found this term suitable 'for the many words which, linked in pairs by *and* or *or*, are used to convey a single meaning.' Legal language contributed most of them. With many, one of the pair is meaningful and the other a meaningless duplicate – often a synonym or a near-synonym. Among these are *betwixt and between/bits and pieces/gall and wormwood/heart and soul/leaps and bounds/lo and behold/nerve and fibre/rags and tatters/shape or form/sort or kind.*

Fowler listed another group of Siamese twins that consists not of synonyms, but of associated ideas: *bill and coo/bow and scrape/hot and strong/thick and fast.* Yet another set consists of opposites or alternatives: *fast and loose/hither and thither/by hook or by crook/thick and thin/to and fro.* The legal profession contributed those that are most frequently used in India: *aid and abet/each and every/let or hindrance/null and void*. Such twins were much favoured by clerks of the Raj days. They took to penning them in the belief that these lent sonority to their gibberish.

V S Naipaul found journalism in India 'a clerical pursuit'. (Naipaul would have studied English-language papers.) Clerks-turned-hacks who write editorials for English-language papers not only nurture Siamese twins, but also play midwives for new ones, as in this excerpt from a recent editorial in the same 'leading daily':

> While this is quite lamentable, what is much more deplorable is the *tone and tenor* of the replies given by some in the BDA and the BMP, who seem to think that they are accountable to none. The core issue is whether it was *proper and prudent* on the part of these officials in the two public bodies to take such a purely *legalistic and constricted* view of the matter.

The clerical orientation of such hacks shows up all the more in such circumlocutory phrases as *on the part of/in the sphere of/in view of*, etc. strewn all over such writing. 'Whenever a Siamese twin suggests itself to a writer,' said Fowler, 'he should be on his guard; it may be just the phrase he wants, but it is more likely to be one of those clichés that are always lying in wait to fill a vacuum in the brain.' That explains the twins' demand among edit writers: they need vacuous words to fill those vacuums.

New breed

The new breed of meaningless words ushers a new concept. These are supposed to serve as the badge of identity of the 'hep' generation. And these are mouthed *ad nauseam* by the VJs, whose badge of identity is scanty clothing and scantier brains. Their vocabulary is limited. They

have given a new lease of life to the old *you know* and *well*. And they keep chanting their new five: *cool/check it out/far out/like/things like that*. Way back in 1926, Fowler had described *well* as 'a permanent member of the class' of meaningless words.

For *Indlish*-mouthing Indian youth, these 'noises automatically produced' serve the function croaking does among frogs: like calls to like, and those who utter these sounds are accepted among others who do. Among some groups, such meaningless words are also tied up with snobbery. Youth who utter the VJ *mantra*s announce that they have acquired a certain level of westernisation. And that's supposed to imply a certain level of affluence.

This process of instant recognition through use of certain words is a new phenomenon, though it brings to mind the argot among the *thuggees* of India. One *thuggee* found another when he returned the code of greeting that to others sounded like mere ritual: *Salaam, Ali my brother* was returned with *Ali my brother, salaam*. Only, those weren't meaningless words.

IV

USAGE *INDLISH* STYLE

29

She is having two daughters

We unwittingly load the English we write with the stiffness of our written regional languages, and the verbosity of literary Victorian English. During the Victorian period, literary English took on several attributes that are un-English. Some of these were easily absorbed here because they coincided with the way we use our regional languages:

1   the predominance of the noun, which in English ushers a string of prepositions
2   the use of weak verbs, which robs English of its vigour
3   the use of participles, which weakens writing.

In all written Indian languages, we usually leave the noun rigidly as a noun, and add a *do/doing* word after it, instead of modifying the noun into a verb. In English, on the other hand, most nouns can easily be modified into a verb. If we do to the English noun as we do to ours, the noun will drag in prepositions and force indirect and roundabout expressions.

Overuse of prepositions

The following examples show how the predominant noun (italicised) ushers in prepositions (*of/in/by*) and weakens the sentence, and how the same sentence gains in strength and directness if the noun is changed into a verb (italicised):

1 They are hopeful of early *resolution* of the crisis in a couple of days.

Better: They hope to *resolve* the crisis soon/in a couple of days.

2 There are abundant examples of *misbehaviour* towards young girls by older men, and these occur often.

Better: Older men often *misbehave* with young girls; examples abound.

The sentences that give predominance to the noun bring in several prepositions. Their number dwindles when the noun is changed to a verb (italicised in the sentence below it). This eliminates the clutter that often mars the English we write. It also eliminates the roundabout expressions that nouns trailing prepositions bring in.

Weak verbs

Sentences that carry weak verbs, such as *am/are/be/do/ get/is/make/take/was/were*, can often be made stronger if the weak verb is replaced by a strong one. Sentences beginning with *is/are* are often weak, and replacing them helps strengthen statements, as the above examples show. Some more:

1 There are several clues that suggest that the murder was carried out by someone who is an insider.

Better: Several clues suggest the murder was an insider job.

2 Determination of institutional policy *takes place* at the directorial level.

Better: Directors decide institutional policy.

3 When you come to that crossing, take the turn to your right.

Better: Turn right at/after that crossing.

The weak participle

The participle is the weakest form of the verb and its use weakens the English sentence. The most frequently misused participle is 'having'. It inevitably appears in Indian English speech and writing in ways altogether unidiomatic:

1   I am *having* a headache.

    Better: I have a headache.

2   I am *having/running* a temperature.

    Better: I have a fever.

3   The woman said she is *having* two sons and one daughter.

    Better: The woman said she has two sons and a daughter.

The last of those Indian English examples would have only one meaning to a native English speaker: that the woman was speaking while giving birth to two sons and a daughter. Such unidiomatic use of the participle comes from transliterating expressions in our regional languages, most of which permit such use. And such unidiomatic use often gets into news reports because those who work in English-language newspapers often cannot tell *Indlish* from English:

4.   In spite [sic] the Thigala community *having* a population of 40 lakhs in the State, no majority party had ever given a ticket for the members of the community for Assembly elections.

     Better: No major party had ever given a Thigala an Assembly election ticket even though the State has four million Thigalas.

This is not to say that one must always avoid the participle.

What we must remember is that unless used as an adjective (as in 'a rolling stone gathers no moss'), the participle weakens expression and should be avoided where possible. Also, it is not English idiom to keep repeating participles. Nursery rhymes are a pointer:

- Had Little Miss Muffet been *sitting* on her tuffet and *eating* her curd and whey, she wouldn't have violated rules of grammar. But English idiom demanded that she *sat* on her tuffet, eating them.

- Nor would grammar have been violated if Jack and Jill had gone *climbing* up the hill to fetch a pail of water. But idiom has it that they *went* up the hill. And only in the end, to suggest continuity of motion, did Jill come *tumbling* after.

- Little Jack Horner could well have been *sitting* in his corner and *eating* his Christmas pie. But he *sat* in a corner eating it.

Because the participle weakens a sentence, we should avoid beginning with it. We should also avoid repetition of participles in the same sentence, as we often see in news reports:

5. The Congress is open to *forming* a minority coalition government, but the parties *supporting* it should accept its manifesto, party spokesman Kapil Sibal said on Friday.

   Better: The Congress is open to a minority or a coalition set-up, but its supporters should accept its manifesto, Mr Kapil Sibal, party spokesman, said on Friday.

The participle is all too often used to connect (italicised) two actions. This should be avoided at all times. Statements sound more forceful when active verbs are used for each idea:

6. *Promising* to *return* by the next day, he *left* by the morning train.

Better: He *promised* to return the next day, and left by the morning train.

Most sentences gain strength when the participle (italicised in the newspaper report) is replaced by an active verb (italicised in the improved version):

7. *Insisting* that the November 12 1998 'letter' written to the Chief of Army Staff by Brig Surinder Singh does exist, *Outlook* magazine in a press release issued here on Friday alleged that 'the Army is *putting* together a contingency plan to claim that the letter got "lost" en route to the Chief'. . . . *Quoting* 'sources close to the family of Brig Surinder Singh', the magazine claims that the Brigadier stands by 'whatever has been reported in *Outlook*'. And that he has been threatened with a court martial.

Better: In a press release *issued* here on Friday, *Outlook* magazine alleged the Army has planned to claim that Brig Surinder Singh's letter of 12 November 1998 got 'lost' on its way to the Chief of Army Staff. It insisted that the Army has the letter. . . . *Outlook quoted* sources close to the Brigadier's family to substantiate its claim that the senior officer stands by 'whatever has been reported in *Outlook*', and that he has been threatened with a court martial.

30

I have seen that film last week

In listing the characteristics of Indian English, the *Oxford Companion to the English Language* (Oxford, New York: OUP, 1992) says that we Indians have the tendency to:

1   give progressive forms to stative verbs: *Lila is having two books/You must be knowing my cousin-brother*, and to
2   use the present perfect, rather than the simple past: *I have bought the book yesterday.*

If we examined that interesting observation, we'd see that we come across the first error more often in south India, and the second more often in north India. Both relate to the use of *have/having*. I have briefly dealt with our frequent unidiomatic use of the first in 'She Is Having Two Daughters', pp. 175–80. No doubt our grammar books tell us to use only the simple past, never the present perfect, with adverbs that denote time past – not *I have seen that film yesterday*, but *I saw that film yesterday*. And readers would at once recognise that the correct form for 1 would be *Lila has two books/I'm sure* (or, *I suppose*) *you know my cousin*, and for 2, *I bought the book yesterday*. But our grammar books don't explain why we often go wrong in handling this auxiliary.

Are there patterns of usage, or a set of words, in south Indian languages that translate into *having*, and another in north Indian languages that easily translate into *have*? And do these mislead us to unidiomatic English?

The unidiomatic *having* in *Lila is having two books* might in Tamil be traced to *irukku*; in Malayalam to *indu*; in Telugu to *unnaee*, and in Kannada to *ive*. But none of these translate into *have/having*. They are closer to *are/is with*. The south Indian languages, therefore, see the two books more as being *with* Lila, than as Lila possessing/owning them, as *has* implies.

To say those two books *belong* to Lila, we'd have to import the possessive case and we'd then arrive at *Lila udiye* (Tamil); *Lilayude* (Malayalam); *Lila vee* (Telugu) and *Lilandu* (Kannada).

In north Indian languages, we'd have an identical problem: *Lila ke paas do kitaabein hai* (Hindi) would accurately translate into *two books are with Lila*, not that they are *hers*. We'd have to add the genitive case to Lila to convey the sense of possession: *Lila* ki *do* kitaabein hai (Lila has two books). In Bengali, likewise, we cannot convey the sense of possession unless we add the genitive (*Lila*ar).

The problem therefore is not that Indian languages have words or expressions that translate into the ungrammatical or unidiomatic *have/having*, but that they don't have an auxiliary that denotes possession as *have/having* does (as in *Mine to have and to hold from this day forth* – which the bride and groom utter at a church wedding).

The second example (use of the present perfect where the simple past is idiomatic) is more intriguing. All Indian languages have the simple past. Why then this confusion?

The simple Hindi version of the correct form would be *main nay woh kitaab kal kharidi*. But confusion begins when one mentally adds the unnecessary *tha/thi* at the end (to say *main nay woh kitaab kal kharidi thi*) in the belief that it serves more emphatically to convey completion of the action. One then mentally translates that unnecessary *tha/thi* into the present perfect. That's how the unidiomatic *have* intrudes where the simple past suffices.

The dual nature of *have* complicates usage. We need to understand that in most idiomatic uses, *have* does denote possession, but *have* can also imply *receive/suffer/indulge in/share in/cause to be done*, etc. It is when we confuse the usage rule that goes with the sense intended that we arrive at the unidiomatic *have* and *having* in *Indlish*.

Examples of *have* in the sense of 'possession' – *I have two brothers and a sister/She has three children/They have two cars/He has green fingers/He has bats in his belfry/He has ants in his pants*, etc. In all these expressions, one would understand the colloquial sense of *got* – *I have (got) two brothers/he has (got) ants in his pants/they have (got) two cars*, etc. And with none of these would *having* ever be idiomatic. Unfortunately, it is in the sense of *have (got)* that *having* is all too often used in south India.

We can use *have* also to mean

- **receive:** *I have just had a phone call from him to say. . ./I have had no word from him yet/I have no orders for that item yet.*
- **obtain:** *I was told I could have that car for the asking/You can have that fridge for a song, you know.*
- **activity:** *I'll have a shower first/I need to have a long holiday.*

- **suffer:** *I have had enough of her tantrums/I have had this pain for almost a year.*
- **accept:** *I told him I'd return a loan in three days, but he wouldn't have it/I won't have her ordering me about/He said he wouldn't have his daughter return home late at night.*
- **cause** (to be done): *You needn't come all the way; I'll have the cheque collected from your office/He'll have the van pick us up from home/I'll have the papers ready in no time.*
- **experience:** *No, I didn't have any problem finding your house/I have had a restful day.*
- **must:** *You'll have to fill out that form first/The lodge is free, but you'll have to pay for board.*
- **indulge in/enjoy:** *Let's have a ball with this money/Let's have some fun teasing her/Let's have a high old time tonight.*
- **suggest:** *Rumour has it that he ran away with his friend's wife/Legend has it that he killed the lion with his bare hands.*
- **get the better of:** *I have him by the short and curlies/You have me there/They have him by the throat.*
- **deceive:** *How could you pay such a price for that ramshackle car? You have been had!*
- **eat/drink:** *I'll have a beer/I had a drink about an hour ago, and it's gone right to my head/I think I'll have some more of that vindaloo.*
- **settle:** *Let's examine the accounts and have done with it.*
- **harm:** *Kalyan Singh's convinced Mr Vajpayee's followers have it in for him.*

- **wear:** *Her husband won't let her have anything on in bed, not even a handkerchief.*
- **include/contain:** *My house must have two floors/How many pages does that book have?*

English idiom admits *having* mostly with the notion of *indulging/enjoying*, and rarely, with suffering: *He's having a ball while his money lasts/She's interested only in having a good time/He's having it good* (i.e. he is going through a comfortable phase)/*He's having the time of his life/The children are having a whale of a time at the pool.* A rare instance of its idiomatic use with suffering: *He's having one of his bad days, swearing at everything and everyone.*

Other idiomatic uses of *having*: *Is he having a bath now?/Don't disturb him now, he's having his dinner/We're having our house painted/Our new car is having teething troubles/She insists on having* (i.e. delivering) *her baby at home.*

31

This condom costs very less

How often have we come across such an absurd use of *less*? It probably began in Bombay, where the Marathi expressions *khoop kamhi* (often translated as *very less*) and *khoop thode* (more often translated as *a lot less*) got confused thus. That confusion found an echo in other south Indian languages. The Kannada expression *thoomba kadimay* corresponded to the Marathi *khoop kamhi*, as did the Tamil *romba kadachchal*, and the Telegu *chaal kanchi/kanjam*.

Having thus found acceptance, this ungrammatical *Indlish* spread throughout the country. Those who use it habitually are often people who either live, or had spent some time, in Bombay. Of a slow-moving train, they will say 'Its speed is *very less*'; of one's flagging enthusiasm in something, that one's 'interest is *very less*', and so on. Though they might otherwise speak fairly good English, they are so conditioned to accept this aberration that they refuse to reason that if *very* were to go with the comparative (*less* is the comparative of *little*; *least* the superlative), then one might just as well say *very more/very better/very faster/very slower/very quicker*, and so on.

That inexplicable confusion apart, *less* causes problems even among those whose mother tongue is English. Such confusion most often lies in when to use *fewer*, and when to use *less*. The basic rule isn't difficult to remember. *Less* goes with notions of *quantity* and *amount*:

> I can buy that for *less* than you paid for it.

> Many six-year-olds can do the Rubic's cube in *less* time than most adults.

> The taxi driver returned *less* money than he ought to have.

> Let's see if we can't get that done with *less* noise and trouble.

Fewer is idiomatic when we mean *number*, unqualified by a numeral word such as *three/five/fifty*, etc.

> There seemed to be *fewer* cars on Chittaranjan Avenue this afternoon.

> With industry shattered, there are *fewer* job opportunities in Calcutta now.

> The hawkers say few people visit their new stalls, and *fewer* buy anything from them.

A useful tip: *less* is usually idiomatic where we would not use a plural noun. For example,

> I'd like *less* sugar in my tea, please.

> Given your blood pressure reading, you'd better get used to *less* salt in your food, you know.

> You eat *less* rice than a child of five!

With none of those nouns (*sugar/salt/rice*) would we ever use the plural form. But with nouns for which we'd use the plural form, we should opt for *fewer*:

> After each budget, he smokes *fewer* cigarettes for about a month, and then reverts to his two packets a day.

> He never said no to borrowers, and so has *fewer* books on his shelves.

Honda declared it would produce *fewer* cars at its UK plant, but ruled out retrenchment.

We do use the plural form for such nouns (*cigarette/book/car*) and hence they take *fewer*, not *less*.

To test that rough-and-ready rule, we could combine such nouns in the same sentence:

He gets *fewer* shirts made now, and spends *less* time before the mirror.

He has *fewer* customers at his shop nowadays, and makes *less* money than he used to.

Mr Rao is less important now, and so has *fewer* hangers-on.

The boss said he wanted the job done with less noise and *fewer* hitches.

He has *less* money to spend now, and far *fewer* friends.

The terrorists were left with *fewer* guns and *less* ammunition.

In each of those sentences, *less* goes with a noun we'd not use in the plural form, and *fewer* with a noun that we would use in the plural. But one must not observe that rough-and-ready rule blindly, without caring for the sense intended. In a sentence such as 'Many people in India earn less than Rs 300 a month', one must not opt for *fewer* just because *rupees* is in the plural. Implied by 'Rs 300' is a total sum, not three hundred units of Re 1.

By the same reasoning, it would be correct to say 'Serampore is *less* than 50 miles from Calcutta by road' and not '*fewer* than 50 miles'. Although in the plural, '50 miles' carries the sense of the total distance, not 50 individual miles.

Confusion over the correct use of *less/lower/fewer/smaller* shows up most frequently in English-language papers. Here are two examples:

1 Erratic maintenance and functioning of the four
   crematoria over the last eight to 10 months has made
   their use even *less*.

Had this reporter known that *people* use a crematorium, he
could have solved his problem with 'Erratic . . . 10 months
means that fewer people use them'.

2 Government said in the Lok Sabha it may be more
   profitable for traders to import sugar from Pakistan in
   view of *less* transport cost.

Obviously, neither this parliament reporter, nor the sub-
editor who handled his copy, was familiar with the idiomatic
'lower transport cost'. Frederick T Wood puts it down
simply:

> Do not speak of *a less price*, or *a less number*. Say *a lower
> price* and *a smaller number*. But 'The number was less than
> we expected' is correct, since . . . we are comparing two
> numbers thought of as mathematical quantities.'
>   (*Current English Usage*, Macmillan, 1962)

To return to the headline: *very* is used with the positive
degree, never the comparative. 'This . . . costs very *little*'
would be correct English, as would 'The price of this . . . is
very *low*' (both *little* and *low* being the positive degree). The
Bombay version (*very less*) is absurd and ungrammatical.

We in India need to remember that usage long ago
narrowed down to the more specific *smaller, fewer, lower*
from the wider *less*. Also, that we need to be on guard
against using translations of regional expressions or idioms
(such as *khoop kamhi*) that go against English grammar and
idiom.

Lesser than

This expression, as all grammar books make clear, is a double comparative. Its use should be restricted to mean the less serious/the less important/the less harmful of two things. In usage now obsolete, the expression was common in contexts where we would today use *smaller than/less important than*. Shakespeare uses it in the old sense when the three witches greet Macbeth and Banquo:

> FIRST WITCH: *Lesser* than Macbeth, and greater.
> SECOND WITCH: Not so happy, yet much happier.
> THIRD WITCH: Thou shalt get kings, though thou be none; so all hail, Macbeth and Banquo!

Today, it is not an everyday expression and should be reserved for what has emotional content. Thus, it would be wrong today to say that Vilayat Khan felt he had been offered *a lesser prize*, but it would be correct to say he felt he was offered *a smaller prize* than he deserved.

'Tell me no/say no'

The absurd translation of another regional expression that has acquired all-India status is the tag 'Tell me no?/say no?' This began as literal translation of the Hindi tag questions *Arrey, bolo naa?/Arrey bolo bhi toe?* But it has moved, like the salwar-kurta, from the Hindi heartland to the Deccan, and is heard most often in the *Hindlish* speech of English-medium school students.

The difference between tag questions in English and our regional languages is discussed in 'Lover, You Are Very That Thing', pp. 303–9. English has no tag question equivalent to *arrey bolo naa?/arrey bolo bhi toe?* The closest one could adduce is 'Will you tell me?/Would you care to tell me?' But these carry a slightly accusing tone not implied by *bolo naa*, which more often than not conveys exasperation! Forcing the idiom of one language into another can only lead to the absurd. And surely, the only meaning the English translation can convey is that one is being nagged to say 'no'. The most that can elicit, surely, is an obliging 'no!'

32

On Sunday, I went to my native

Exasperated at each batch of her students coming up with the same *Indlish* expressions, a college teacher has composed a letter to identify the more familiar ones. We might use her 'model letter' as a convenient chart:

My name is Mohan Kumar. I *am coming* from a very large family *having five brothers and two sisters*. Two of my brothers are *elder to me*. I am *third eldest* in *my family*. I *am qualified* as a software engineer currently *employed with* MNC. My brothers and *myself* are *put up* in Bangalore. My parents and sisters are *residing* at our *native place*.

At present my father is busy trying to *finalise* my marriage. He is looking for a suitable alliance. I am very much *tensed up* because the girl he will choose may not be able to *adjust to* me. Since I am *having* a job with *a* MNC I would like to marry a *modern type of* girl who is *social* and can move about with me. But since my father is very orthodox I will have to bow down to his wishes and marry *the girl of his choice*.

As per our custom the marriage will be held in our *native place*. *Mostly* the marriage date will be *fixed for* the last week of January. Please keep yourself free. I will be distributing cards to friends and relations in Bangalore after the marriage date is *finalised*.

Please don't *mistake me* if I do not join you this evening. I am *on the look out* for a *larger accommodation* and the estate agent is taking me every evening to show some houses/flats. So far nothing suitable has turned up. Yesterday I saw a good flat, but the *backside* veranda does not have sufficient space to *hang clothes*.

Since I am planning to *go in for* a big fridge and some modern kitchen appliances, I want a flat with a big kitchen *also*. There should *even* be enough space to store the *cooking vessels* and other utensils. Plus, of course, a spacious hall to accommodate my new 29-inch colour TV and big sofa set. If it is *nearby to the office* it will be ideal. Then I can *go by walk to* the office daily and I don't have to worry about getting *stuck up* in traffic jams. Plus I can *save up on* petrol *also*. My fuel bills will be *very less* compared to what it is now.

Thank you for giving me a patient hearing. I am looking forward to continuing our friendship.

We could group the *Indlish* there into

- translation of 'manufactured' expressions
- errors of preposition
- errors of usage

The unidiomatic use of the present continuous tense in *I am coming from a very large family* and *having five brothers and two sisters* have been dealt with in 'She Is Having Two Daughters', pp. 175–80.

The question we need to ask is: do we use the present continuous tense in the equivalent in our regional languages? No, we don't. Why then do we switch to this form in English? The answer must lie in the pidgin that Indian clerks working for the East India Company devised. Between them, they manufactured absurd English equivalents for what they supposed were idioms in our regional languages. In Calcutta, some such clerks ran *pathshalas*, where they 'sold' each

English word they had picked up from British merchants. Their 'buyers' were middlemen who wished to trade with the Company. Something similar must have happened at Madras, the Company's other important centre. (And that's how English initially percolated to the people.)

We never use in our regional languages terms corresponding to such *Indlish* as *elder to me/third eldest in my family/I am qualified as/currently employed with/My brothers and myself are put up in/My parents and sisters are residing at our native place.* If we correctly translated the corresponding Indian-language expressions, we'd get *older than I/I am the third/I am a software engineer/now working for/my brothers and I live in/my parents and my sisters live in our village.*

Company clerks' 'manufacture' is obvious in such preposterous expressions as *native place.* Neither in Bengali nor in Kannada do we use the equivalent of *native* when we refer to the place where we were born. What we say translates correctly as 'my village/our village/home village/home town/our town'. And yet, if he switches to English when he returns from his village, the Kannadiga invariably says, 'I went to my native.' And 'they went to their natives' is a familiar expression throughout south India.

Where did this absurdity begin? The answer lies in Company clerks' pidgin. Among such absurd expressions, we may include *modern type of/cooking vessels and other utensils.* These betray a fool's attempt to affect precision, with little thought to his own idiom, and less acquaintance with the idiom of English.

The real problem with *Indlish* is that such rubbish became automatic expressions, which circulate to this day. Correspondents and sub-editors in English-language

newspapers, who absorbed these as students, and never questioned them, do the greatest harm by keeping such pidgin circulating.

* * * *

Errors of preposition (caused again by ignorance among Company clerks) led to such *Indlish* as *put up in/backside/nearby to/go by walk/stuck up/save up*. One may ask a friend to *put* him *up* for the night; one does not *put up in* there.

Though Americans do use *back of* where British usage demands *behind*, *backside* means the buttocks to Englishmen and Americans alike. (This expression among their Indian clerks must have caused endless mirth among officers of the Company.)

The use of *nearby to* for *near* betrays ignorance. But *go by walk* for the verb *walk* can be traced to the dependence on the noun in all Indian languages, against the dominance of the verb in English (discussed in 'Jest *Choop* and *Chel*', pp. 264–9).

With many English idioms, a change of preposition changes the sense. In Indian idioms, meaning changes with each change of the verb after the noun. (Consider the Bengali idioms *haath karaa/haath othano/haath neoa* or the Hindi *sar uthana/sar jhukana/sar denaa, sar bechna*, etc.)

Adding *up* after English verbs is often redundant and, in some idioms, changes the sense. One may get *caught* in a traffic jam, but people label someone as *stuck-up* if he is snobbish. If one walks to office, one could save *on* petrol, but could save *up* for a rainy day with wise investments. One might feel *tense*, and *tense up* over impending danger, but would achieve only nonsense if he said he was *tensed up*, or *tensed*. Errors through confusion with some Indian-language idioms, as in *very less*, have been dealt with in 'This Condom Costs Very Less', pp. 187–93. We need to reconsider our indulgence of Indian English, and recognise the truth: *Indlish* did NOT evolve; most of it was manufactured by East India Company's pen-pushers.

33

Write it today *itself* and post it tomorrow *itself*

Of the various forms of *Indlish* that get into our English-language newspapers, perhaps the most jarring is the use of reflexive pronouns for emphasis that is unidiomatic in English, and unnecessary in any language.

A reflexive pronoun is correctly used when the object and subject of a verb refer to the same person or thing, or when the action done by the subject turns back (reflects) upon the subject: 'She cried *herself* to sleep'/'The city defended *itself* from attack.'

Emphasis reflexive pronouns (or 'emphatic pronouns') are often used to emphasise that an action is done by one particular person *instead of* another: 'Please don't wash my cup; I'll do it *myself*'/'She was trying to calm Mrs X, but I noticed she *herself* was very upset.'

English-language papers in south India place the 'emphatic pronoun' after names of persons and places, specified time or day, and facts that need no emphasis. In north Indian papers, the redundant emphasis usually comes after some significant detail that is already conspicuous and needs no such prop. More often than not, what looks like the emphatic pronoun in news reports doesn't function like one. In none of these examples picked at random from editorials and news items was the emphatic pronoun necessary:

> Rural Development Minister . . . told reporters that . . . the government would write to the State Election Commission tomorrow *itself* that it might go ahead with the process of fixing the date for the elections . . . since the notification was being issued today *itself*, the commission . . . may hold the elections even in the first week of June.

> Speaker . . . assured that he would ensure that the minister would immediately send an officer to Hassan today *itself*.

The reader need only read those excerpts aloud after deleting *itself* at each place to realise how absurd such 'non-functional' emphatic pronouns render *Indlish*. Where does this habit come from?

In most south Indian languages, such emphasis is accepted as idiomatic. The words *tannay* (Malayalam) and *taan* (Tamil) are used for an emphasis that is mistranslated into *itself* and *only* (mistranslated, because neither *itself* nor *only* are used in the same way as *tannay* or *taan*).

There is no discernible pattern in when those words translate into *itself* nor in what contexts they mean *only*. Those whose first language is Malayalam tend to prefer translating *tannay* into *itself*; those who speak Tamil seem to think *only* conveys the emphasis intended by *taan* (perhaps because they are used to the emphasis they effect through the Tamil *mattum*, which translates into *only*).

Going by logic, words denoting specific time such as *yesterday, today, tomorrow* should need no emphasis. But most Indian languages add such emphasis after specifying day or time. Compare *aaj hee* (Hindi); *aaj-ee/aaj-kayee* (Bengali).

Obviously, the need to add the emphasis is created by

our flexible syntax, and by the need we feel to fill the vacuum created in writing by the missing intonation of speech. The rigid syntax of English does not tolerate the 'non-functional emphatic pronoun' that mistranslation has made a characteristic of *Indlish*. The acceptance of such *Indlish* leads to emphatic pronouns being added after names of people and places:

> On the face of it, the constitution of Administrative Reforms Commission (ARC) for Karnataka . . . needs to be welcomed even though it is doubtful to what extent its recommendations would be implemented. . . . There is bound to be scepticism . . . . Because experimentation . . . in the past by Mr A D Gorawala during . . . Mr Morarji Desai (at the Centre) and Mr Hanumanthaiya *himself* (again at the Centre) did not seem to have yielded the results. . . . For instance, in Karnataka *itself*, it was with good intentions that efficiency audit bureaus was [sic] set up twice but the outcome was not much.

What purpose do *himself* and *itself* serve in that editorial excerpt, or in this news item:

> The BJP Goa General Secretary['s] . . . open criticism of the Francisco-Sardinha government's handling of the state police department and other issues, have puzzled its co-alition partner . . . . Chief Minister Francisco Sardinha *himself* seemed puzzled by . . . outburst.

Did the reporter have reason to believe that unless he added the emphatic pronoun, the reader might attribute Mr Sardinha's puzzlement to someone else? The emphatic pronoun placed after a person's name is always redundant unless it is used to emphasise that an action is done by one particular person *instead of* another. No such sense is conveyed here:

> Ms Uma Bharati seems to be in trouble. Today was the fourth day of her indefinite fast. . . . Ms Bharati *herself* admits that she had not received the party chief['s] blessings.

The only plausible explanation for *herself*: the reporter expected someone other than Ms Bharati to admit that, and was thrilled that she did so instead!

When such meaningless use of emphatic pronouns is accepted, they start popping up everywhere:

> It's summer time – vacation time for students and donation time for parents. This year . . . the donation market has hit an all time high with some prestigious schools charging as much as Rs 50,000 plus for a lower kindergarten seat. . . . While parents *themselves* shell out exorbitant amount to secure admission for their wards in prestigious schools . . . . But parents complain that the admission process in some CSE and CBSE schools were [sic] completed in January *itself*, donation paid and seats secured . . . .

The reader can only conclude that the reporter has information that it is normal for people *other than* parents to shell out the donations. And if the admissions were completed in January, what did *itself* add to the parents' suspicion?

The use of emphatic pronouns after significant facts or details can only weaken the impact:

> Former chief minister J H Patel today sought to make it clear that he would be actively participating in the party affairs. . . . He said the party's national presidentship *itself* was offered to him some time ago, but he rejected it.

English-language newspapers will keep *Indlish* circulating, and we shall therefore always have to sort out confusion created by the non-functional emphatic pronoun:

Write it today itself *and post it tomorrow* itself

The meeting of Bangalore Rural Zilla Panchayat was formally adjourned today . . . calling the meeting . . . others defended the move pointing out that the assembly session *itself* was going on.

The Bangalore Metropolitan Transport Corporation's (BMTC) efforts to augment its inadequate fleet has received a set back. . . . The cost of operation for every bus is Rs 14.50 for the BMTC *itself* with its own infrastructure.

A RTO agent has lodged a complaint . . . that a ten-member gang posing as sleuths of the City Crime Branch had kidnapped her husband. . . . The police are verifying whether . . . was picked up by the police *themselves* for questioning.

Excavations through weathered rock would require extensive shoring and support measures, besides at locations where hard rock *itself* appears at shallow depth there is no other alternative than to [sic] resort to blasting.

34

People have different different tastes

We seldom examine how certain words in English have acquired among us connotations wider than they had before they landed in India.

This is roughly how it happens: the translation of a word leads us to associate with it other words close to the Indian language equivalent. We then load the English word with equivalents of connotations it never had. One such word is *different*. The word is correctly used to distinguish something or somebody from another (*His views are different from those of his friends/This cloth may look similar to that, but it has a different texture and weave/Calcutta's problems are different from those of most other metros*). It translates correctly into *bhinno/onnyo* (Bengali); *annya/bhinnya/aur kuchch* (Hindi). The Bengali translation brings in associations of *bibhinnyo/naanaa* and these lead us on to *preethak*, and again to *bibidho/bohu/anek*. We then begin to load *different* with these connotations, though these would correctly translate into *various/several*, *separate*, and *many*, rather than *different*. This is why those who speak Bengali often use *different* where *various/several/separate/many* would be appropriate.

An identical process takes place with all other Indian languages. Those who speak Hindi load *different* with connotations equivalent to *alag/anek/bahut saray*, which would more accurately translate into *separate/many/various/multifarious*. In south Indian languages too, a similar process loads *different* with connotations of *bhinnya/vibhinnam* (Kannada and Malayalam); *halavu/halavaru* (Kannada for *several/many*); *pala pala/otthiri* (Malayalam for *various*) *oru paadu* (Malayalam for *several*); *vevveru/palavere* (Tamil for *several/various*), and so on.

In English, the use of *different* is restricted to connotations of *unlikeness*, and words such as *several/many/various/separate* carry out the functions that we too often dump on *different*. In Indian languages, words for *several/various* often blur.

Four broad patterns in the way we misuse *different*:

1 when it fulfils no function, and is altogether redundant (this defect appears in British usage too)
2 when it is misused for *some/several/many*
3 when it is misused for *separate*
4 when its meaning is confused with other expressions.

In our English-language newspapers, and TV and radio bulletins, the redundant *different* invariably shows up in accounts of accidents and crime, as in this excerpt:

> Ten people were killed and 33 others were injured in three different road accidents in the State since last night.

Only to reporters, sub-editors, and news readers could the omission of *different* mean that the 10 were killed in 'three *same* accident'. A newsreader recently informed TV viewers of some people being killed in *tintee preethak durghatanay* (three separate accidents). She emphasised *preethak*, lest listeners miss it and believe they were killed in three *same* accident!

Newspapers in English-speaking countries come up with the redundant *different* especially when a number of something is mentioned, as in 'He wrote three different books on marketing strategy.' The excerpt below fits into this pattern:

> The BMP has proposed to install more than 1,000 world-class bus-shelters in six different models in the city in the next one year.

One can only wonder whether the omission of *different* could ever imply six *same* models to anyone!

> Four Nepalis, three of them members of one family, and a special branch sub-inspector were among seven people killed in different incidents in Assam since Wednesday night.

The sense here is served better by *some*, though the message would be intact if that word, as well as 'in different incidents' were omitted, to read '. . . among seven killed in Assam since . . .'.

In our English-language newspaper reports, *different* all too often elbows out the more appropriate *various*:

> With housing being declared as a priority sector, the State government has planned to construct two lakh houses for the houseless . . . . Staing this at . . . Housing Minister Q I said the houses would be built under different schemes like the rural and urban Ashraya schemes, Ambedkar Yojana . . . .

The context demands substitution of *different* by *various* to read '. . . built as part of various schemes, such as . . .'.

> Eleven people were killed on Sunday, and an equal number injured when lightning struck them in different parts of the district which was lashed by heavy rain.

The sense intended demands *various* instead of *different*.

> Mr Shetty denies that there was any *difference* in the [High
> School Masters'] association. . . . The constituency with over
> 16,000 voters (teachers of the high school and above) has
> been returning candidates of *different* parties in the last three
> elections.

The first italicised word needs to be replaced with *(were any)*
differences (to mean difference of opinion/dispute), and the
second, with *various*.

> There should be decentralisation of the judicial administra-
> tion considering *the number of* cases pending before the
> *different* courts in the country, Mr Kumar felt.

Replacing the two words italicised with *various* makes the
intended sense clear.

> Considering the incidents of attacks on the minorities in
> *different* parts of the country like the Sikhs and Pandits
> in Kashmir and those from outside the state in the north-
> eastern states, there was a sustained campaign in disturbing
> the harmony in the country, he added.

The sense needs *various* instead of *different*, and the
language needs overhaul.

Reports in our English-language papers bristle with
different when the intended sense is *several/various* as in
these excerpts:

> Leaders of *different* political parties today condemned the
> hoisting of a flag to mark the formation of Northern
> Karnataka state. . . . Addressing *separate* press conferences
> here, they declared that they were opposed to dividing the
> State.

The *separate* only betrays confusion in the mind of the writer: it's possible, but highly improbable, that leaders of *several/various* parties would get together and address the same press conference.

> Prominent Khalistani ideaologues [sic] settled abroad, Jagjit Singh Chauhan and US-based Ganga Singh Dhillon[,] have been secretly hobnobbing with *the different* Gurdwara Management committees and radical groups in India imploring them to send Sikh jathas to Pakistan.

The intention clearly is to use the plural sense, and hence the two italicised words need to be replaced by *various/several*.

> Regarding the recent spree [sic; read: *spate*] of bomb blasts in churches in *different* states, Mr Kumar said it might be the hand of anti-national elements backed by the ISI.

The need to replace *different* with *several* is only too obvious.

Occasionally, news items carry *different* only because the appropriate expression eludes the reporter or the sub-editor:

> Releasing the letter at a press conference here, State BJP President BSY – defended his party's decision. The government has been imposing its views on the Opposition on *different* issues.

The intended meaning would have been served by '. . . imposing its views too often on the Opposition'.

A repetition of *different* usually betrays carelessness with the language:

> Regarding . . . the debacle of the BJP in the just concluded zilla and taluk panchayat polls, the Union Minister said the reasons for the defeat of the BJP in *different* elections like in assembly, parliament or ZP TP elections were *different*. They had to be studied, he added.

That needs overhaul; perhaps: 'The reasons for the BJP's defeat in assembly, parliament, or ZP and TP elections were varied, and needed to be studied, the minister said'.

V

THOSE TROUBLESOME MIDGETS

35

I also don't like that film

The flexible syntax of Indian languages allows varied arrangement of words in the same sentence without change in meaning. Intonation fills in emphasis and nuance. And all Indian languages are spoken with musical intonation. But when we must write, we keep feeling the need for devices to fill in for the missing intonation. A mere rearrangement of words would make little difference to emphasis, given our flexible syntax.

One tempting device is to import extra words to convey the emphasis intended. This leads to the use of adverbs and adjectives more often for emphasis than for precise meaning. Among words most misused thus are *also, as, both, only*.

Also

Perhaps few words in the English language are as often misunderstood and misused in India as this midget. Reports and editorials in English-language newspapers bristle with the redundant and the slovenly *also*. Example:

> Some RJD members, whose party is *also* against the Bill in its present form, were *also* present at the Press Conference.

> Governor V S Rama Devi observed that 'unnecessary delay *also* amounts to corruption in judiciary'.

> Basic literacy would be compulsorily enforced through the
> panchayats and family planning would *also* be compulsorily
> enforced.

The first two illustrate the meaninglessness of the redundant
also in newspaper reports. The third shows that the slovenly
reporter forgot and then tried to paste on with a meaningless
also what he should have placed after *literacy* (to read 'Basic
literacy and family planning would be enforced through the
panchayats').

We all too often forget that *also* has meanings other than
too. Other senses in which it is used:

1 *In addition to/as well as*

> He is the proprietor of this newspaper house, and is also
> the sole agent here for Hyundai cars.
>
> I am tired; I am also hungry.

2 *Likewise*

> We could distribute these papers among the teachers; we
> could also distribute them among students who might be
> interested in such issues.

3 *Besides* – as an afterthought

> Do remember to buy the meat. Also, since you'll be
> going that way, could you call on the plumber? [Such
> afterthought may be all right in speech, but a writer needs
> to get his thoughts organised before writing them.]

The sense of *too* in Indian languages is served either by
an independent word, or a suffix such *as -bhi* in Hindi.
To say *take this* also *with you*, for instance, one would
add the suffix to a noun or pronoun (Hindi: *Isay bhi saath
lay lo)*; *-o* (Bengali: *Etao saathay nao)*; *-bhi/madhya* (Oriya:
Saita madhya nai jayaa); *pun* (Marathi: *Hay pun gheyna*

zaa); or use a separate word, such as *kooda* (Kannada: *Idannu kooda ninna jothe thegedukondu hogu*). Tamil and Malayalam would admit both a suffix (-*yum/um*), and a separate word (*kooda/koodi/koode*). Informal speech might even admit both in the same sentence (Malayalam: *idum koodi eduthu kondu pogoo*; Tamil: *ide-yum eduthukol-lide/kooda eduthukol*).

Often, such a suffix or word is used in Indian languages solely for emphasis. In English, *also* rarely admits emphasis (as in *They also serve who only stand and wait*). But such words or suffixes in Indian languages do not admit the other senses of *also* – namely, *besides/in addition to/likewise*. Indian languages would have other words to serve those meanings (e.g. *aur/iskay alaawa* in Hindi; *aye chcharaa/taa chcharaa/byatita* in Bengali; *au chchada/eha betito* in Oriya; *hyacha shivai* in Marathi; *adhi matto alla* in Tamil; *adhe alladhe* in Malayalam, etc.).

This would explain why *also* is used in such a restricted way, and all too often for unnecessary emphasis in *Indlish*. Its use in English-language newspaper reports and editorials is often meaningless. Some examples:

> Several churches are gearing up to welcome the new millennium year. The Holy Ghost Church in . . . is *also* conducting midnight mass in Tamil, Kannada and English.

After the introductory sentence, the reader expects – and gets – highlights of what each church plans to do. Why does one of them need *also*? It conveys nothing.

> He [the Karnataka Forest Minister] said that the government will take all steps to conserve the existing forest lands. The government will *also not allow* destruction of trees in Western Ghats, he said.

Here, *also* is used with a negative notion. To justify the sense of *too*, the preceding sentence should have handed out a negative notion similar to 'will not allow'. And had such a negative notion been presented, the correct form would have required 'Nor will the government allow . . .'. Negative verbs take *not . . . either/neither/nor*, and not *not also/also not*. For example:

> 'Did you like that film?'
> 'No, I didn't.'
> 'I didn't like it either/Nor did I/Neither did I.' (Not '*I didn't like it also/I also didn't like it.*')

And yet, editorials in the same paper bristle with such unidiomatic negatives:

> The BJP still has not resolved . . . and decided whether it should be a party of governance in the plural society or be an uncompromising sectarian political movement. . . . Mr L K Advani's clarification at the session *also would not* have helped to clear this confusion.

The correct form would require *Mr Advani's clarifications . . . would not have helped either . . ./Nor would Mr Advani's clarifications have helped . . . .*

> What is unfortunately lacking among our educational administrators is the lack of sincerity and earnestness . . . there is *also no monitoring* in the present system and many teachers are apparently not taking their jobs seriously.

Correct: *There is no monitoring . . . nor do many teachers take their jobs seriously.*

Almost every report in the paper employs either a meaningless *also* or its unidiomatic negative use:

> The village, which has come up where the earlier Chalburga

village existed before it was destroyed by the earthquake, *also does not have* temples of any caste or religion.

Here *also* is redundant and has been used with no intent other than misconceived emphasis; it needs to be replaced by *The village . . . has no temple . . .*, etc.

Writers betray their ignorance when they use *also* along with the very words that are its other senses (*likewise/in addition to/moreover/as well as/besides*):

The take off of the . . . flight from Delhi was delayed due to heavy fog. . . . Earlier, another . . . flight from Bangalore was *also* delayed due to *the same* reason.

Here *the same reason* makes *also* altogether redundant. It should read: *Another . . . flight was delayed for the same reason.*

In addition, a board displaying the time when works will be complete will *also* be put up . at the worksite, he said.

In addition to is synonymous with one sense of *also* and the context demanded neither. The sentence would read better as *He said he would have the deadline for each item of the work displayed on a board.*

36

He is equally as good as . . .

Clarity demands that we use words for their precise meaning. Our message becomes muddled when we use words that can imply various meanings. The obvious way out is to choose a synonym that serves the intended sense without ambiguity.

The word *as* causes problems when it is used:

1   to mean *because/for/since* (each of those three would be more precise), and
2   in varied senses in the same context.

These news briefs from a single page of a leading newapaper leave the reader guessing after the meaning of *as*:

> Eighteen students of a middle school at . . . were hospitalised *as* they vomited after partaking of noon meal.
> [meaning: *after*]

> Four people, including three women, were killed and three seriously injured when a train hit their car *as* they were attempting to cross a level crossing near Saharanpur. [meaning: *when*]

> Air services at the capital's Indira Gandhi Airport, which came to a grinding halt . . . due to dense fog, resumed . . . *as* visibility improved. [meaning: *after*]

Confusion worsens when *as* is used in varied senses (though not wrong) in the same report, as here:

According to the Census Directorate, the 2001 census will be carried in a detailed manner *as* compared to the previous census [meaning: nil; *as* needs to be deleted] . . . The Directorate said that it is very essential to have co-ordinate effort *as* a lot of details have to be collected from each house [meaning: *because*]. . . . *As* a preliminary step, listing of number of houses throughout the State will be carried out from May 8 to June 6 [meaning: *in the way of/manner of*]. . . . The [Census coordination] committee will have the Director of the Census Directorate *as* the convenor and the secretaries of prominent departments *as* members [meaning: *in the capacity of*].

Eric Partridge said:

[Such practice] is heavily taxed – grossly overworked – by many writers, who are apparently enamoured of its brevity; often *as* is ambiguous ('he could not work as he was ill in bed') . . . *As* is colloquial both for . . . *because*, and for . . . *for*; either of which is to be preferred to *as* in good writing and dignified speech.

(*Usage and Abusage*, Great Britain: Hamish Hamilton, 1947)

Let us look at some *as*-phrases peculiar to *Indlish*:

As also

This is unnecessarily used where *and/as well as* would be idiomatic:

Parents of one of the air hostesses . . . on board the hijacked flight . . . have appealed to the Prime Minister . . . to ensure safety of their daughter *as also* other passengers.

As because

How this 'twosome' became part of the East India Company clerk's vocabulary only research can reveal. It remains

confined to clerks and typists, and is still handed down to them by the 'commercial colleges' they train at. It appears inevitably in leave applications clerks write:

> I beg to state that I shall not be able to attend office on Wednesday, *as because* I shall have to arrange the *sradh* ceremony of my . . . .

As it is

Derives from transliteration of such expressions as *aisay toe* (Hindi); *akayi toe/emnitayi* (Bengali), etc. used for emphasis. Its use is often meaningless, as in this excerpt from an editorial:

> The attempts to disturb communal amity in Chikmagalur District . . . are most deplorable. . . . This is a matter of deep concern since the communal situation in the district was, *as it is*, quite tense.

As per

In Calcutta, this expression stays confined to clerks in government and merchant offices. These excerpts from reports show how English-language newspapers nurture such East India Company clerks' lingo:

> Panchayat Raj Minister . . . today declared that he would quit office if the gram panchayat elections were not held *as per* schedule . . . this year . . . 'Chief Minister . . . is in favour of holding elections *as per* schedule . . . .' He said there was nothing which was hindering the holding of elections *as per* schedule.

> Referring to the Mysore Palace Acquisition Act, brought in by the previous Janata Dal regime, Mr Wodeyar said legislations were changed *as per* the political postures of different governments.

> In an open ended on-line poll, where the surfers were given
> the choice to vote *as per* their own choice, Sarat Chandra
> Chatterjee polled 7,456 votes to emerge the winner.

Over 50 years ago, Eric Partridge condemned this expression
as 'such horrible *commercialese* that even merchant princes
are less than riotously happy when their secretaries wish
it on them' (*Usage and Abusage*, Great Britain: Hamish
Hamilton, 1947).

As from

This had a legitimate use, though it is seldom used correctly.
Its use in the sense of *with effect from* is wrong; *from* alone
suffices to serve that notion. The correct use would mean
with retrospective effect from: 'Primary teachers will be paid
according to the new scale as from April 1998.'

As and when

This Siamese twin was adopted by Raj-day administrators
as more grand than *when*, even though *when* is all the
expression conveys. Since reporters depend on official
handouts, they carry the Siamese twins into their writing
too, as in this news item:

> Most of the women [from Pakistan] came to the country
> on visitors' visas, got married . . . and stayed on, getting
> extension of the visas *as and when* required.

As to

English-language newspaper editorials perpetuate several
roundabout *as*-phrases, all of them of Victorian vintage.
These fall into two patterns: *as to* followed by a noun, and
as to followed by an adverb. The *as to* of the first group

betrays that the writer has not bothered to search for the appropriate preposition, for which he makes this phrase do duty. For example,

> The dealer could give no idea *as to* the date when he would receive the next consignment of such cutlery. [Replace *as to* with *about* or *of*.]

The *as to* of the second pattern (*as to* how/*as to* whether/*as to* when/*as to* why) is altogether redundant:

> Mr Advani gave no indication *as to* when India would make the evidence public. [Delete *as to*.]

Equally as

The use of *as* alongside *equally* creates the error of logic Fowler called 'an illiterate tautology' (*A Dictionary of Modern English Usage*, OUP, 1926). Where no comparison is expressed within the same sentence, Fowler advised, we should use *equally* alone, and when we do imply a comparison, *as* alone.

> The Taliban authorities were *equally as* perturbed over the killing of helpless hostages, and took a firm stand. [Omit *as*.]

> The Taliban authorities said they were *equally as eager as* India to get the hostages released. [Omit *equally*.]

As a general rule, *as* is redundant after *equally*: two men may be *equally* strong/*equally* good/*equally* bad, not *equally as* strong, etc. Alternative expressions: one may be *just as good/just as bad*, or *as good as/as bad as* the other.

Even as

A valid expression that English-language newspapers have battered out of shape. The correct meaning is *at the very moment that/at the same time as* something else happened. But its use in Indian newspapers conveys no sense of simultaneity, as in this excerpt from an editorial:

> The political picture in Pondicherry continues to be hazy *even as* there is growing indication that the Tamil Manila Congress and the Congress are likely to come together to form an alternative government.

Many news reports begin with it and achieve nonsense:

> *Even as* the agony of the 150-odd passengers on board the hijacked Indian Airlines aircraft *continues* at the Kandahar airport in Afghanistan for the seventh day, popular and expert opinion *was* fully in favour of rejecting the hijackers' demand outright.

> *Even as* the striking students in Andhra Pradesh have decided to intensify their ongoing agitation . . . against the government policies, Chief Minister . . . has defended the awarding of marks to students participating in the programme.

37

No parking *both* sides

Few determiners cause errors of logic as often as does *both*. This tiny word has foxed English-speaking people ever since they borrowed it from Norsemen. It is difficult to pin down an exact equivalent for *both* in Indian languages. Most Indian equivalents would come close to *the two of us/we two*. *Both* looks at the two together; *the two* looks at each of them separately. Also, *we both* focuses on the two together, but *both of us* looks at the two separately. Such logical niceties can, and often do, cause confusion.

In *Indlish*, we often meet:

1 *both* used where *each/either* is required
2 the illogical *both*
3 the redundant *both*
4 *both* used with a negative expression
5 *both* used where *the two* would be appropriate
6 *both* at the wrong position.

These categories are arbitrary and I list them only for convenience. All of them are caused by illogical or muddled thinking.

No parking *both* sides

Eric Partridge cites the example '*There is a garage on* both *sides of the street*', which, he says, should be *There is a*

garage on each *side of the street* – 'unless the author means
that a garage is partly on one, partly on the other side
of the street' (*Usage and Abusage*, Great Britain: Hamish
Hamilton, 1947).

One might still find some old traffic signs in Calcutta
that warned car owners against parking at some places. The
sign read '*No parking* both *sides*' – better conveyed by '*No
parking on* either *side*'. This ties up with *both* used with a
negative expression.

The illogical *both*

But *both* is illogically used for *each/either* also in contexts
where no negative notion is implied, as these excerpts from
news items and editorials show:

> Mr Chautala's statement that *both* parties would have a
> *separate* poll manifesto for the Assembly elections scheduled
> for March, *too* has irked the BJP leaders.

An absurdity: *each* party might have a *separate* manifesto,
both of them can't. The message is clearer as 'Mr Chautala's
statement that *each party* would have *its own* manifesto . . .
has irked BJP leaders.'

An analogous error of logic ushers in *both* where *each*
+ verb + *other* would serve one's meaning:

> The border agreement signed by China and Vietnam is a
> significant milestone in relations between the two countries
> . . . there were serious differences on the border too with *both*
> accusing *each other* of incursions.

This editorial writer achieves the ludicrous: one accuses
another or *the other*, so that *both* has no place. The intended
meaning is served by '. . . there were serious differences . . .
with *each* accusing *the other* of incursions'.

Both individual and joint statements

The redundant *both* comes in whenever the word is used in the same context with *alike/as well as/at once/between/equally*. This, said Fowler, 'is at least a fault of style, and at worst (e.g. with *between*) an illogicality' (*A Dictionary of Modern English Usage*, OUP, 1926).

Some examples:

> The Karnataka Administrative Tribunal passed an order directing the State government to treat *both* teachers and engineers *alike* and to give the benefits given to teachers to engineers *also*.

This reporter has packed *both*, *alike* and *also* in the same sentence. Logical thinking might have prompted him to write 'directing . . . to extend the benefits to teachers and engineers *alike*'.

> In *both* individual *as well as* joint statements, the party leaders have stated that it was not appropriate to focus suspicion on any particular community.

This is a gross error of logic: the reporter sees an identicality in *statements*, even though he says they differ in nature – namely, joint and individual. The omission of *both* helps sense.

The redundant *both* is dragged in also by hazy thinking:

> Under terms of the definitive deal, which has been approved unanimously by *both* boards of directors, Time Warner and America Online stock will be converted to . . . .

Surely, no deal can be worked out unless the directors approve its terms. The entire parenthetic clause containing *both* is redundant and the sentence should read: 'According to the terms of their deal, Time Warner and . . . converted to . . . .'

Both parties are not keen

Muddled thinking places *both* with plural verb in negative statements that require *each/either/neither/nor* + singular verb:

> He declined to go into strategic aspects of bilateral ties, particularly the defence cooperation between the two [Israel and India]. For, there were 'compulsions' on *both* sides *not* to discuss it publicly, he added.

Surely, that sense is better served by 'For *each* side had its own compulsions against public discussion, he added'.

> According to reports, *both* parties are *not* keen on being seen to have brought down a government which still has its term to complete.

What this editorial writer meant was '*neither* party is keen to be seen as having brought down a government . . .'.

> Mr Swando said the negotiations are being held in Korea and the Indian subsidiaries of *both* the companies [General Motor and Daewoo] are *not* included in the discussions.

The business writer's meaning would have been clear had he written '. . . and the Indian subsidiary of neither company has been included . . .' or '. . . and each company has excluded its Indian subsidiary from the discussions'.

Both the Patnaiks

Often, *both* is used where *the two* would be appropriate:

> If sources in the Congress and the BJD are to be believed, trusted aides of *both* the Patnaiks [J B and Naveen] have already short-listed a few constituencies for their party chiefs.

There is no justification for using *both* with rivals who cannot be thought of together; 'aides of *the two* Patnaiks' is what the confused editorial writer intended.

> Launching the party's campaign . . . he [Om Prakash Chautala] said '*both* the parties will contest elections together'.

Mr Chautala must have said what translates correctly into 'the two parties will . . .'.

Confusion in the writer's mind over *both* and *the two* can lead to nonsense such as this:

> A small high level group comprising Dr—, member (Finance Commission), Dr—, member (Planning Commission) and other officials from *both* commissions have been formed to sort out the issues and adoption of unified approach by *both* commissions.
>
> The high-level group involving officials from *both* commissions would be meeting soon to evolve modalities for a unified approach in this matter by *both* commissions.

What must have been meant: 'A small high-level committee comprising . . . and other officials from *the two* panels has been formed to suggest a joint action plan. This committee will meet soon.'

Wrong position of *both*

Both in the wrong position betrays that the writer does not understand that wrong placing of a word can alter sense, given the rigid syntax of English:

> *Both* the old man [Augusto Pinochet] and the young boy [Elian, Cuban refugee] are responsible for their life; ideological predilections and national prejudices should be allowed no role to play.

The writer of this piece obviously does not understand that *both* must go with the word/s that indicate common ground:

'The old man and the young boy are *both* responsible for their lives.' That raises the question how a six-year-old can be *responsible* for his life. But then editorial writers in English-language papers go more by sound than sense.

38

Balancing with *both*

Let's turn to the correct use of *both*. All usage rules have their controversies, and some rules on the use of *both* are still debated. First, the rules that are accepted:

Position of *both*

Confusion usually occurs about the position of the verb that is common to the two nouns that *both* sees together. The easy way out is to remember to place the common verb before, and the nouns after *both*:

> The rebel MLAs said they would keep their distance from *both* the BJP and the Congress.

The message in that sentence is that a breakaway group (number of MLAs not stated) had decided that their strategy would be to distance themselves from those two parties. The emphasis is on their strategy. That message would change if, as one often sees in news reports, *both* were placed before or after the subject.

'*Both* the rebel MLAs said . . .' would mean there were *two* MLAs and they had agreed on this strategy. That shifts the emphasis from the strategy to their agreement, when the original message emphasised the *strategy* the group (not two of them) had decided on.

'The rebel MLAs *both* said . . .' would mean that two particular MLAs (who have already been mentioned) took the same stand on strategy. That shifts the emphasis to the two MLAs and leaves unclear whether they spoke for a group. This arrangement could also mean there were two MLAs, not a group.

Both . . . and

In the first example *both* is followed by a noun (*the BJP*). The rule of parallel construction demands the same treatment for *and* – as in the example (the Congress). But this rule is often forgotten and one notices *both* followed by one part of speech and *and* by quite another. That leaves a sentence unbalanced, as here:

> The new version [of scooters] would be upgraded *both* technologically *and* in its look . . . a company official said.

This example from a business-and-finance page report is typical of the unbalanced construction one sees in newspapers. Here, *both* is followed by an adverb; *and* by a phrase that has a preposition and a noun. One way to ensure parallel construction would be to place a similar phrase with a noun after *both*:

> The new version would be an improvement *both* in technology *and* in appearance.

This rule of parallel construction applies to all other correlative expressions, such as *not . . . but*; *not only . . . but also*; *either . . . or*; *neither . . . nor*; *first . . . second . . . third*, etc.

On this there is no controversy, and we might look at what Sir Ernest Gowers said 50 years ago:

When using *both* . . . *and*, be careful that these words are in their right positions and carry equal weight. Nothing that comes between the *both* and the *and* can be regarded as carried on after the *and*. If words are to be carried on after the *and* they must precede the *both*; if they do not precede the *both* they must be repeated after the *and*. For instance:

He was *both deaf to* argument and entreaty.

Since *deaf to* comes after *both*, it cannot be 'understood' again after *and*. We must adjust the balance in one of the following ways:

He was both deaf to argument and unmoved by entreaty.
He was deaf both *to* argument and *to* entreaty.
He was deaf to both argument and entreaty.

Here is a sentence where the unbalanced *both* puts the reader off the scent:

Staff may seek rewards and satisfaction from both their superiors and their clients.

This seems to say that there are two superiors, from both of whom, as well as from their clients, the staff may seek rewards. But that is not what the writer meant; he should have written 'both from their superiors . . .'.

An extreme example of the unbalanced *both*:

The proposed sale must be both sanctioned by the Minister and the price must be approved by the District Valuer.

(*The Complete Plain Words*, 1954)

Both/both of

The placing of *of* after *both* often causes confusion. Should one say 'Both sailors were drunk' or 'Both *of* the sailors were drunk'? 'Both sisters were pretty' or 'Both *of* the sisters were pretty'?

Omission of *of* after *both* always sounds better and emphasises looking at the two together. But placing *of* after *both* is not wrong practice. Which to use depends on the sense intended. If we think of the two together, we should omit *of*. If we speak of them as individuals, we may insert *of* after *both*. That means we should follow up 'both sailors were drunk' with what both did together, or in a similar fashion:

> Both sailors were drunk; both sang aloud and swayed clumsily to keep their balance.

But:

> Both *of* the sailors were drunk. One waved a bottle of hooch and screeched invectives at some invisible enemy; the other reeled a bit, but was silent and pensive, as though dead to the world.

The same reasoning applies to the use of pronouns.

> Both his sons went to Doon School.

But

> Though both *of* his sons had grown up, he was worried about how the second would fare, naive as he was.

The first looks at the two sons together; the second looks at them individually.

Us *both*/*both of us*

In placing pronouns after *both of*, usage admits *both of you*/*both of us*/*both of them* as correct. Eric Partridge said *you both*/*us both*/*them both*/*they both* were incorrect, but *admitted* that 'one often hears all of them, except *they both*' (*Usage and Abusage*, Great Britain: Hamish

Hamilton, 1947). But the 1998 Indian reprint of Longman dictionary admits 'They both started speaking together.' And so does Frederick T Wood in *Current English Usage* (Macmillan, 1962).

Both/both the

Closely related is the placing of *the* after both. To go by the example cited, do we say 'Both sailors were drunk' or 'Both *the* sailors were drunk'? Surely, if we were thinking of the two together, it would be better to omit *the*. Some idiomatic examples:

> The bickering will go on till both sides [India and Pakistan] see the need to reach agreement.

> Both his parents are diabetics, and doctors say he has 70% chance of turning diabetic before he reaches 40.

> I think I'll buy both books.

One all too often sees the ill-placed *the* after *both* in newspaper reports, as here:

> The decision to this effect gains significance as the management and the workers union had reached an understanding on January 6 this year to resume work at both *the* units of the company [Sahagunj and Ambattur units of Dunlop].

One need only read that aloud without *the* and feel the improvement its omission makes. A simple rule: if we place *the* before the first noun after *both*, so should we before the second, as in the example cited at 'Position of *Both*'. If only one plural noun follows *both* (as above), we should omit *the*.

39

Only where it belongs

The placing and misplacing of *only* in a sentence has been much debated. Fowler quoted a letter from someone who found fault with the placing of *only*: 'I read the other day', the correspondent complained, 'of a man who "only died a week ago", as if he could have done anything more striking or final; what was meant by the writer was that "he died only a week ago".'

Fowler frowned on the critic: 'There speaks one of those friends from whom the English language may well pray to be saved, one of the modern precisians who have more zeal than discretion, and wish to restrain liberty.' Fowler went on to say:

> There is an orthodox position for the adverb, easily determined in case of need; to choose another position that may spoil or obscure the meaning is bad; but a change of position that has no such effect except technically is not only justified by historical and colloquial usage but often demanded by rhetorical needs.
>
> (*A Dictionary of Modern English Usage*, OUP, 1926)

But Eric Partridge (in *Usage and Abusage*, Great Britain: Hamish Hamilton, 1947) sided with the 'precisian' when he insisted that the expression 'We only heard it yesterday' should be 'We heard it only yesterday'. He said:

Shakespeare makes this mistake in

> The summer's flower is to the summer sweet
> Though to itself it *only* live and die.

There is also ambiguity in the use of *only* where *alone* would be clearer, as in Nesfield's example from Johnson (Letter to Rev. Mr White), 'No book has been published since your departure[,] of which much notice is taken. Faction *only* fills the town with pamphlets, and greater subjects are forgotten.' Nesfield takes 'only' to be an adjective qualifying 'faction', but might it not be an adverb qualifying 'fills'? Coleridge, a careful writer, at least once committed a misplacement: 'The wise only possess ideas; the greater part of mankind are possessed by them' ('Notes of Robinson Crusoe', 1830): properly, 'only the wise'. Even G K Chesterton fell into the error of a misplaced *only*, as in 'His black coat looked as if it were only black by being too dense a purple. His black beard looked as if it were only black by being too deep a blue.'

(*The Man Who Was Thursday*)

We in India need to be more concerned with the kind of misplacing of *only* that, in Fowler's words, 'may spoil or obscure the meaning'. Given the rigid syntax of English – as opposed to the flexible syntax of Indian languages – the message in many an English sentence can change with each shift in the placing of *only*. The message intended by *I have only a hundred rupees on me* would change entirely if we were to shift *only* to the beginning and say *Only I have a hundred rupees on me*. The first says I have no more than this; the second, that I alone in my group have the amount (implying that others with me have either little or no money at all).

Let's look at the change of message with each shift in the position of *only* in the same sentence:

Laloo said he needed the support of *only* the Yadavs. (Message: If he had their support, it wouldn't matter if non-Yadavs didn't vote for him.)

Laloo said he needed *only* the support of the Yadavs. (Message becomes unclear; it could mean he was confident about support from other groups, and now needed only the Yadavs' assurance.)

Laloo said he *only* needed the support of the Yadavs. (Message is unclear; perhaps the same as in the second example.)

Laloo said *only* he needed the support of the Yadavs. (Message: He alone needed such support; the other contenders had support among other groups.)

Laloo *only* said he needed the support of the Yadavs. (Message: To a question – perhaps about his chances of success – Laloo said this was what he still needed to ensure success.)

Only Laloo said he needed the support of the Yadavs. (Message: Laloo alone said this; none of the other contenders did.)

A shift in the position of *only* could change the message sharply even in a short and simple sentence. Compare *He is an only child* (message: he has no siblings) with *He is only a child* (message: and therefore we should be tender and indulgent). The debate about the correct placing of *only* in a sentence becomes meaningless unless one defines which function of *only* one means. For *only* can function as an adverb, an adjective, and also as a conjunction. The rigid syntax of English demands that related words be placed close to each other. And by that rule, *only* should stay close to the verb it qualifies when it acts as an adverb.

Confusion would result if, when we intend to use *only* as an adverb, we were to shift it to where it would seem to be an adjective. This accounts for the changes in Laloo's message. We have only to examine those sentences closely to find that the message keeps changing as *only* serves now as an adjective and again as an adverb, relating now with one word, and again with another.

Arguments over the placing of *only* overlook the role intonation plays. In the informal spoken form of any language, intonation makes the message clear, even though the arrangement of words may be somewhat faulty. Intonation *cannot* be conveyed in the written form of a language, and precise arrangement of words therefore becomes important.

Given its rigid syntax, word arrangement becomes all the more important in written English. And, with all due reverence for Fowler, what he considers 'justified by . . . colloquial usage' may not always serve clarity in writing. The *Concise Oxford Dictionary* (compiled by the Fowler brothers) says:

> In informal English, *only* is usually placed between the subject and the verb, regardless of what it refers to (e.g. I only want to talk to you); in more formal English it is often placed more exactly, especially to avoid ambiguity (e.g. I want to talk only to you). In speech, intonation usually serves to clarify the sense.

Let's look at a few idiomatic sentences where *only* acts as an adverb:

> Police warned the suspect his silence would *only* make matters worse. (*Only* here means *merely* and qualifies *make . . . worse.*)

The man said he wanted *only* overripe apples to make his cider. (Meaning: *solely*; qualifies *overripe*)

Only the US President can press the nuclear button. (Meaning: *exclusively*; qualifies *US . . . can press*)

The man looked tired and said he *only* wanted to sit for a while. (Meaning: *nothing else besides*; qualifies *wanted to . . . a while*)

These make clear that *only* relates not merely to a single word that may be a verb or an adjective, but often to a phrase or part of a sentence. The correct position of *only* should be dictated more by the sense intended, than by rules of grammar. We should so position *only* in a sentence that there can be no ambiguity.

40

Clinton even took care to get photographed . . .

We often bring in redundancy in our speech and writing with words we use to emphasise what needs no emphasis. All too often, the need we feel to emphasise an idea is misconceived: its expression would be clearer if we omitted words we use solely for emphasis. Among these are *actually*, *also*, *definitely*, *even*, *only* and *really*. Of them, *actually* and *really* long ago joined the list of meaningless words and became what Fowler termed 'noises automatically produced' (discussed in 'Words without Meaning', pp. 167–72).

Earlier, I dealt with the misuse of *also* and *only* in *Indlish*. Yet another word that keeps appearing needlessly in our writing is *even*.

Eric Partridge put it across emphatically: '*Even* (like *actually*, *definitely* and *really*) is often used where there is no need for it, with the result that instead of the desired emphasis, there is weakness' (*Usage and Abusage*, Great Britain: Hamish Hamilton, 1947).

Reports and editorials in English-language newspapers in India bristle with

- the redundant *even*
- the mystifying *even*

- *even* where *also/too* is meant
- the absurd *even*
- the wrongly placed *even*.

Most often, the redundant *even* and the mystifying *even* overlap and leave us wondering why the word was used at all. The mystifying *even* creeps into pompous editorials, as this excerpt shows:

> In the atmosphere of conflict of interests and mutual suspicion, words and actions carry *even* meanings which otherwise they would not have.

The *even* in that sentence can only confuse the reader. Whatever did the author mean? If *even* were deleted from that sentence and *can* inserted after *actions*, the sentence would perhaps convey the meaning intended. But then, hacks who write editorials for English-language papers often have no message in mind, and one's guess could be wide of the mark.

The reader can only wonder at the significance of *even* in this excerpt from another editorial in the same paper:

> But in Bihar the Governor, Mr Vinod Pande, did not have any justification to invite Mr Nitish Kumar to form the government. . . . Mr Pande cannot *even* plead an error of judgment. The figures were there all for him to add up.

Here, the omission of *even* makes the message forceful; its insertion brings in obfuscation and weakness – a good example of the redundant *even*.

Sometimes, *even* is used when some other word (such as *also/too*) would be more appropriate:

> This is the story of Karnataka during the latter half of 1999. Nothing significant happened during the first half and this holds good *even* for the international airport.

The message would be clearer here if *even* were deleted and *too* placed after *airport*.

Court reports in newspapers often leave the reader guessing:

> He noted that *even* after considering all the evidence, the petitioner has only violated the norms and procedure, which do not prima facie constitute any offence under Section 13(1) (d) of the Prevention of Corruption Act.

That sentence can only mean that the judge *noticed* ('noted') that the petitioner (not the judge) had *considered* all the evidence, and had concluded that he had committed no offence. Since that cannot make sense, one can only go by guesswork and reword that into sense after omitting *even*:

> He said that the evidence amounted to a violation of procedure. That alone did not constitute an offence.

Not to be outdone by court reporters, news reporters do their bit to baffle the reader with the absurd *even*:

> India's Foreign Office had expressed its opposition to any meeting between Hurriyat leaders and Mr Clinton and *even* communicated its views to Washington.

The *even* here is a gross absurdity. The Foreign Office can always present its views to Washington. Did the reporter have reason to believe that the Foreign Office had achieved some feat of derring-do?

A report in the same paper had this sentence:

> Mr Clinton spent about two hours watching the marble structure. He *even* took care to get photographed before the Taj with his daughter Chelsea.

Only the reporter can explain what kind of care he saw

Mr Clinton take for it to need that *even*. In this excerpt from another of the paper's reports, the author decides to go one up on his colleagues: he first imports the redundant *even* and follows up with the absurd *even*:

> Janata Dal (U) floor leader . . . raised several technical objections . . . and leader of the Opposition . . . demanded that the Opposition members should be allowed to express their reservations *even* before the introduction of the bill. . . . *Even* the Speaker endorsed their opinion.

Placing of *even*

As with *only*, the misplacing of *even* can change the sense intended. Fowler, who took a liberal stand on the placing of *only* (as discussed in '*Only* Where It Belongs', pp. 241–6), is more strict on the placing of *even*. Fowler said:

> [The placing of adverbs] is a matter partly of idiom and partly of sense; *even* is one of those whose placing is important to the sense. *Even I did not see him on Monday* implies that I was more likely to see him than anyone else was. *I did not even see him on Monday* implies that I had expected not only to see him, but also to speak to him. *I did not see even him on Monday* implies that he was the person I expected to see. *I did not see him even on Monday* implies that Monday was the day on which I expected to see him.
>
> (*A Dictionary of Modern English Usage*, OUP, 1926)

This excerpt from yet another report in the same 'leading daily' shows an example of the misplaced *even*:

> Though the displaced vendors have a tale of woes to narrate, the common village folk is [sic] elated at the visit [Mr Clinton's]. . . . The village now gets round-the-clock power supply. All its 150 telephones which were erratic are now 'perfect'. 'Earlier we could not *even* get connected to

Jaipur,' says . . . a final year M A (Hindi) student at the Jaipur University.

What the M A student must have said was that they could not get connected *even* to (a place as close as) Jaipur.

The howlers our English-language paper reporters achieve with *even as* have already been discussed in 'He Is Equally as Good as', pp. 221–7. A valid expression these papers do not use is *even so*. Fowler said:

> [That phrase] often serves as a conveniently short reminder to the reader that the contention before him is not the strongest that could be advanced. . . . But some writers become so attached to this convenience that they resort to it when it is a convenience to them and an inconvenience to their readers, i.e. when it takes a reader some time to discover what exactly the writer means by it.

The last sentence fits the bill accurately for our reporters' use of *even*.

VI

MOTHER TONGUE, OTHER TONGUE

41

Let's plainspeak

When Bangalore was to have a cyber park built to encourage new IT companies to set up shop, this is how the city's leading English-language daily served the news:

> Highly-placed sources in the commerce and industries department said the cyberpark *facility* envisages *facilitating* start-up IT ventures to have *comprehensive infrastructure facilities* to enable commencement of software development operations in a short duration. . . . The park would provide *facilities* like modular office space, uninterrupted power supply, water supply, telecom and hardware support *facilities*, banking *facilities* and a business centre.

What sense does that make to the average reader? Why do we write like this? The answer lies in the *mantra* syndrome that afflicts every Indian. It's rooted in our culture. It allows our priests to mutter Sanskrit *mantra*s that neither they nor the devotees understand. It's what helps our *neta*s get away with all the pompous blather they mouth at election rallies. The nature of the disease: neither message nor meaning matters; only sound does. Sonorousness is all. That explains the sound and fury every Indian politician cultivates.

With the English language in India, there's the added problem of the Victorian legacy that hangs like a dead albatross around each educated Indian's neck. The educated Indian is schooled in archaic Victorian English. And the Victorians consciously tried to imitate the blather of German scholars of their time. Karl Popper, acknowledged as the major influence in modern philosophy and political thought, had this to say about this German cult of incomprehensibility:

> Many years ago, I used to warn my students against the widespread idea that one goes to college in order to learn how to talk and write 'impressively' and incomprehensibly. At the time, many students came to college with this ridiculous aim in mind, especially in Germany. . . . They unconsciously learn that highly obscure and difficult language is the intellectual value par excellence. . . .
>
> Thus arose the cult of incomprehensibility, of 'impressive' and high-sounding language. This was intensified by the (for laymen) impenetrable and impressive formalism of mathematics. I suggest that in some of the more ambitious social sciences and philosophies, especially in Germany, the traditional game, which has largely become the unconscious and unquestioned standard, is to state the utmost trivialities in high-sounding language.
>
> (Karl R Popper, *The Myth of the Framework*, London & New York: Routledge, 1996)

Our addiction to *mantra* destroys our resistance to blather devoid of meaning. When archaic Victorian English aggravates this, we become incapable of producing anything but the obfuscating gibberish that English-language newspapers in India serve every day. And this is what every college student absorbs into his system.

If we agree that informal language makes our writing more readable, why do we torture our readers with what's

fuddy-duddy? How can we keep our writing from turning into the meaningless jabber of government office clerks?

As long ago as 1949, Rudolph Flesch tried to answer these questions. Over-formal English, he said, was 'typically . . . the language of minor clerks, secondary officials, cogs in some social machine. It is their psychological substitute for personal importance. The farther towards the bottom, the thicker the coat of assumed dignity.' And the secret of lively language, he said, was simple: 'Stop being stuffy and talk like a human being – that's that!' Write simple; write plain. Of course we've all heard that advice before. But why do we find that simple advice so difficult to follow?

What we've not done seriously is take a close look at the nature of the English language. What's never attempted in our schools and colleges is getting students to understand how the English language behaves, contrasted with how the Indian languages do. If we did, we'd find that there are broadly four major areas in which the English language behaves almost opposite Indian languages. If we could remember these four areas, we could then easily revise what we write and ensure that it reads like contemporary English, rather than the archaic gibberish we got from the Raj days.

42

The lady with mahogany legs

A Bangalore paper's report on pre-election grouses in a political party included this sentence:

> Mr Krishna said the committees had been dissolved by him in view of serious complaints that loyal partymen had been ignored while constituting them earlier.

That left the reader wondering how loyal partymen are 'constituted'. Had the reader the time to unravel that puzzle, he would have guessed that the intended meaning was that loyal partymen had been ignored when those committees were set up (constituted).

Why do so many reports in our English-language papers include such confusing sentences? Why do their authors think we have time to unravel these puzzles? The answer: neither those who write them, nor those who edit them, seem to understand that people cannot write efficiently in a borrowed tongue unless they understand how that language behaves. In at least four major areas, English behaves the polar opposite of all written Indian languages.

Syntax

All Indian languages have an immensely flexible syntax, so that we can keep changing the arrangement of words in a sentence, without much harm to sense. Thus, we could say *main nay aaj kuchch nahin khayaa* (I didn't eat anything today), or change the position of those words without changing the message, and say: *kuchch nahin khayaa main nay aaj/aaj nahin kuchch khayaa main nay/nahin kuchch khayaa main nay aaj*, and so on.

But if we were to try this with words in the English version, most such combinations would amount to nonsense. (Try *anything haven't today I eaten/Today haven't eaten anything I*, etc. for sense.) Contrasted with Indian languages, the syntax of English is very rigid. Often, there is only one way that words in an English sentence may be arranged to best convey the sense intended. A change in the arrangement could change the meaning altogether, or render it nonsense.

Consider this classified advertisement in a newspaper:

Wanted a piano for a lady with mahogany legs

Only one arrangement of those words can most efficiently get the intended meaning across:

Wanted for a lady a piano with mahogany legs

Any other arrangement would need punctuation, or sound awkward, or take away sense.

Because we don't have this problem with the flexible syntax of Indian languages, we forget to check what we write in English for errors of syntax. Unless we work out for ourselves an easy way to tackle the rigidity of English syntax, that lady will always put her mahogany foot in the English we write. The easiest way to keep her at bay: we must revise our sentences to see that we do not separate related words or ideas; that words or ideas that belong together, stay together.

Those mahogany legs belong to the piano. Place them with the piano. The word 'wanted' goes with the lady. Place them close and everything automatically falls into place. If we apply that simple principle to the convoluted sentence in the Bangalore paper, we get:

> Mr Krishna said he had dissolved the committees because of complaints that when they were set up loyal partymen were ignored.

That arrangement relates the committees with 'set up' (constituted) and the complaints with ignoring the loyalists – ideas that belong together.

Errors of syntax create howlers. Trouble is, after the reader has had his laugh, he justifiably becomes contemptuous of those who work for the paper that provides such entertainment. Some more howlers from the same paper:

> Mr Revanasiddaiah said Mr Manjunath had expressed his willingness to contribute the amount in a letter written to him.

How does one contribute money in a letter? Does the reporter mean that he would send a cheque? It takes the reader some effort to work out that the letter conveyed not the amount, but his willingness to contribute. And that message would have been crystal clear had the reporter not separated related words and said:

> Mr R said that in his letter, Mr M had expressed his willingness to contribute the amount.

Here's another:

> Cabinet Ministers waited in vain in the Cabinet Hall for Mr Patel to arrive from 11 am to 2.30 pm.

That left the reader wondering whether Mr Patel had turned snail and was inching his way to the hall over all of three-and-a-half hours! With better understanding of syntax, the reporter and sub-editor would have attributed those three-and-a-half hours to the waiting ministers:

> The ministers waited between 11 am and 2.30 pm for Mr Patel to arrive at the Cabinet hall.

The context would have made clear that their wait was futile – 'in vain'.

43

Jest *choop* and *chel*

Because we in India inherited the legacy of literary Victorian English (which perverted the way English always worked), we do not notice the difference between the way we use the noun, and the way the English use the verb. In all written Indian languages, we retain the noun rigidly as a noun and instead of modifying it into a verb when needed, we add a 'do' or a 'doing' word after it. The Hindi equivalents are *kurna/karke/kijiye*, etc., and the Bengali, *koray/koroon/korchchi*, etc.

With only a few everyday words do we transform the noun into a verb, as *khao* from *khanaa*; *jao* from *janaa*. We have no verbs for most of the Sanskrit words we use, nor for many of those derived from Sanskrit. And so, though we may modify the noun *khana* and say *tum khao/aap khayiye*, or *aap jaayiye*, we'd have to fall back on the 'do'/'doing' word if we used the Sanskrit words *bhojan/aahaar* and say *aap bhojan kijiye/aap aahaar kijiye*. Neither *bhojan* nor *aahaar* can be transformed into a verb. We cannot say *tum bhojano/aap aahaariye*.

English differs from all written Indian languages most in this: all English nouns readily change into a verb and often the noun serves also as the verb. Thus, a man can *man* a boat, and a mother can *mother* her child, even though he might feel he's grown up and needs no more mothering!

In written Indian languages, the noun dominates every sentence; in the English sentence, the verb is the most important word. The difference becomes obvious when the Englishman tries pidgin Hindi. Kipling gives a rare insight into this in one of his stories about young British soldiers in Simla: they are at a pub, where their tiresome old colonel keeps flirting with young girls they want to chat up. They keep buying the colonel drinks till he is sloshed and bundle him into a horse carriage. This is how one of them uses pidgin Hindi (italicised) to tell the coachman to rush and dump the colonel back in the barracks:

> Now look 'ere ye bloke, *av* he *bolos* anything, jest ye *choop* and *chel*. And the *chooper* ye *choops*, and the *jilder* ye *chels*, the more *kooshy* will the sahib be. And 'ere's a rupee fer ye.

Accustomed to obtaining his verbs from nouns, the British soldier saw no need to tag the 'do' or 'doing' word like *rahna* (*choop rahna/chaltey rahna*). Contrast Kipling's illustration with the way we must keep tagging the 'do' or 'doing' word every time we wish to suggest any action: *koshish karna/chestaa koro* (not just *try*); *phone karna/phone koro* (not just *phone*), and so on.

The English sentence has always operated on the verb. But literary Victorian English changed all that. Because the Victorian gentleman wished to show off his little learning, he affected Latinate words. And this landed him in the same problem that we face with words that are *tatsama* (unaltered from Sanskrit) and *tadbhava* (derived from Sanskrit): these borrowings are limited to the noun; we do not use the corresponding verb. What that does to Indian languages,

Latinate words do to English: where the verb isn't borrowed or can't be fashioned, one needs to keep adding those 'do' or 'doing' words.

We can be direct if we use the everyday word *smell*, and say: 'She smells nice.' But if we were to use the Latinate *fragrance*, we'd no longer be able to be as brief, because the verb for *fragrance* hasn't been borrowed from Latin. We couldn't say 'She *fragrances* nice', and we'd have to add the 'doing' word and become roundabout to express the same idea: 'She exudes a pleasant fragrance.'

The result: Victorian writing perverted the directness that is the *dharma* of English, and took on roundabout forms of expression. No wonder Indian Brahmins, steeped in stilted Sanskritised languages, took to it like ducks to water.

Through his sketch of Mr Micawber in *David Copperfield*, Dickens lampooned the un-English pomposity that crept into Victorian prose. Mr Micawber had a phobia: that he might utter plain English, instead of the pompous variety that was supposed to distinguish the educated Victorian gentleman. And so Micawber always wrote out lengthy letters, which he read out to impress his audience. That guaranteed that he never uttered plain English. An excerpt:

> I am at present engaged, my dear Copperfield, in the *sale* of corn upon commission. It is not an *avocation* of a remunerative *description* – in other words, it does not pay – and some temporary *embarrassments* of a pecuniary *nature* have been the consequence. I am, however, delighted to add that I have now an immediate *prospect* of something turning up (I am not at liberty to say in what *direction*), which I trust will enable me to provide, both for myself and for your friend Traddles, in whom I have an unaffected interest. (96 words)

That string of adjective-laden nouns (italicised), has made for roundabout expressions. It's the kind of writing one finds in English-language newspaper editorials, memos by government officials, and drab textbooks.

One needs only to convert the nouns where possible into verbs, and delete the silly adjectives, to arrive at contemporary English. If we apply that principle to Micawber's letter, this is what we get:

> I now *sell* corn on commission, Copperfield, but it *doesn't pay* and I'*m* in debt. But something's about to turn up soon (I *can't give* you the details yet), that I believe will *solve* all problems both for me and for your friend Traddles. I'*m* rather fond of him. (48 words)

Micawber's note has now shed half its load. And this has been achieved only through changing his nouns into verbs (italicised) and deleting unnecessary adjectives. And here's the rub: Dickens invented Micawber to poke fun at pompous Victorian language. But Micawber has become a role model for those who churn out editorials for English-language newspapers in India; as here:

> Another major *disaster* so soon after last month's *accident* highlights the inexcusable *failure* of the Railways in ensuring the requisite *alertness* for precluding a *disaster* which has claimed so many *victims*. (31 words)

If we change some of those nouns (italicised) to verbs, and delete the overblown adjectives (*major, inexcusable, requisite*) we could get something more readable:

> Another accident so soon after last month's only proves that the railways can't stay alert enough to prevent such disasters. (20 words)

If we wish to write contemporary English, we need only to switch from the Victorian way of writing with a string of adjective-laden nouns and work with verbs freed of their burden of adverbs. That will make our writing direct and forceful, which is the strength of plain English.

44

Enemy fire had been responded to

Roundabout expression is ingrained in our feudal culture that frowns upon directness. On this count, English and written Indian languages are at loggerheads. All written Indian languages nurture the passive expression as elegant and formal. English, on the other hand, always sounds vigorous when the active voice is used; the passive voice often renders the English sentence weak.

Most passive expressions commonly used in all Indian languages are alien to English: *Yeh kaam mujhse nahin ho payegaa/ei kaaj amaar dwara hawbey naa* goes down well in Hindi/Bengali. But *This work cannot be done by me* is altogether un-English.

Because reporters write, and sub-editors pass, passive sentences modelled on our regional languages, our English-language newspaper reports often read quaint and un-English. The daily Army briefing over the Kargil skirmish in 1999 treated readers to un-English passives such as this:

> The army spokesman noted that enemy fire *had been responded to* by the Indian artillery and as per radio intercepts, the enemy has suffered some casualties.

Had the reporter and the sub-editor known that English does not work well in the passive, they would have translated that *Indlish* to read:

> The army spokesman said Indian artillery responded to enemy fire and, to go by radio intercepts, hit some intruders.

Reports by senior analysts, too, were couched in the passive:

> India would like political affirmation from Pakistan on ending terrorism sponsored by it through various means before the two countries sat down for talks, the Foreign Office spokesperson said here today.

Translated into the active voice that contemporary English demands, that would read:

> The Foreign Office spokesperson said that before the talks begin, India wants Pakistan's promise to stop sponsoring terrorism.

The un-English use of the passive voice belongs to *commercialese*, or commercial English, which is defined as 'words and phrases used in commercial offices and avoided by other self-respecting people'.

Unfortunately for us, English arrived here through British merchants and seeped into Indian society through the *baboos* who worked for the East India Company. Indians have always been sceptical of the literary aspirations of their *baniyas*, but never questioned the kind of English they kept picking up from the British *baniyas*.

To this day, Indian English retains all the quaint words and forms of expression rejected long ago in England as *commercialese (advise/as per/be in receipt of/beg to state/ your good self/your esteemed favour/in receipt of your favour of the 9th inst., etc.)*

Perhaps *commercialese,* with its ornate and fawning expressions, echoed the over-formal fawning expressions Indians cultivated as *durbari* (court language) during Muslim rule. The combination of the flavour of *commercialese* and *durbari* brought about what can never be used to convey message or meaning efficiently, for each of those ingredients was used always to pad utterances with meaningless verbiage. It made for a perverse language, which placed form before matter, and mannerism before message.

To this day, the older generation of Indians venerate hideous *commercialese* as 'high flown' English and will not be convinced that such language is treated only with contempt by those whose mother tongue it is.

Madras and Calcutta were the two important administrative centres of the East India Company. And in these cities, *commercialese* seeped in deepest among the middle classes, who were the first Indians to seek jobs with the company. It's no coincidence therefore that the older newspapers printed from these two cities did – and still do – the most to keep *commercialese* afloat. A veteran of Madras refuses to deviate into any semblance of contemporary English. The news reports and editorials in these papers, passive to the point of effeteness, and strewn with fossil expressions, read like pieces penned by East India Company *baboo*s. An example:

> Under the amended Protocol II of the International Convention on Certain Weapons, the use of landmines and booby traps and other similar devices are prohibited from being used against civilians. Indiscriminate use of these weapons and use to cause unnecessary suffering are also prohibited. Advance warning to civilians is necessary.

Rid of the passive verbs, that translates into:

> The amended Protocol II . . . Weapons bans the use of
> landmines and booby traps against civilians. It also bans
> their indiscriminate use, and lays down that civilians must
> be warned about where these have been laid.

Unless we understand that excessive use of the passive voice
is un-English, and switch to the active voice, we shall not
write contemporary English.

45

The complexity arises from the fact that . . .

The biggest difference between English and all written Indian languages lies in the way each evolved. All written Indian languages consciously shunned dialects, veered away from speech forms, and tilted towards Sanskrit. But written English began as a written dialect, and retained speech forms.

When Chaucer began writing around 1387, there was no standard written English, and Chaucer wrote in the dialect of his East Midland region. And English has retained the simplicity, directness and informality that are the essence of dialects everywhere.

Because educated Indians picked up only the sick variant they saw in literary Victorian English, their perception of the English language remains warped. They do not understand that plain language and closeness to speech are so much the *dharma* of English that all authors who veered away from speech doomed their work to oblivion.

We still read only those writers whose prose kept close to the speech forms of their day. Authors such as Francis Bacon, who cultivated an artificial and elaborate style (*The Advancement of Learning*, 1605), have been forgotten, even though Bacon was considered a revolutionary in his day. But we still read Shakespeare (who wrote his last plays by 1608–1613), for his language is earthy and unpretentious.

We still read Daniel Defoe's story in plain English (*Robinson Crusoe*, 1719) and Jonathan Swift's racy satire (*Gulliver's Travels*, 1726). But how many read Dr Johnson (1709–1784), who was the spirit behind the move towards Latinate English and Latin models of prose writing (with his string of abstract nouns and epigrams)? Yet Swift wrote during the same neo-classical phase in English literature as Dr Johnson.

The English language has always resisted formalism, and each move away from plain speech has always led to a counter move to restore plain language. The revolt against literary Victorian English began during the Victorian period. Dickens caricatured its pomposity; Kipling moved away from it altogether. Queen Victoria died in 1901. And in 1906, the Fowler brothers presented the English-speaking world with their *King's English*. They condemned the bloated language that English had become during her reign and laid down these simple rules for effective writing:

> Prefer the familiar word to the far-fetched.
> Prefer the concrete word to the abstract.
> Prefer the single word to the circumlocution.
> Prefer the short word to the long.
> Prefer the Saxon word to the Romance.

Those rules named (on the right in each) the five most telling symptoms of the disease that plagued literary Victorian English. All we need do is ensure that our writing has the five qualities on the left in each rule. (By 'Romance' languages, they meant all languages descended from Latin: Italian, French, Spanish.)

The complexity arises from the fact that . . .

A sick pomposity creeps into what Indians utter and write in English. We need only remember Rudolph Flesch's advice: 'All you need is to stop being stuffy, and talk like a human being; that's that!' (*The Art of Readable Writing*). Stuffiness is common to our speeches, reports, public notices and announcements, textbooks, newspaper reports and editorials. If it's in English, it'll reek of East India Company *baboo* English, or sound stiff and bookish. Here's the first paragraph of a book by an eminent NGO leader. It opens with what he delivered as his speech at a seminar:

> Sustainable development is multi-dimensioned. Hence though it occurs frequently in current discourse, it is by no means easy to define. To different people it conveys different meanings and its interpretation is often contextual. The complexity arises from the fact that both the key elements, 'sustainability' and 'development', themselves have several ramifications. Perhaps it would be more meaningful to first define 'development' and then proceed to examine its sustainability from different angles.

He delivered a long speech in this bookish vein without bothering about its effect on his audience. If to that kind of speech and writing we apply the principles the Fowler brothers laid down, and follow Rudolph Flesch's advice, we'd get something like this:

> We've all heard the term 'sustainable development' bandied about. Can we define it? If we tried, we'd agree that the problem is that each of those two words has more than one connotation. Let's then first define 'development'. And then let's see whether it's 'sustainable'.

That contains all the author's ideas, in about half his words. The roundabout and bookish expressions have been removed. And now it takes on an informal directness that addresses the listener. It also becomes more reader-friendly. Agree? The easiest way to achieve this is to follow speech forms.

The same stuffiness gets into our newspaper reports that quote stuffy officials and politicians, as here:

> Mr Murthy alleged that dictatorial attitude had reached a flashpoint in the Congress and internal democracy had faded away. Though dictatorial attitude existed in the party earlier also, the present dictatorial attitude was a self-interested one which did not have any concern for the country or the party, he added.

Besides the bad English, we need to attend to the stuffiness, to make it sound more human:

> Mr Murthy said bossism (or *bossiness*) had peaked in the Congress and stifled internal democracy. The party had seen bossism in the past too. But today's self-serving party bosses cared for neither the party, nor the country.

'Why do we speak and write the way we do?' Rudolph Flesch agonised over the stiff formalism of Victorian English. 'Why aren't our books and letters and speeches full of racy, colloquial, rhythmical, personal language?'

Why, indeed? Flesch provided an answer:

> The answer goes far beyond grammar and usage; it even goes beyond psychology. Language is a social affair; we use it according to the social situation we are in. . . . We write stilted English because we unconsciously assume that this is expected of us in the position we happen to fill, or the organisation we belong to.

And how do we get out of this habit? Flesch said:

> Like everyone else, you spend your life in a world filled with all kinds of bureaucratic, technical, or legal gobbledygook.

The only way to fight it is active, daily, unceasing resistance. You must learn to replace every *prior to* by *before*; every *subsequently* by *later*, every *we are endeavouring to ascertain* by *we are trying to find out*. It takes years until this becomes an invariable habit and you automatically translate jargon into English.

46

The point is sought to be evaded

In the active voice, the doer/agent comes first; the action after ('*I* ate that piece of cake'). The passive voice reverses that order ('That piece of cake was eaten by *me*'). The passive voice, then, either diminishes the importance of the doer, or evades mentioning him in such constructions as 'That piece of cake was eaten'. English sounds best in the active voice; the passive often drags in roundabout expressions, and weakens our writing. George Orwell advised writers to 'never use the passive voice when you can use the active'. And yet, for all that, the passive voice does prove useful in five situations:

1   When the person at the receiving end is more important than the doer/agent: we'd surely prefer the passive in *Mr Bal Thackeray was today bitten by a rabid dog* to the active-voice version, which would make the dog more important than Mr Thackeray (*A rabid dog today bit Mr Bal Thackeray*).

2   When we do not/cannot know the doer/agent: *The man was found murdered in his hotel room/They came back from their holiday, to find their house burgled.*

3   When the doer is not important, only the action is: *Gas cylinder regulators should be switched off after cooking*

is done/Corroded power cables should be replaced as quickly as possible.

4 When the doer/agent is too obvious to need naming: *The goonda was arrested and charged with manslaughter/Laloo was defeated on home turf.* Naming the police in the first sentence, or voters in the second, would sound awkward (and the active-voice version, *Police arrested the goonda . . ./Voters abandoned Laloo . . .,* would be wordier).

5 When the accepted manner of writing on science, technology, or academic subjects demands that the doer remain faceless: *A portion of the sediment was treated with hydrochloric acid and the precipitate analysed/The tumour was excised and tissue samples were sent for biopsy.*

This impersonal fifth manner, unfortunately, has escaped from textbooks and become the staple of government office communication. And when this circulates freely and is absorbed, it gets into letters, memos, news reports and editorials, and turns all writing effete. Most government officers follow fossil formats of the Raj days and end up with the kind of impersonal passives Churchill told British bureaucrats to avoid. As long ago as 1945, Churchill invited Sir Ernest Gowers to go through official correspondence and suggest guidelines for a people-friendly style. Said Gowers:

> The use of the impersonal passive, with its formal, unsympathetic phrases, such as 'it is felt', 'it is regretted', 'it is appreciated', is a sure sign that the wrong note has been struck. It gives the reader the impression that he is dealing with robots rather than human beings. How feeble is the sentence 'It is thought that you will now have received the

form of agreement', compared with 'I expect you will have received the form of agreement by now'.

(*The Complete Plain Words*, 1948)

The Indian bureaucrat bloats his letters with impersonal passives. In asking people or organisations to submit some papers as part of official routine, the government officer affects a ludicrous pompousness:

> It is recommended that . . . papers be arranged to reach the undersigned on or before 31 July '99.
>
> It has been notified that . . . papers are to be arranged to reach the undersigned . . . .

The reader is never told who made such a recommendation, nor who notified whom. Such *officialese* leads to what Fowler called the double passive.

The double passive is popular with bureaucrats because it helps evade the point (in *bureaucratese*, that would read: *The point is sought to be evaded*). Almost 90 per cent of all official letters that hop tables in the pecking order begin sentences with double passives made out of verbs such as *attempt* (*The project is* attempted *to be started by the month of December* . . .), *proposed* (*The project is* proposed *to be scheduled for trial run* . . .) and out of a host of others, such as *endeavour, hope, intend.*

During Raj days, such evasive and lifeless writing was paraded as propriety, and seeped into all forms of communication. Here are some defects the passive voice causes:

Verbosity

The passive voice inflates 95 in every 100 sentences. That's in the active voice. Its passive-voice version would read:

95 in every 100 sentences become inflated when the passive
voice is used.

Wordiness mars all writing; the unnecessary passive voice
drains writing of life. When we must serve several ideas in a
sentence, wordiness slows the reader's ability to take in the
message, as in this one from an editorial on the tasks ahead
of Mr Vajpayee:

> Contending claims from the partners of the National
> Democratic Alliance for inclusion in the ministry and on the
> allocation of portfolios, apart from demands from within his
> own party, will have to be handled to the satisfaction of all
> claimants. (40 words)

The active voice would make the intended message clearer:

> He will face contending claims for ministerial berths and
> portfolios from Alliance partners and partymen alike, and
> will have to satisfy everybody. (22 words)

Circumlocution

The passive leads to a roundabout way of saying things.
Authors of editorials fall back on passives because they think
the style is more grandiloquent:

> While the BJP's allies has [sic] grown in number and strength,
> a larger question mark *may have been formed* against the
> stability of the 24-party government, to *be installed* soon,
> and its ability to provide effective governance.

The use of the active voice here cannot help readability
unless the writer explains how a question mark or a comma
or an exclamation mark of any size *forms* over stability or
instability of a government. English-language newspapers in
India circulate such drivel, and readers can hardly be blamed
for absorbing this ludicrous language.

The sum of verbosity and circomlocution: statements in the passive voice lose directness and slacken the reader's pace. But we in India need to ponder whether the passive voice is not deeply ingrained in our thinking. When on the battlefield Arjuna broke down and said he couldn't kill his kinsfolk, Krishna told him he must view himself not as the doer of any action, but only as a passive agent (*Nimitta maatram bhava, Savyasachi*). Perhaps the passive voice comes easily to us because our fatalism prompts us to suffer, rather than act – and to equate suffering with action.

47

May the lowliest be permitted . . .

If only we'd research how written Indian languages absorbed the mannerisms of eighteenth-century written English, especially, *commercialese*, formal Raj-day Bengali and Tamil correspondence would yield rich pickings (Calcutta and Madras were the East India Company's important administrative centres).

Letters Bengali estate managers wrote to their *zamindar*s show equivalents forced for such mannerisms of the British merchants as *beg to state/may it please your honour/may it be placed on record/your humble servant*. The *nayeb/dewan* would spatter his letters with such impersonal passives as *kortey agnya hoke* (may it be ordered/permitted) and sign off with a flourish of servile humility, such as *awdhomaadham* (lower than the lowliest). That flourish became the standard ending for all letters.

Formal Tamil too adopted such equivalents as *arasarin anaipadi korikai niraiveruvudaga* (may it be permitted), and double passives such as *arasarin anai pirappikkapadu vadaaga* (may it be allowed to be ordered). An incurable *Anglophilia* and absorption of *commercialese* make Tamils and Bengalis kin.

The impersonal passive wasn't new to Indian languages. During Muslim rule, north Indian languages moved away from the sharp directness of Sanskrit. *Durbari* (court language) nurtured the impersonal passive, and cultivated the ornamental hyperbole of Persian.

South Indian languages adopted the circumlocution and impersonality dictated by feudal Brahminical custom. Eighteenth-century *commercialese* reinforced both. Once one Indian language accepted the debasement of *commercialese*, the affectation spread like a pestilence through all our regional languages.

Karnataka, for instance, saw little of Muslim rule (except for brief spells in regions under the Bahmani sultans, and then Hyder Ali and Tipu Sultan), and less of the East India Company. And yet to this day, official circulars in Kannada often begin with such impersonal double passives as *e suttole mulaka tamagay tiliya padi suvudu enendaray* (what is sought to be informed to you through this circular is . . .).

The passive voice dominated literary Victorian English. Not till the 1940s did writers on style begin their strident condemnation of it. Fowler condemned as a 'monstrosity' the use of the double passive (as in *The point is sought to be evaded*), but was milder about the impersonal passive (*it is felt/it is believed*). Constructions in the impersonal passive, Fowler said in *A Dictionary of Modern English Usage* (OUP, 1926), were 'dear to those who write official and business letters. . . . But when one person is addressing another it often amounts to a pusillanimous shrinking from responsibility.'

Contrast that mildness with William Zinsser's language 50 years later: 'The difference between an active-verb style and a passive-verb style – in pace, clarity, and vigour – is the

difference between life and death for a writer' (*On Writing Well*, HarperCollins, 6th ed. 1998).

Obviously, as the pace of life quickened, writers woke up to the sloth of the passive. The post-War years sped communication. That snuffed out formalism and gave clarity of message priority. The passive voice often means wordiness and roundabout expressions that slow comprehension. And hence the renewed post-Victorian emphasis on economy of expression, and the insistence on plain English, stripped of frills and ornamentation, and the strident call for writing in the active voice.

Writers in Indian regional languages today shun the passive. But Indians who write in English cling to it. Official letters reek of it, and so do textbooks, newspaper reports, articles and editorials. The obvious explanation: Indians wallow in archaic English.

A thoughtful article on reservation for scheduled castes and tribes begins with this sentence (*The Hindu*, 16 October 1999):

> Two successive verdicts *issued by* the Supreme Court recently on reservation has [sic] added to the apprehensions *felt by* many that there is a concerted attempt to do away with this social welfare measure altogether. (34 words)

Besides the obvious passive in *issued by/felt by*, the sentence carries weak verbs and impersonal passives. Its wordiness confuses even the author, who uses *has* where she needs *have* (to agree with the plural *verdicts*). The active voice would have made it easier for her to write her message, and for the reader to grasp it quickly:

> The Supreme Court's two recent verdicts have fuelled fears about a concerted move to scupper reservation. (16 words)

Readers might say that version changes more than merely the passive voice. True. To be concise, we must shun all that ushers in the passive:

1   All verbs formed from *to be* (*am/are/is/was/were/be/will be/being/been*) are weak and usher in passive constructions whenever used with past participles: *I have been told/I was given to understand/The refugees were being fed gruel*. Common to all those expressions is an absence of the doer, who should be the subject of a sentence in the active voice.

2   Other weak verbs we should use judiciously: *do, get, make, take*. These will bring in wordiness and weaken a sentence: *You should have taken the right turn at that crossing* sheds two words even if we retain the passive voice, but replace *taken* with a stronger verb: *You should have turned right at that crossing*.

3   A string of nouns often ushers in the passive and more often, slows comprehension through wordiness. Changing a noun where possible into an active verb adds muscle to writing. Compare '*Determination* of foreign *policy* takes place at the expert advisory *committee level*' (nouns italicised) with *An experts committee decides foreign policy*.

4   The doer/agent of an action is the subject of the sentence in the active voice. Where the action comes immediately after the doer, the sentence gains clarity. In the recast sentence, tying the doer (*committee*) with the action (*decides*) brought in the active voice.

These two simple rules would help keep out the avoidable passive:

1   In sentences that lack an active verb, change a noun into an active verb.

2   Place that verb after the doer/agent of the sentence.

But the simple point is this: when we speak, we use the active voice in 90 per cent of our sentences; when we write, we need only follow the same pattern.

48

Can you give me one glass of water?

There are many misconceptions about the use of the articles (*a/an*, *the*). Let's begin with what we so often hear about the use of the indefinite article (*a/an*) – that we must use *an* before words that begin with vowels (*a*, *e*, *i*, *o*, *u*). Too many teachers tell their pupils just that, without making clear that *vowel* and *consonant* are phonetic terms – NOT, repeat *not*, letters. Pupils would be less confused if teachers told them to use *an* not when a word begins with a certain letter, but when it begins with a vowel sound.

A word may begin with one of the five vowel letters, but would still take *a* if in pronouncing it we began with a consonant sound: *a* one-time wrestler (not *an*); *a* one-armed bandit (not *an*). In pronouncing *one*, we begin with a consonant sound approaching *w* (as in *won*).

Conversely, abbreviations might begin with consonant letters, but would take *an* if in pronouncing the first initial, we begin with a vowel sound: 'He's *an* FCI employee' (not *a* FCI employee, though we'd use *a* if we pronounced the words those initials stand for – 'He's *a* Food Corporation of India employee').

And so, we'd say 'He obtained *an* LLB from . . .' (not *a* LLB, though '*a* Bachelor's degree in law'); 'He has *an* MA from BHU' (not *a* MA, though 'He has *a* Master's degree . . .'); '*An* NCC cadet did this' (not *a* NCC cadet); 'He's *an* RBI officer' (but 'He's *a* Reserve Bank of India officer'); 'He's *an* ST candidate' (but 'He's *a* Scheduled Tribe candidate'). Even though F, L, M, N, R and S are consonant letters, we use *an* before those abbreviations because we begin with vowel sounds: *eff-see-eye/ell-ell-bee/emm aye/enn-see-see/are-bee-eye/ess-tee*.

But why such a rule? We'd understand the need for *an* if we tried to do without it and uttered two vowel sounds in succession in our sentences: *a* ass, *a* egg, *a* iguana, *a* olive, *a* oar, *a* hour, and then contrast the ease we'd find if we replaced each *a* with *an*. (Contrast '*A* washerman had *a* ass/He stole *a* egg from the nest' with '*A* washerman had *an* ass/He stole *an* egg from the nest'.) A simple guide: when in doubt over *a/an*, we must go by our ears, not by our eyes.

In a letter to a newspaper, a reader says he has often noticed *an* before words beginning with *u*, 'particularly *unique*, though we know *a* is used when *u* is pronounced *yoo*.' He is right, and the error he has noticed only confirms the misconception created by the ruling that we must use *an* before 'words beginning with vowels'. The *Concise Oxford Dictionary* settles such doubt with '*a* unique thing or person'.

Words beginning with *u/eu*, pronounced with the consonant *y* sound (as in *yoo*) take *a*: *a* university/*a* Unit Trust Certificate/*a* utopian theory/*a* European identity/*a* euthanasia lobby. Words that begin with *u* take *an* only when we begin with the vowel sound of *u* – *an* umbrella/*an* uncharitable remark/*an* upright person, etc.

Not numeral

A common Indian error equates the indefinite article (*a/an*) with *one*. Neither *a* nor *an* does duty for *one*. The word *one* emphasises the singular number; *a/an* doesn't.

To avoid this error, considered a characteristic of Indian English, we need only ask ourselves if we'd use *some* when we mean the plural sense. If the answer is yes, then we should use *a/an*, rather than *one*. But if the answer is we'd use two, three or greater numerals, then we should use *one*.

We correctly use *one* when we have the singular number in mind. We misplace that emphasis when we say 'Give me *one* glass of water', for we mean not one glass as opposed to two glasses, but some water to drink. Going by that test, we should ask for *a/some* light in a dark room (not *one* light); *a* ship to sail in, or *a* car to go places, and *a* hot meal at the end of *a* journey (and not *one* ship/*one* car/ *one* hot meal/*one* journey). In those expressions, the idea of number is vague.

But we'd be right to insist on *one* post for *one* party member; on *one* spouse for each (assuming we do not want polygamy and polyandry); on *one* vote for each citizen, and *one* law for all. The emphasis in each is clearly on the singular number, and we must therefore use *one*, rather than *a/an*.

Position switch

The articles are demonstrative adjectives, and like other adjectives, they precede the nouns they qualify. But when used beside *many*, *quite*, *such* and *what*, *a/an* switches position and follows those adjectives. Wordsworth saw *a* good many daffodils; Gray spoke of 'full many *a* flower' being born to blush unseen. We speak of *a* good feeling, or *a* bad feeling, but The Carpenters sang 'Such a feeling's comin' over me'. One could miss *a* good opportunity, but the article would come later in 'What *an* opportunity that was/Quite *an* opportunity'.

A/an also switches position when *as, how, so, too* precede adjectives: one speaks of another as being 'as good *a* man as any', though the normal position of the article is '*a* good man'. Similarly: 'How wonderful *a* man he was' (against the normal 'He was a wonderful man'); 'I have yet to see *so* spectacular an event' (against the normal 'It was a spectacular event'); 'I don't wish to place too strong *an* emphasis on this' (against the normal '*a* strong emphasis').

49

That leaves us none the wiser than . . .

No Indian language has the definite article (*the*), which belongs to Latin-derived languages, such as Italian, Spanish and French. In English, it exists as a relic of the Norman occupation, when Latin and French were imposed on Anglo-Saxon subjects (see page 3). Arabic is the only language Indians are familiar with and which uses something similar (*al*).

People say they find the articles 'confusing'. The only shortcut to learning to use a language is to hear it spoken. BBC and CNN programmes on cable TV make that possible.

A discussion on when to use and when to omit the articles would be redundant: the *Concise Oxford Dictionary* gives a compact set of rules. Most readers will be familiar with the grammar book by Wren & Martin. Let's instead take a look at some common errors.

Errors creep in frequently in comparisons, especially when *than* follows the comparative. These tips might be useful:

Rule 1

The indefinite article should *not* be used with the comparative degree in such expressions as 'India has had no better *a* batsman than Sachin'. But it would be correct to use the article with the positive degree: 'India has never had as good *a* batsman as Sachin.'

- Following that rule, we should not use the indefinite article (*a/an*) in such expressions as 'Laloo is more *a* buffoon than *an* administrator'. Omit both *a* and *an*. (Wren & Martin favours use of the first article and omission of the second 'when two nouns refer to the same person or thing', as in the example cited. But the omission of both adds force to the intended meaning.) In speech, one often hears '. . . is more of *a* buffoon than . . .'. This is a permissible colloquialism, though less forceful.

- Nor should the definite article (*the*) be used if *than* follows the comparative: 'Our salaries have gone up, but inflation leaves us none the richer *than* in the sixties' is wrong. We must omit *the* and amend that to read '. . . leaves us *no richer than* . . .'.

- Ditto with expressions such as 'That left us *none the wiser than* before' (amend to '. . . *no wiser than* . . .'). In many such expressions, unless the phrase or clause after *than* gives some information, as in the first example, one could stop before *than*, without any harm to sense ('That left us no wiser').

- When *the* is used with the comparative, it takes on the sense of 'thereby', or 'by so much'. As the Duchess said to Alice: 'And the moral of that is – "the more there is of mine, the less there is of yours".' Such repetition of the article is idiomatic when we compare or contrast ideas: 'The more I learn, the more I discover my ignorance.'

Rule 2

The other frequent error creeps in when the article is used with *both* and *or*. The definite article (*the*) should be repeated for each noun after *both*. 'Both *the* management and *the* union accepted the wage board recommendation' is correct. Wrong: 'Both the BJP and Shiv Sena said in their manifestoes that . . .' (insert *the* before Shiv Sena).

Rule 3

The article should be repeated before each noun on either side of *or*, if they are alternatives, but not when we use *or* merely to give a second name for the first noun: 'Would you take the train at 8.30 or the bus at 10?' is correct. But the article should not be repeated here: 'George Fox founded *the* Society of Friends, or *the* Quakers, as they came to be known.' (Omit the second article, which precedes another name for the same community).

Rule 4

In a series of nouns that are dissimilar or separate entities, one should use *the* before each noun: 'And who you think they were? *The* butcher, *the* baker, *the* candle-stick maker.' Such sentences take a plural verb.

Rule 5

A single *the* and a singular verb should be used if two nouns are joined by *and*, but thought of as going together: 'The grit and raw courage of our jawans is what won in Kargil' is correct, not 'The grit and the raw courage *are* . . .' because those two qualities are thought of together.

Rule 6

An article is placed before such collectives as *dozen*, *hundred* and *thousand* only when the expression is in the singular: 'Eggs come cheaper by *the* dozen' (not 'dozens')/'The rats followed the Pied Piper by *the* hundred' (not 'hundreds' nor 'thousands'). The article must be omitted if the plural form is used: 'Rats followed the Pied Piper in hundreds and thousands.'

The definite article is used with the plural only when we refer to the years of a century: 'Frills were very much the fashion in *the* nineteen hundreds' (meaning the twentieth century).

Should the definite article be repeated before *prison* in this sentence: 'Finding the warden asleep, the convict escaped from prison'? Wren & Martin answers this question with the rule that the article is used if we mean the specific place or building, when we use words such as *school*, *church*, *bed*, *table*, *hospital*, *market*, *prison*. Going by that rule, *prison* does need the article. But it wouldn't if you referred to the normal activity or purpose of a prison: 'The undertrial was sent back to prison'/'He was in prison for a year'.

50

Lover, you are very that thing

How many readers would endorse the argument that because Indians have been using English for over two centuries, it's high time we accepted it as an Indian language and stopped viewing it as a foreign one? One problem that argument ignores is that 'Indian English' can and does have as many variants as our major regional languages. English in each region takes on expressions peculiar to the language dominant in it. And so, following our national anthem, we'd have to recognise at least *Punjlish*, *Sindhlish*, *Gujlish*, *Marathlish*, *Tamlish*, *Orlish*, *Benglish*, *Kannadlish*, *Himachalish*, and of course, *Hindlish*.

Given our regional chauvinism, a discussion on this would deviate all too easily to jokes about the way certain English words are pronounced in each region. Let's instead examine how we arrive at unidiomatic English, or un-English expressions.

We must recognise that *Indlish* will sound distorted in proportion as we literally translate what we think in our mother tongues. Westernised Indians who believe they do their thinking in English refuse to acknowledge that they do much of that in *Indlish*.

Distortion results also when we translate idioms of one regional language into another. Hence jokes about the way

Bengalis, Tamils and Punjabis speak, pronounce or intone Hindi. A popular TV serial ('*Zaban sambhal ke*') uses this to imitate a BBC serial ('Mind Your Language') on how Italians, Frenchmen, Poles, etc. speak, pronounce and intone English.

We may trace *Indlish* distortions to syntax and grammar, and also to literal translation of idioms peculiar to a region:

Asking questions

No Indian language requires us to do anything more than insert the equivalent of *why* when we move from a statement to a question. The arrangement of words in a statement remains unaltered in the question, except for such insertion. Thus the word arrangement in *tum huss rahay ho* (you are laughing) remains unaltered when we place *kyon* (why) either before or after *tum (tum kyon huss rahay ho?)*. But English demands a bit more than that. The auxiliary verb must switch position and precede the subject when we frame a question: *You* are *laughing* must change to *Why* are *you laughing?* Because no Indian language requires such subject/auxiliary inversion, a common *Indlish* error is to frame questions without it: *What I can do for you?/What your name is?/Why you are crying?/Where you are going?/Who you will vote for?/He has paid his bill?*

Indlish question tags

Closely allied is the habit of adding a question tag to sentences, which is common to all Indian languages: *hai na?* (Hindi), *taina?* (Bengali); *allay?* (Malayalam); *illiya?* (Tamil);

alwa? (Kannada), etc. The *Indlish* versions – *So you really want this, yes?/You like him very much, no?/This variety of rice is very good, is it?* – are not idiomatic English.

But that is not to say question tags aren't used in English: *You're bent on getting this, aren't you?/You like him very much, don't you?/This variety of rice is very good, wouldn't you say?* These are some idiomatic question tags widely used in conversation. (The pre-Victorian *I think I did that rather well, what?* is now outmoded.)

The difference: the *Indlish* question tags (*yes?/no?/isn't it?*) are generalised, and are tagged on to statements indiscriminately. The idiomatic English question tags are subject- and verb-specific – *She is rather pretty, isn't she?/They sound angry, don't they?/I'm rather good at conning, aren't I?/You wouldn't want that to happen, would you?*

This thing and *that thing*

All languages have 'conversational props' we fall back on when we search for the right word, or expression: *yeh/woh/woh kya hai* (Hindi); *eeaye/eta holo giye* (Bengali); *idu/adu* (Kannada); *ida/ada* (Tamil and Malayalam), etc. None of these props mean anything more specific than 'er . . ./umm . . .' even though *yeh/woh* and *idu/adu*, etc. translate into *this/this thing* and *that/that thing* in normal conversation.

Translating the prop into *this thing/that thing* has become a widespread habit, especially among those who speak Hindi. Those who argue that Indian English should have its own flavour would then find *You are very that thing* an acceptable equivalent of the Bollywood coy-girl pout,

Aap bade woh hain, and *Lover, you are very that thing* as acceptable Indian English for the film song *Baalmaa, tu bada woh hai.*

Perhaps because such *Indlish* is gaining currency, a Hindi-speaking woman said to another at a husband-bashing session in *Indlish: You know, my husband's that thing is very this thing* (when the context required something like *You know, my husband's temper is something nasty*).

Conversational English has many such props: *er . . . / um . . . you know . . . /well . . ./like . . ./kind of . . . .* So does every conversational language. But if such props are translated, specific meaning intrudes where it was never intended. And this leads to the absurd.

This itself

The immensely flexible syntax of Indian languages creates a need for emphasis that the rigid syntax of English does not demand. This leads most often to either redundancy or unidiomatic use of words to emphasise a point. Because the word arrangement in sentences in Indian languages can be changed without altering meaning (as discussed on pages 259–60), we are left with the feeling that a sentence we have uttered does not quite emphasise what we had in mind. We then add a word or phrase that we feel would do the job better. The rigid syntax of English demands only a change in word arrangement or intonation.

The most frequent violation of idiom is caused by the use of reflexive pronouns (*myself, himself, herself, itself, ourselves, themselves,* etc.) to emphasise a point that needs no such emphasis in English. These pronouns are correctly used when the verb denotes an action that turns back

(reflects) to the subject (*I hurt myself/She cried herself to sleep/He drank himself silly*). Use of these reflexive pronouns only to emphasise a point is un-English.

But because of their flexible syntax, all Indian languages allow such use, and admit certain words that are used solely for emphasis. The result: we translate such usage into English and come up with unidiomatic expressions, such as 'That book is in our college library *itself*' (against the idiomatic 'We have that book in our college library'); 'This *itself* proves his guilt' (against 'This proves/establishes his guilt'); 'They said the place *itself* was terrible' (against 'They felt the place was a hell-hole/mess'), etc.

Like that only

All Indian languages permit some words or suffixes to be used only for emphasis: *-hee* (Hindi: as in *Yehee hai* right choice baby); *ei/etai* (Bengali: as in *etai ucheet* – this is the right thing to do); *-ay* (Kannada: as in *adhay/heegay/avanay* – that only/like this only/he only); *taan* (Tamil: as in *Avan appidi taan* – he is like that only); *tannay* (Malayalam: as in *Adu tannaay /Avan tannay* – that only/like this only/he only), etc.

The use of *only* to arrive at that emphasis isn't idiomatic English. The word *only* is used in English more often for exclusion (as in 'He drinks *only* rum'/'I need *only* this bit of information', where the sense is: this/that and no other). The use of *only* solely for emphasis is rare, and mostly amounts to a redundancy permitted in conversation (as in 'We've only just begun').

But the unidiomatic use of *only* for emphasis is a character-istic of *Indlish*: *They are like that only* (for 'That's how they behave')/*Children behave like that only* (for 'But that's how children behave')/*That only is the problem* (for 'That's the problem'), etc.

51

Why worry about small small things?

Because English and Indian languages differ widely in behaviour, some of our ways of expression can never be recreated in English. *Indlish* sounds ludicrous when we recreate the reduplication that all Indian languages permit either for musical effect or for emphasis:

Hindi

- *chhoti chhoti baaton* (trivial issues/trifles)
- *chori chori* (stealthily)
- *baaton baaton mein* (in the course of a chat)

Bengali

- *chhoto chhoto katha* (trivial issues/trifles)
- *choopi choopi* (stealthily)
- *kathay kathay* (in the course of a chat)
- *kaanay kaanay* (whisper)
- *mookhay mookhay* (by word of mouth)

Oriya

- *bada bada katha* (big talk)
- *kahu kahu kahidela* (in the course of a chat)
- *astay astay kar* (take it easy)

Tamil

- *chinna chinnaa asai* (little dreams)
- *vanna vanna pookkal* (colourful flowers)
- *odi odi va* (run here)
- *parandu parandu po* (fly there)

Malayalam

- *kochchu kochchu karyangal* (trivial issues/trifles)
- *kayttu kayttu mathiyayi* (my ears are stuffed with it)
- *vegam vegam pokaam* (let's go fast)

Telugu

- *chala chala bagunadi* (very very good)
- *ekku ekku ga* (more and more)
- *pitchi pitchi ga matladaku* (don't rant like a madman)
- *daba daba ga panichayandi* (work fast)

Kannada

- *hannu hannu muduka* (grand old man)
- *chikka chikka makkalu* (little children)
- *bega bega ba/odi odi ba* (run here)

Marathi

- *chotya chotya goshti* (trivial issues/trifles)
- *kadhi kadhi* (sometimes)
- *khare khare sang* (come out with the truth)

All those expressions are idiomatic and lend music to our regional languages. The translation alongside each is inadequate: it carries neither the music nor the effect, and almost nothing of the connotation. No translation can convey the flavour of any of those expressions.

English does not permit reduplication for meaningful effect. The few examples that English does permit achieve little more than meaningless sound-effects in:

- finger rhymes for babies (*this little pig said wee wee wee*)
- animal sounds (*baa-baa/moo-moo/meow-meow/quack-quack*)
- nursery rhymes (*twinkle twinkle little star/hey diddle diddle, the cat and the fiddle*)
- light songs *(in a gilly-gilly house . . .)*

English permits the replication (not reduplication) of a sound-effect *(hickory dickory dock . . ./. . . and there in the wood a piggy-wiggy stood)*, or the close repetition of words in songs (*in a tiny house by a tiny stream, where a lovely girl had a lovely dream*).

In some poems, words are repeated for heightened effect (*In vain I weep to him that cannot hear, and weep the more because I weep in vain*: Coleridge), or a whole line is repeated in refrain (*For I have promises to keep, and miles to go before I sleep. And miles to go before I sleep*: Robert Frost). In English, the closest to reduplication would be those few rhyming pairs used in informal adult speech to emphasise an idea, usually derogatory. Unlike the Indian expression that repeats the identical word, the English word pairs with:

1 a word that replicates the sound of the first, but with a change in the initial consonant (*argy-bargy*; *fuddy-duddy*; *fuzzy-wuzzy*; *harum-scarum*; *heebie-jeebies*; *helter-skelter*; *higgledy-piggledy*; *hoity-toity*; *hotch-potch*; *hurly-burly*; *itsy-bitsy*; *miminy-piminy*; *namby-pamby*; *niminy-piminy*; *nitty-gritty*; *razzle-dazzle*; *roly-poly*; *teeny weeny*)

2 a word that begins with the same consonant sound, but
changes a vowel within (*dilly-dally*; *flip-flop*; *flim-flam*;
hee-haw; *hip-hop*; *mish-mash*; *see-saw*; *tip-top*; *tittle-
tattle*; *whim-wham*; *wiggle-woggle*; *wishy-washy*).

Often, only the first word may carry the meaning intended;
the second may have no meaning or existence independent
of the combination (*fuzzy-wuzzy*). With a few, neither of the
pair may have a meaning, and neither is used alone (*fuddy-
duddy*; *hoity-toity*; *niminy-piminy*). Others may retain the
sense of neither when each of the pair has an independent
meaning (*hip-hop*; *hurly-burly*).

Readers will at once recognise that all Indian languages
have such imitative rhyming pairs too, made with similar
changes in the initial consonant or vowel sounds: such
a term for *things around you*, for instance, would be
aas *paas* (Hindi), *aashay paashay* (Bengali); *pakha pakhi*
(Oriya); *sutta mutta/akkaa pakkaa* (Kannada); *ikkada
akkada* (Telugu); *akkam pakkam* (Tamil); *aviday ividay*
(Malayalam); *aazu baazu* (Marathi), etc.

But Indians often recreate in English the reduplication
they are accustomed to use in their languages, and this
has led to what Englishmen consider a comical feature of
Indlish. In its list of features of Indian English, the *Oxford
Companion to the English Language* (OUP, 1992) includes
'Reduplication used for emphasis and to indicate a distribu-
tive meaning: *I bought some small small things*; *Why don't
you give them one one piece of cake?*' Because they never
use reduplication, and only rarely a replication, Englishmen
are unable to understand why Indians use such expressions
as The teacher warned the children that 'She would give

them *one one* slap'/'Such *little little* things can cause *big big* problems'/'I want a *same same* dress as yours'/'She was saying *some some* things'/'Why don't you pay them *ten ten* rupees each?'

Reduplication enlivens Indian languages. But let's recognise that if English doesn't permit it, we mustn't import it. That can only make such 'translations' ludicrous.

VII

Your Reader Deserves Better

52

Make me see

A man who went on to become a managing editor of *The New York Times* began as a writer for a paper with a circulation of only 9,000, and an editor who was blind. Gene Roberts acknowledges that his blind editor taught him the secret of effective writing. When he showed up for work in the morning, Henry Belk, editor, would call Roberts over, and tell him that his writing wasn't descriptive enough. 'Make me see,' he would order. Roberts says:

> It took me years to appreciate it, but there is no better admonition to the writer than 'Make me see'. There is no truer blueprint for successful writing than making your readers see. It is the essence of great writing.

In India, as elsewhere, literature of the oral tradition cultivated this quality. The enduring quality of the *Ramayana* and *Mahabharata* lies in the way generations of listeners sat enthralled as a *kathak* recited those epics. Bengal had the *kathak thakur*, who embellished myths and legends with vivid description. It was his skill at weaving description that transformed his story-telling into movies for his audience. Writers who hone this skill endure. Abanindranath Tagore gave Bengali children technicolour prose (in *Booro Aangla*). The earliest attempt at creative writing in Bengali (*Hutom pyanchaar nakshaa*) gave us the 'word sketches' we still examine for a glimpse of Company-day north Calcutta.

Creative writing in all our regional languages has sought to bring into prose the descriptive power of our oral tradition. This quality is absent in the English that Indians write. The hotch-potch of *commercialese, officialese* and *legalese* that passes for English in India can never serve as a medium for creative writing. In our English-language papers, attempts at description show not fresh pictures, but ready-made frames. Poverty of language makes for poverty of thought and skill. There is no attempt to look minutely and describe things in fresh language. The writer grabs a few clichés to suggest familiar settings. A sample from page 1 of an edition of *The New Indian Express*:

> The scene is *almost picture perfect*: mist *hugs the tips* of trees, *cattle* are *returning home*, *dusk streaks the sky*, pink behind the *forested peaks*. But today the Bargu hills look *menacing*, the dense Satyamangalam forest is *full of foreboding*.
>
> For somewhere behind those peaks sits Kannada icon Rajkumar whose abduction by Veerappan has entered its sixth week bringing two states *down on their knees*, their people *pushed to the brink*.

Not one of those italicised phrases and words is fresh; each is either a familiar frame (*cattle returning home/forested peaks/menacing/full of foreboding*), or a threadbare expression (*down on their knees/pushed to the brink*).

Graphic description in writing is a skill the West has cultivated and encouraged over centuries. A special quality of this craft is attention to detail. A sample from a popular novel:

Last night I dreamt I went to Manderley again. It seemed to me I stood by the iron gate leading to the drive, and for a while I could not enter, for the way was barred to me. There was a padlock and a chain upon the gate. I called in my dream to the lodge-keeper, and had no answer, and peering closer through the rusted spokes of the gate, I saw that the lodge was uninhabited.

No smoke came from the chimney, and the little lattice windows gaped forlorn. Then, like all dreamers, I was possessed of a sudden with supernatural powers and passed like a spirit through the barrier before me. The drive wound away in front of me, twisting and turning as it had always done, but as I advanced I was aware that a change had come upon it; it was narrow and unkept, not the drive that we had known. At first I was puzzled and did not understand, and it was only when I bent my head to avoid the low swinging branch of a tree that I realised what had happened. Nature had come into her own again and, little by little, in her stealthy, insidious way had encroached upon the drive with long tenacious fingers.

That opening of *Rebecca* (by Daphne du Maurier, 1938) is a glimpse into this craft of concentrating on detail to create pictures with words.

Some readers might feel it is unfair to compare du Maurier's exquisite prose with writing by a journalist whose mother tongue isn't English. Let's then turn to Bengali prose. Here's a loose translation of an excerpt from Parashuram's spoof on our faith in rebirth. In *Bhushondir maathay*, he describes the plight of *Shibu*, a lovelorn ghost, smitten by three she-ghosts:

The tail-end of *Falgun*. A southern breeze quavers over a bend in the Ganga. The sun god, after floundering for a while, has just gone under. The scent of *ghentu* bloom has smothered the entire stretch of *Bhushondir maath*.

> Shibu's *bael* tree has sprouted new shoots. At some distance, the mature pod of an *Akondo* bursts and a mist of cotton rises in the breeze, then the fibres begin to land on Shibu, like the shimmering skeletons of so many spiders. A yellow butterfly flits through his phantom form. A black dung-beetle keeps whirring around him. On a *babool* tree not far away, a pair of jackdaws sits close. The male preens its mate's neck and the hen, eyes shut, now and again croaks in throaty delight. A toad, just awakened, clambers its way out of a bole of the *bael* tree, rests its pop-eyes on Shibu, and jeers at him. Some crickets were tuning for the evening's chorus; they find their scale and begin chirring in unison.
>
> Though he no longer possessed a body of flesh and blood, death hadn't changed his nature. Shibu felt forlorn. The cavity that once housed his heart, filled and went thump-thump.

No translation can ever match Parashuram's finesse, but even that weak rendering will serve to prove his attention to precise detail. Effective writing in any language will carry this quality.

Can detail be overdone? How much detail should one pack into his writing? A veteran journalist tells us:

> Unless the main purpose of a piece is to be descriptive, colour is best doled out in small helpings here and there rather than in long, unbroken passages. You can tell readers an awful lot in a series of small asides, remarks made in passing and in the occasional sentence. The thing you have to watch is where you place these. The fact that the person you were quoting is red-haired and collects stamps is worth recording somewhere, but probably not . . . immediately after you have them calling on the government to resign.
>
> Relevance is the key. Introduce description where it helps, not where it is incongruous. More detailed descriptions of a certain person or place are, however, best given in one part

of the story and not sprinkled through it. It is irritating to read a piece where, every time someone is mentioned, you are thrown another little crumb of description about them.

(David Randall. *The Universal Journalist*. London: Pluto Press, 1996)

53

Show, don't tell

Here's how *The New Indian Express*, Bangalore, narrates a recent massacre in a village in Bihar:

> For Bihar, the story was *sickeningly familiar*. As villagers in tiny Narkopi went around doing their shopping on the afternoon of September 13 at the weekly bazaar, around 50 armed men *struck*. The *shootout* lasted hours, by the end of which six were dead and many grievously injured. The villagers turned to the police, and the latter 'turned away'.
>
> 'We requested the police to open fire to disperse them, but the police remained mute,' says a villager, Mohammed Ismail.

That leaves the reader wondering:

1 If the police remained mute, who were the parties to the 'shootout' (which means a gun-battle between at least two parties)?
2 Where were the six shot dead? – in their homes/inside shops in the bazaar?
3 What exactly was the scene?
4 Where were the policemen who 'turned away'? – in the thana/in tea shops?/at siesta?
5 Who were the six killed: men/women/children?
6 How many were the 'many grievously injured'?

That report begins with a pretentious editorial comment,

and answers none of those questions. Did the reporter go about the village blindfolded? Obviously, he never went anywhere near that village, and only sprinkled a few ready-made phrases on the crumbs he picked up from police, or perhaps from regional-language papers that are far more enterprising. The absence of visual detail, and vague phrases such as *around 50 men struck* (at what?); *the shootout* (between whom?); *many grievously injured* (how many?) give him away. Contrast that with this report in *The Times*, London, on a massacre of Palestinians at a refugee camp at Chatila in 1982:

> Down a laneway to our right, not more than fifty yards from the entrance, there lay a pile of corpses.
>
> There were more than a dozen of them, young men whose arms and legs had become entangled with each other in the agony of death. All had been shot at point-blank range through the right or left cheek, the bullet tearing away a line of flesh up to the ear and entering the brain. Some had vivid crimson scars down the left side of their throats. One had been castrated. Their eyes were open and the flies had only just begun to gather. The youngest was perhaps only twelve or thirteen years old.
>
> On the other side of the main road, up a track through the rubble, we found the bodies of five women and several children. The women were middle-aged, and their corpses lay draped over a pile of rubble. One lay on her back, her dress torn open, and the head of a little girl emerging from behind her. The girl had short, dark curly hair and her eyes were staring at us and there was a frown on her face. She was dead.

The difference:

1 The reader is able to see the horror of the massacre through the writer's eyes.

2 The details are those only someone up close could have gathered.

3 The writer does not comment on the horror, or show emotion.

That leads us to these conclusions:

- Narrative writing is effective when it does not strive for effect.
- Effect is diluted if the writer butts in with his comments.

And that again leads us to an important principle of good writing – that we should try to show the reader the horror, the drama, the action; not serve a preface telling him it's horror-filled, or dramatic, or action-packed. Melvin Mencher of Columbia University, and guru of American journalists, puts that principle in three simple words: 'Show; don't tell.' He explains:

> In our effort to find some guides to help us write well, we might start with Leo Tolstoy who, in describing the strength of his masterwork, *War and Peace*, said, 'I don't tell; I don't explain. I show; I let my characters talk for me.' . . . Show, don't tell. Telling not only makes for dull reading, it makes readers passive. Showing engages readers by making them visualise, draw conclusions, experience insights. . . . Good writers let the words and the actions of their subjects do the work. John Ciardi says, 'Make it happen; don't talk about its happening.'
>
> (Melvin Mencher. *News Reporting and Writing*. 8th ed. Boston: McGraw-Hill, 2000)

Reporters in our English-language papers most often practise just the opposite. Here's a typical news item:

> Eight persons were killed and nine others injured in a *ghastly road mishap* on the National Highway 4 . . . in the early

hours today when a matador van collided with a lorry.

    The injured include two women and two children and the condition of three of the injured is said to be critical. The occupants of the van were proceeding to . . . from Bangalore carrying the body of a *deceased relative* when the *mishap* occurred. Those killed in the accident include . . . .

Some problems with that item:

1 A mishap is at most a minor, unlucky accident. A mishap may cause injuries. It cannot cause multiple deaths. Just how does a mishap become 'ghastly'?

2 What was 'ghastly' – the battered van/the scene of the accident/the way their bodies lay in the van? The reader can see nothing.

3 Were only those in the van killed and injured, or were some in the lorry also among them? The reader isn't told. If only those in the van were killed, the reader might have seen it in a new light: this was Death's van, if as many as eight of those carrying a corpse (to the crematorium?) were to become corpses before journey's end. Not a happy thought, but one that might have justified 'ghastly'.

4 What kind of kinship is implied by '*deceased* relative'? Would they have been carrying his 'body' if he were alive?

The reporter need not have mentioned Death's van; the idea would have suggested itself to the reader had he only narrated the facts and let the reader react:

> Eight of about 20 people accompanying a corpse to the crematorium were killed, when their van collided with a lorry on National Highway 4.

Our English-language newspaper reports almost always begin not with the news, but with fetid phrases of comment: *In a bizarre incident . . ./In a dramatic incident . . ./ In a piquant development . . ./In a rare incident . . . .* And since what follows is almost always what the reporter's been told, not what he's seen, he can show nothing.

A veteran journalist's tip:

> If the events in the story are stark and horrific, resist the temptation to over-write. Not that you should over-write in any situation, but the lure to do so is always greater when your material is extraordinary. Let the events themselves make the impact. . . . Do not . . . write that the story is 'sensational', 'disturbing', 'extraordinary'. Present the story without such comment and let the reader judge.
>
> (David Randall. *The Universal Journalist.* London: Pluto Press, 1996)

54

The role people play

This is the way two articles begin on the same page of the *Sunday Herald*, 1 October 2000:

1   Rivers flowing through various valleys, plains and mountains usually have to travel long distances before merging with the sea. Sometimes rivers mysteriously vanish leaving behind only evidences of their existence. And with the river, the history associated with it, civilizations associated with it also vanish. It is not very difficult to establish the route of the river but, putting together its history and the civilizations associated with it is a difficult task. Saraswati is one such river which has vanished.

2   The boatman urged us in Hindi, 'Take some water in your hand, sprinkle it on your head.' We were sailing along the river Ganga in Varanasi on [sic] a small boat. As we began our journey from Tulasi Ghat, the middle-aged boatman told us about the holy city Varanasi and its famous ghats on the bank of the holy river Ganga. But all along the journey, I saw carcasses of cattle, sewage points from where polluted water entered directly into the river and a row of bodies on Harishchandra and Manikarnika Ghats.

The blurb says the writer of the first piece examines the question whether the Saraswati 'is still flowing beneath the *prayag* at Allahabad, as the *local population believes*'. But 80 words into it, the reader finds not a single one of that population. It's the dreary school essay. The reader is served geography textbook fare; some theories, and myths. The blurb is based on a sentence in the second last paragraph: 'Interestingly, the local population believes . . . .'

The writer of the second piece sees the Ganga 'as polluted as it was years ago', but begins with the boatman's faith in the holiness of the putrid water. His first 91 words succeed in getting the reader interested enough to read on. Later, when he asks about the Ganga Action Plan, the boatman tells him, '*Sare ke sare paise kha liye saab*' (they ate all the money). He then points to Rajendra Ghat, where a city sewage canal pours into the river: he isn't stupid; he understands.

The writer of the Saraswati piece will protest that this is an academic exercise. But that's what's wrong with it. Too many writers believe they need only regurgitate some bookish facts, and presto, their writing becomes profound! They never bother to ask what technique would get the reader interested in the profundity they wish to dispense. The blurb tried to add interest by talking about the belief among the local people. Had the writer begun with someone voicing that widespread belief (perhaps, some old pundit who dismisses geologists and cites Sanskrit texts), the human voice might have aroused interest.

Whether it's a newspaper article, or a news item, a short story, or a novel, only human interest will keep the reader going. No reader takes in chunks of the abstract with relish. And yet, the abstract and the abstruse can be made palatable

NO ENTRY

ABSTRACTION

??

Sandgit

if it is served with some human interest. The trouble with most of what passes for 'intellectual' writing is that it touches neither the mind, nor the intellect. A writer tells us:

> Details should drive out generality. Everything should be related to human beings. The great escape should be made from mere intellectualism, with its universal essences, to concrete particulars, the smell of human breath, the sound of voices, the stir of living.
>
> (C E Montague. *A Writer's Notes on His Trade.* Pelican, 1949)

Few writers have done this as successfully as Parashuram (Rajshekhar Basu). His short stories have delved into beliefs, notions and obsessions. But he brought these to the reader through convincing sketches of living and breathing men and women who clung to those notions and obsessions.

In '*Atal Baboor Ontim Chintaa*' (The last thoughts of Atal Baboo), he takes us into the mind of a dying businessman, who shoos out relatives, and asks his doctor to bluntly tell him how much time he has, for he wishes to examine his life's 'balance-sheet'.

Parashuram's story begins with a few remarks the dying man makes, and those others make about him. These are so pointed that we are able to see the man. We identify with him and follow his reflections on his life, pleasures and pain, rebirth, and life after death. These border on the philosophical, but are never abstruse. He hovers between consciousness and black-outs, and leads us on:

> Atal Baboo tried to resist a haze and said to himself: no, there can be no rebirth, no heaven, no world of spirits. Where would he go? After death, the body disintegrates and blends with the five elements. Does the dead man's mind blend into

a world-mind too? And if it does, what happens to one's identity? 'I am Atal Choudhury' – shall I retain this sense?

The author keeps himself out till Atal Baboo dies. He comes in with only two sentences at the end:

> Only Atal Baboo knows where he's gone. Or perhaps not even he knows.

People breathe life into what we write. The guru of British journalists explains:

> People can recognise themselves in stories about particulars. The abstract is another world. It requires an effort of imagination to transport ourselves there. The writer should bring it to us. . . . At the end of the line of every seemingly abstract proposal there is a group and an individual.
>
> A 'domestic accommodation improvement programme' comes out as government money for people willing to spend more of their own on house repairs. 'The deterioration of the traffic situation' comes out as your wife caught in a traffic jam taking the children to school . . . an 'inevitable amount of redundancy' is the sack for 66 men.
>
> (Harold Evans. *Newsman's English*. London:
> Heinemann, 1972)

William Zinsser tells us how not to write:

> Nouns that express a concept are commonly used in bad writing instead of verbs that tell what somebody did. Here are three typical dead sentences:
>
> > The common reaction is incredulous laughter.
> > Bemused cynicism isn't the only response to the old system.
> > The current campus hostility is a symptom of the change.
>
> What is so eerie about these sentences is that they have no people in them. They also have no working verbs – only 'is' or

'isn't'. The reader can't visualize anybody performing some activity; all the meaning lies in impersonal nouns that embody a vague concept: 'reaction', 'cynicism', 'response', 'hostility'. Turn these cold sentences around. Get people doing things:

> Most people just laugh with disbelief.
> Some people respond to the old system by turning cynical; others say . . . .
> It's easy to notice the change – you can see how angry all the students are.

My revised sentences aren't jumping with vigour, partly because the material I'm trying to knead into shape is shapeless dough. But at least they have real people and real verbs. Don't get caught holding a bag full of abstract nouns. You'll sink to the bottom of the lake and never be seen again.

(On Writing Well. 6th edition)

55
Tell me a story

The way two magazine articles on bonded labour begin:

1   Although there are no recent studies or data available for the extent of bonded labour in India, it is fairly common knowledge that the practice continues to exist even after five decades of independence and despite the Bonded Labour System (Abolition) Act, 1976.

    Bonded labour has long been declared illegal in free India. The Constitution ensures this in Articles 21, 23 and 46 (Directive Principles of State Policy) and the Supreme Court has interpreted the Right to Life as the right to live with human dignity. This should, therefore, include protection of workers – men, women and children – against abuse, providing them the opportunities and facilities to develop in a healthy manner, with freedom and dignity.

2   Venkatesh, a 58-year-old Dalit, has not come to terms with freedom. The 15-kg iron chain that clung to his ankles for two years is gone and his lean frame has suddenly become unbearably light. 'It is a strange feeling. It is like coming out of water,' he laughs, showing his tobacco-stained teeth. His walk is measured and cautious; curiously similar to an infant taking his first steps.

    Ever since he can remember, Venkatesh has been crushing stones for a living. His father came to Mysore from the semi-arid Rayalaseema region of Andhra

Pradesh as part of the labour force that built the Krishnaraja Sagar dam. The family settled there and worked in stone quarries in and around Mandya.

Four years ago, Venkatesh began working in a stone quarry at Arakere near Srirangapatnam, the capital of Tipu Sultan. . . . From dawn to dusk, he crushed half a tractor load of jelly stones for Rs 55.

The first excerpt speaks of bonded labour in India; the second focuses on a bonded labourer. We might read the first for the information it serves, but we're drawn to the second for the portrait of a man just freed from the chain his employer clamped on him. Our reaction to those two excerpts should raise these questions:

- Are we drawn to the second piece because it reads like a story?
- Are we drawn to it because it tells the story of *a* man?
- Would we have felt just as interested had it told the story of *an* animal freed from captivity?
- Do we feel less inclined to read the first piece because it doesn't read like a story?
- Do we feel that the first piece dispenses cold facts that might concern men, but doesn't tell the story of *a* particular man?
- Would we have felt the same if it had similarly treated the theme of keeping animals in captivity?

Most readers will answer 'yes' to all those questions. And that should lead us to these broad conclusions:

- That we all read avidly what reads like a story
- That we are instantly drawn to a story about *a* man and his condition; not equally strongly to a story about man and his condition

- That we react the same way to stories about *an* animal, *a* bird; rather than animals and birds in general

People who write learned articles, treatises, dissertations, might feel offended: does this mean their efforts are in vain? Mustn't their presentations be read for the information, knowledge, thought-provoking ideas, or arguments that they serve, often with scholarship and insight?

The problem with much of the writing we see in books, magazines, and newspapers is that too many writers feel they would be demeaning themselves if they strove to write in a way that might awaken popular interest.

Such opponents of 'popular writing' ignore how the human mind behaves. Our minds latch on to the concrete; not to generalities. Subhas Mukhopadhya explains this behaviour in his poem, '*Michchiler sei ekti mookh*'. In it he wonders how his mind keeps coming back to that one angry face in a procession of protesters; how that man's face, and his clenched fist, are etched in his memory, and all else is a haze.

Here's how an article in the Magazine supplement of *The Hindu*, began:

> Internationally, there is an increased interest in addressing the issue of trafficking. It is generally presumed that legislative proposals addressing this issue are designed to protect persons crossing borders from the possible harms, violence and exploitation they may experience in the course of crossing borders. However, an analysis of the Trafficking Victims Protection Act, 2000, now pending before the U.S. Senate, reveals that such legislation is not only anti-migration, directed at curtailing the crossing of borders, but is also anti-women and directed against developing

countries, as demonstrated through its moralistic and punitive provisions.

Does the reader feel eager to continue with what is so generalised? Let's turn to the opening of a *Time* magazine feature on the anti-people ways of powerful and corrupt officials in China:

> The moment the light went off in the small room in Fenghuo village, Wu Fang knew something terrible was going to happen to her. Three women from the village rushed in, knocked Wu Fang to the floor and began stripping her. Then her husband threw sulfuric acid on her face, chest and thighs. She let out a long cry. The women held her down, rubbing the acid onto her face and breasts, disfiguring her horribly for the rest of her life. . . .
>
> Worse than the memory of the pain is the wall of silence that immediately fell around the village chiefs who were implicated in the attack. Powerful and arrogant, these officials from Fenghuo village in northwestern Shaanxi province have consistently blocked Wu's attempts to bring them to justice. . . . For centuries China's rulers have struggled with corruption and lawlessness across their empire. Entire dynasties have collapsed after losing control over unruly provincial governors, warlords and self-enriching local officials.
>
> Today the Communist Party is facing the same nightmares – rampant corruption by officials at all levels, and growing discontent among ordinary people over the unaccountability of those who rule them. . . . So explosive has the problem become that President Jiang Zemin has acknowledged it threatens the future of his government.

Rudolph Flesch said long ago:

> Only stories are really readable . . . factual exposition is done best by story-telling. If you want to convey information

effectively, you'd better make sure of characters, drama, conflict, a plot, and a denouement. . . .

But what do you do if there simply is no human-interest story connected with the subject? . . . If there are no people visible on the scene, it's your business to put them there.

(*The Art of Readable Writing*. Harper & Row, 1949)

Those who doubt this can be done with abstruse subjects need only recall the way religious dogmas are presented through Nachiketa's questions and Yama's answers in the *Kathopanishad*.

Flesch began his chapter ('How to Be Human Though Factual') with a quote from E B White: 'Don't write about man; write about *a* man.'

56

Dodging visual detail

This is how a journalist began *Looking for Durga* in an article in *The Sunday Statesman* in 2000:

> In less than five minutes, the water rose from the rain-swept glistening asphalt in Southern Avenue – first levelling it with the concrete pavement, and then rushing towards the heavy double-panelled glass and teakwood doors of the Academy. Bits of shattered earthen cups, concave plates made of dry *sal* leaves sewn together, marigold petals and dog turd swirled up, bobbing slowly in the ashen water, rippling in cross-currents on the pavement.

We don't often find such visual detail in English that Indians write. Much of what we read contains either scant visual detail, or 'blended' description – the author's impressions blended with his reactions.

More than 90 per cent of what we read today is non-fiction. That's the trend the world over. And English non-fiction in India has kept away from objective description. Writers who excel at it convey what they see, touch, taste, smell and hear. Most writers concentrate on visual detail; others try to work in sounds and smells, and still others, also touch and taste.

Here's how Gerald Durrell begins his reminiscences of boyhood in *My Family and Other Animals*:

July had been blown out like a candle by a biting wind that ushered in a leaden August sky. A sharp, stinging drizzle fell, billowing into opaque grey sheets when the wind caught it. Along the Bournemouth sea-front the beach-huts turned blank wooden faces towards the greeny-grey, froth-chained sea that leapt eagerly at the cement bulwark of the shore. The gulls had been tumbled inland over the town, and they now drifted above the house-tops on taut wings, whining peevishly. It was the sort of weather calculated to try anyone's endurance.

Durrell keeps himself out of his August day painting. If we were to split hairs, we'd say he isn't really out: his similes and metaphors bring him in. Fresh similes and metaphors are the measure of a writer's skill. To be fresh, they must be born exclusively of that writer's imagination. And in that sense, a good writer cannot be truly out of his piece.

But is there then little difference between that objective description and this excerpt from D H Lawrence's essay on New Mexico:

I think New Mexico was the greatest experience from the outside world that I have ever had. It certainly changed me forever. . . .

But in this article, I don't want to deal with the everyday or superficial aspect of New Mexico, outside the cellophane wrapping. . . . What concerns me is what he is – or what he *seems to me to be*, in his ancient, ancient race-self and religious-self.

For the Red Indian *seems to me* much older than Greeks or Hindus or any Europeans or even Egyptians. . . . That is to say, he is a remnant of the most deeply religious race still living. *So it seems to me. . . .*

You can feel it, the atmosphere of it, around the pueblos. Not, of course, when the place is crowded with sightseers and motorcars. But go to Taos pueblo on some brilliant snowy morning and see the white figures on the roof: or come riding through at dusk on some windy evening, when the black skirts of the silent women blow around the white wide boots, and you will feel the old, old roots of human consciousness still reaching down to depths we know nothing of: and of which, only too often, we are jealous. It seems it will not be long before the pueblos are uprooted.

D H Lawrence is not even trying to be objective; he wants to tell us his impressions and his reaction to what he sees.

Few writers of the non-fiction that our magazines, journals and newspapers serve us each day bother with visual detail of any kind. They ladle an overdose of abstractions, ideas and facts. Their chief ingredients are:

- exposition (to explain, analyse, or clarify something)
- argument (to convince the reader of a thesis)
- persuasion (to push the reader to accept the writer's conclusions).

Aren't we missing an important ingredient? Or have writers decided that visual detail belongs to fiction, and has no place in non-fiction? That certainly is the stance most of our English-language paper journalists adopt. Can descriptive writing enrich non-fiction?

Here is how a news agency reporter wrote his eye-witness account of the execution in October 1917 of Mata Hari, dancer, accused by the French of being a German agent:

> Mata Hari was not bound and she was not blindfolded. (She refused to wear one.) She stood gazing steadfastly at her executioners when the priest, the nuns and her lawyer stepped away from her.
>
> The officer in command of the firing squad, who had been watching his men like a hawk that none might examine his

rifle and try to find out whether he was destined to fire the blank cartridge which was in the breech of one rifle, seemed relieved that the business would soon be over.

A sharp, crackling command, and the file of twelve men assumed rigid positions at attention. Another command, and their rifles were at their shoulders; each man gazed down his barrel at the breast of the woman which was the target. She did not move a muscle.

The under-officer in charge had moved to a position where from the corners of their eyes they could see him. His sword was extended in the air.

It dropped. The sun – by this time up – flashed on the burnished blade as it described an arc in falling. Simultaneously the sound of the volley rang out. Flame and a tiny puff of greyish smoke issued from the muzzle of each rifle. Automatically the men dropped their arms.

At the report Mata Hari fell. She did not die as actors and moving picture stars would have us believe that people die when they are shot. She did not throw up her hands nor did she plunge straight forward or straight back.

Instead she seemed to collapse. Slowly, inertly, she settled to her knees, her head always up, and without the slightest change of expression on her face. For the fraction of a second it seemed she tottered there, on her knees, gazing directly at those who had taken her life. Then she fell backward, bending at the waist, with her legs doubled up beneath her. She lay prone, motionless, with her face turned toward the sky.

A non-commissioned officer, who accompanied a lieutenant, drew his revolver from the big black holster strapped about his waist. Bending over, he placed the muzzle of the revolver almost – but not quite – against the left temple of the spy. He pulled the trigger, and the bullet tore into the brain of the woman.

Mata Hari was surely dead.

Doesn't that description – part of Henry Wales's report for the International News Service – convince us that

- able description enriches all prose (fiction or non-fiction)?
- description calls for skill, and is therefore avoided by the unskilled?

57

Writer, be quiet!

If we agree that descriptive writing would enrich the non-fiction we read, we could go on to examine where the little that we do see goes wrong.

The two glaring defects that keep occurring in our English-language publications:

- Descriptive prose all too often turns purple.
- Wasteful, prefatory comments interrupt 'seeing'.

Because of our orientation to literary Victorian English, we in India remain admirers of purple prose – the florid and fanciful style that begins as a patch and then threatens to become the main fabric of a piece of writing. As a sample, here's Oscar Wilde's purple patch:

> There are few of us who have not sometimes wakened before dawn, either after one of those dreamless nights that make us almost enamoured of death, or one of those nights of horror and misshapen joy, when through the chambers of the brain sweep phantoms more terrible than reality itself, and instinct with that vivid life that lurks in all grotesques, and that lends to Gothic art its enduring vitality, this art being, one might fancy, especially the art of those whose minds have been troubled with the malady of reverie.
>
> (*The Picture of Dorian Gray*, 1890)

Indians who write English non-fiction generally avoid

descriptive prose. But it shows up now and again in pieces on nature and wildlife.

M Krishnan, whose column on wildlife ('Country Notebook') many readers of *The Statesman* have appreciated, is an exception: he excels in accurate description in plain English. An essay in his collection *Nature's Spokesman* mocks the way Indian writers on wildlife or *shikar* nosedive for purple prose of Victorian vintage. He begins in this tongue-in-cheek manner:

> The wretched thing about being a naturalist is that one is so handicapped in one's expression. A big-game hunter now, or an explorer, can afford a sense of style.

Krishnan then writes in what he calls the '*shikar* literature style' about his encounter with a python:

> There was an ineffable assurance of peace in that sylvan retreat. The morning sun, filtered by the green canopy high overhead, illumined the scene with a soft, clear effulgence. The young grass underfoot cushioned each footfall like a carpet, and was as innocent of guile, the still vistas, flanked by the great gnarled boles, seemed inviolable in their ancient calm, and somewhere at hand an iora was calling flutily to its mate.
>
> (*Nature's Spokesman*, OUP, 2000)

Let's now look at the second common defect – wasteful 'prefaces' and comments that mar descriptive prose. An excerpt from an article about elephant herd behaviour in the magazine supplement of *The Hindu* in 2000:

> As we approached the bend slowly and looked at the expanse of water . . . we realised, *rather excitedly*, that there was a solitary elephant on the slope. The huge, glistening animal was coming down the intruding and jutting slope in measured

treads, often looking back at something on the other side of the slope that was not yet visible to us. . . .

The elephant was a large female which seemed lost in contemplation for what seemed to us like eons. *Well, this was really* only 10 suspense-packed minutes. Then she lumbered to the edge of the water. Gingerly, she put a leg in the water as though testing it and then trumpeted shrilly. *To our untutored ways,* it seemed to be a kind of signal. *We waited with bated breath.*

Our patience was rewarded when we saw a herd appear from behind the slope and moving towards the lady.

To cap our joy, we saw a newborn calf, unsteady on its legs. Often he (or was it a she? We never got to know) was kept on the straight path by the friendly trunks all around, guiding and encouraging it.

As the herd came within 30 metres of the leader, she entered the waters and started swimming powerfully across to the other side, a stretch of about 400 metres. *We wondered what would happen next* as the herd stood quietly near the shore. She reached and lifted her trunk – perhaps a signal to the others that the line was clear. Then another large elephant entered the water, statuesque and commanding. We *realised in retrospect* that though the pilot had gone across, the rearguard wanted to be doubly sure that the coast was clear before the herd crossed over.

The grand drama began. As the second female got into the lake and the herd followed slowly, we wondered what the calf would do, unsteady on its feet and perhaps having the first glimpse of the world. The answer was *revealed to us in all grandeur.*

The baby was placed in the middle of the herd and allowed to keep his legs just below the surface of the water. *From that distance, we were not sure whether it was attempting to swim but found that* it was kept going as though on a raft made by the protective trunks of the others. *We stared dumbstruck,* until the herd crossed over to the leader and deposited the baby on the bank to resume his wobbly, lovable gait.

Wouldn't readers agree that the prefatory comments (*The grand drama began/. . . was revealed to us in all grandeur,* etc.) only spoil what could have been a gripping narrative with good descriptive passages in plain English? Readers need only delete all the phrases and sentences italicised and give that another reading.

The purpose of descriptive prose is lost if the writer keeps butting in with needless prefatory comments (the most common defects of reports in our English-language papers). Such irritants violate the basic rule of effective writing we discussed in 'Show, Don't Tell', pp. 325–30. The reader needs to be left in peace so that he can 'see' in his mind's eye the picture the writer seeks to draw.

Here's a sample of descriptive writing that is effective because its writer doesn't butt in with unnecessary comments – even though he never steps out of his narrative:

> Dipping low across her muscled back, her hair twirled out in two spikes like radio antennae. Washed pots and pans lay stacked on one side, clothes on the other, and between her knees she gripped her toddler son. She cuddled him while scooping up a saucepanful of water and dumping it on his head. He howled as if his world had disappeared, screamed as the soap ran into his eyes, gurgled for air in the final rinse and then, the moment it was over, opened his eyes, beamed at us and clapped his hands. We all clapped back and she kissed him, but overcome with such success, he dived for cover, sinking his head between her breasts.
>
> ('The Congo Dinosaur' by Redmond O'Hanlon. *The Body.* Granta 39, Spring 1992)

58

The sound of talk

Talking of what's lacking in English non-fiction written in India, talking is another element – dialogue, I mean.

All the stories we heard as children were full of dialogue. We *heard* what the fox said to persuade the tiger to re-enter the cage the Brahmin had freed it from, and what the tiger said to justify his decision to gobble his benefactor. We all remember what the ants *told* the grasshopper, who'd only fiddled the whole summer, while they'd worked to save food for the winter. Dialogue and description made those tales live – and often, dialogue was the more important device.

Certainly, our magazine writers do try to use conversation. But here they have a genuine problem. They must translate into English what is spoken in an Indian language. And much of that you just can't convey through translation. What our academics, scientists, doctors, technicians and politicians say poses little problem. Most of them throw in an English word after every two in an Indian language. But quoting someone who speaks throughout in a regional language or a dialect is another matter. Translation often drains dialogue of life.

Frontline, October 2000, quoted Gujjar herdsmen of Himachal Pradesh, who were ordered off the high altitude *dhars* (meadows). The decision followed reports that terrorists were using Gujjar *deras* (stone shelters). They were denied access to *dhars* higher than the defence posts. That meant hundreds of families had to share pastures, creating enormous hardship. Some quotes:

> 'We had to *pack a hundred animals into space meant for 30,*' says herdsman Najjar Ismail, 'and because of the shortage of fodder and space, I lost four of my 28 buffaloes.'
>
> 'When we left our meadows in Tissa after the Satrundi killings,' says Noor Mohammad of Bardi Ka village, 'the locals warned us not to come back. They said we were all terrorists. *The next year, when we went back to a lower pasture, the security personnel harassed us, asking for information about terrorists which we did not have.* Our women were scared to go out into the forests to search for wood and fodder. So this year we decided there was no point going back.'

Well-edited, certainly. But how many of us utter as neat a clause or as complicated a sentence as the ones I've italicised? Does that sound like talk?

Certainly, no writer could have accurately translated Noor Mohammad's words into English without loss of colour. Breaking up the italicised sentence into fragments might have made it sound like talk. The herdsman hadn't worked for an English-language publication, and so would surely not have spoken in parenthetic clauses and compound sentences that are the bane of Indian English writing.

How is dialogue handled in translations from fiction? Here's an excerpt from Ismat Chugtai's *Sacred Duty*, translated from Urdu by Tahira Naqvi and Syeda S. Hameed:

> The girl's mother seethed with fury. She suggested, '*Kill the boy and throw his body in the lawn so he can turn into compost.*'

'Are you out of your mind? Just be patient and see what happens. Tashar is Samina's husband now. *Proposal and acceptance, whether it be in our language or any other, has already taken place*; they are now husband and wife. And both are dear to us.'

That evening the marquee was set up again and invitations went out to all the important people in the city.

Tashar became agitated when he was told to convert. Fearfully he glanced first at Siddiqi Saheb and then at Jawad Saheb, mentally planning an escape route through the window, no doubt.

'Papa, what's this nonsense? *First it was Papaji who forced me to become Hindu, telling me to recite all kinds of holy hymns that sounded like gibberish, and now you've started this farce.* We refuse to be part of your games. As soon as we return to Allahabad we'll be forced to dip again, have more photographs taken, and . . . .'

The girl's mother began to cry at this point, and Siddiqi Saheb floundered. 'There's only one way out,' he said, clasping his wife's hand, 'let's go and drown ourselves in the Jamuna.'

'How can you drown, Papa, you know how to swim. You'll probably let Mummy drown and come out of the water yourself, all nice and clean for your girlfriend, Miss Farzana.'

'Sami, be quiet!' Tashar scolded Samina. 'Papa, I mean Siddiqi Saheb, I'm ready to be a Muslim.'

'Shut up, you fool! I'm not ready to be re-converted.'

'Woe is me! Kill them both and bury them.' It was the mother. 'What an ungrateful daughter. He's ready to be a Muslim, and this miserable creature has decided to be troublesome!'

Surely, much of that does sound like talk. The first italicised sentence is able to convey the comic too. The second and third italicised sentences might have sounded more conversational had they been broken up with *and* at the right places. But those who have heard Urdu can recognise much that rings true.

Does that mean that translators of fiction do a much better job of presenting dialogue? Or does it mean that our English non-fiction writers (specifically, journalists) see no use for dialogue?

Our English-language papers prove every day that their reporters have no ear for dialogue (nor, for that matter, language skill of any sort). A senior reporter once quoted Mr Jyoti Basu thus:

> 'The softening of stand by the United Front Government in case of policy matters related to the public sector undertak-ings in view of strong protest from the Left parties is a right step in a right direction.'

Most readers will at once recognise the absurdity: Mr Basu's utterances are fragments and incomplete sentences. Nor does Mr Basu utter such hideous *baboo* English in hiccupy parenthetic clauses – which most reporters churn out every day.

The reporter wrote that 'fictitious quote' in June 1996 – more than 30 years after journalists in the USA had experimented with bringing into non-fiction all the literary devices that made fiction lively. The 'New Journalism' wave of the 1960s established that accurate non-fiction can be written with techniques we usually associate with the short story and the novel. Reporting colourful dialogue accurately was a technique New Journalism pioneers insisted on.

The New Journalism wave has changed the way daily reports are written. An American crime reporter interviewed a young woman about to face trial for having shot her lover dead. She'd acted in fury, after he suddenly slapped her. The conventional newspaper story would have begun with the date set for the trial and then given the reader a summary of the charges. But this is how the crime reporter (who is a woman) began:

> The man she loved slapped her face. Furious, she says she told him never, ever to do that again. 'What are you going to do, kill me?' he asked, and handed her a gun. 'Here, kill me,' he challenged. She did.

The report then moved on to details like the charge and the date of the trial. The report was brief and accurate, as newspaper reports should be. But it had the flavour of a short story.

59

The power of dialogue

We have already talked about the importance the New Journalists in the USA of the 1960s gave to dialogue. Was it a conscious decision? Tom Wolfe, a pioneer of New Journalism, explains:

> If you follow the progress of the New Journalism closely through the 1960s, you see an interesting thing happening. You see journalists learning the techniques of realism – particularly of the sort found in Fielding, Smollett, Balzac, Dickens and Gogol – from scratch. By trial and error, by 'instinct' rather than theory, journalists began to discover the devices that gave the realistic novel its unique power, variously known as its 'immediacy', its 'concrete reality', its 'emotional involvement', its 'gripping' or 'absorbing' quality.
>
> This extraordinary power was derived mainly from just four devices they discovered. The basic one was scene-by-scene construction . . . and *record the dialogue in full*, which was *device number two*. Magazine writers, like the early novelists, learned by trial and error something that has since been demonstrated in academic studies: namely, *that realistic dialogue involves the reader more completely than any other single device*. It also *establishes and defines character more quickly and effectively than any other single device*. (Dickens has a way of fixing a character in your mind so that you have the feeling he has described every inch of his appearance – only to go back and discover that he actually took care of

the physical description in two or three sentences; *the rest he has accomplished with dialogue.*)

('Seizing the Power', *The New Journalism*. London: Picador, 1990)

Our writers, dramatists and journalists have a rich tradition to fall back on. They have the model of the *Kathopanishad*, which presents religious dogmas through dialogue. The *Bhagavad Gita* uses this technique too – a dialogue between Krishna and Arjuna. That tradition presented great thoughts and philosophy through a device we now associate with fiction. Obviously, our ancient writers knew what the new journalists believed they'd discovered – that 'dialogue involves the reader [and the listener too] more completely than any other single device.'

Among others in Bengal, Parashuram (Rajshekhar Basu) often used a framework of fiction and filled in dialogue for his satires and spoofs. A loose translation of excerpts from his *Bhim-Gita*, in which he gets Bhima to present an alternative view of things to Krishna:

> BHIMA: Say, Keshava, what happened to Arjuna before the battle began today? What were you saying to him? I . . . couldn't hear a word, only saw Arjuna had dropped his weapons and wept; had his palms before you, and gaped like a madman . . .
> KRISHNA: Nothing of consequence. He'd seen elders and close relatives on either side . . . became soft . . . said he didn't want to fight.
> BHIMA: Arjun's always been like that. Gets namby-pamby every now and again . . . And what did you say to him?
> KRISHNA: I said: you are a Kshatriya, and it's your duty to fight in a holy war . . . if you win, you rule a kingdom; if you die, you go straight to heaven.

BHIMA: Absolutely! And did that knock sense into Arjuna?

KRISHNA: Not easily . . . I said, just do your duty without any thought of return. And then I explained *Karmayoga*, *Jnanayoga*, *Bhaktiyoga*, etc. I had to lecture almost two hours . . .

BHIMA: Has Arjuna forgotten what kind of torture Dur-yodhan's gang heaped on us? I hope you reminded him of that?

KRISHNA: It never really struck me to remind him of that.

* * *

BHIMA: You label anger a vice, do you? You're supposed to be a great know-all – we have six vices, right? Ever thought how much we benefit from them?

KRISHNA: But vice must be repressed, surely.

BHIMA: Does repression mean purging? Purge all his vices, and a man turns into stone – that's what's happened to Vyasdeva's son Sukdeva. Women don't even notice him; they bathe right before his gaze!

* * *

BHIMA: Of the six vices, only the first three are necessary. And of the three, the first two – *krodha* and *kaama* – are indispensable. Now I don't suppose I need explain *kaama* to you: people say you've sixteen thousand what's-it . . .

KRISHNA [laughs]: People say you gobble sixteen thousand *laddoo*s every day . . . Let's leave *kaama-tatva* aside; do expound your *krodha-tatva*.

BHIMA: . . . An excess of *krodha* does you no good. Your limbs tremble, you miss your target, it saps fighting skill. But purge *krodha*, and you'll protect neither yourself, nor your kinsmen.

KRISHNA: But surely, one can purge *krodha*, but still fight in self-defence.

BHIMA: Yeah, like one can purge *kaama* and still procreate! Krishna, don't talk crap.

* * *

KRISHNA: But the wise say you must conquer *krodha* with composure.

BHIMA: Govinda, you make me laugh. Why did you kill Kamsa? Why did you take me and Arjuna along to kill Jarasandha? Why did you sever Shishupala's head at the yagna? Why did you incite Arjuna to fight today, when you saw he was without *krodha*? . . . Listen to me. Only when your enemy is a good guy . . . does it make sense to talk about composure and *ahimsa* . . . Remember Biraata (the poor fellow lost two sons in today's battle)? He hurled the dice at Yudhishthira and drew blood. But Yudhishthira showed no anger. Biraata was a good guy and so Yudhishthira's composure worked. But not with Duryodhana. Our Dharmaraja has forgiven him a thousand times, has even affably called him Suyodhana; but all that's done no good. Because Duryodhana isn't noble; he's evil. His brothers, his uncle Shakuni and Karna – that parasite son of a charioteer – they are all equally sub-human. Yudhishtira's patience has only fed their audacity . . .

KRISHNA: Bhimsena, your reasoning is correct. Composure can win over only the noble, but it requires a holy war to conquer the unholy. You are into such a war. But in a holy war, one must abjure *krodha* and revenge . . . That's why I didn't think it necessary to remind Arjuna about Duryodhana's misdeeds.

BHIMA: You goofed . . . you had to lecture for two hours before you could get him to fight. Now if you'd incited his *krodha*, it would've worked at once. You wouldn't have needed *karmayoga*, *jnanyoga*, *bhaktiyoga*, and all the rest of it . . .

That's a weak translation – as all translations of Parashuram are bound to be. But even that, readers will agree, suffices to show how Parashuram relied on nothing but dialogue to put across a viewpoint that through his deft handling of this device turned absorbing and entertaining. That's the importance of dialogue. Many writers have experimented with writing a short story only through dialogue.

60

Utterances no one uttered

About 150 villagers surround 21 armed Naxalites, who want
to whisk away a former militant. Mangali Bhumanna had
left the band and come back to Dahegaon, in Adilabad,
Andhra Pradesh. The Naxalites say the 'deserter' has turned
police informer and want him to come with them. The
villagers say the Naxalites would have to take all of them
along with Mangali. Here's how *The Hindu* staff reporter
described this tense drama in 2000:

> Heated arguments ensued for over 40 minutes. The naxals,
> taken *aback at* the hostile attitude of the villagers, *threatened*
> *that* they would *see how* the locals entered the village. *To this*
> the locals *replied saying* that the forests were not the property
> of the naxals alone, *even they* had every right to go into the
> forests. They dared the naxals to harm them when they *came*
> *into* the forests. *Realising the tense* situation, the naxals tried
> to *settle the issue* and asked the locals *to offer* them food *to*
> *which* they flatly refused.

Apart from the language defects (italicised) typical of the
ineptness of those who work for English-language papers
in India, that rendering dilutes the drama. We aren't told
a word of the 40-minute 'heated arguments'. An accurate
translation of a few significant sentences spoken could have
made all the difference.

But English-language papers in India subscribe to a cult of drabness. All dialogue is either reduced to dull paraphrasing, or what appears within quote marks is faked dialogue. The reason: the quoted sentences are not those uttered by anyone; they're usually lifted from a written statement. The same edition of *The Hindu* wants us to believe that a wildlife activist it interviewed uttered these words:

> 'I have understood the thinking among scientists that wildlife and human habitation must be spatially separate for minimising man-wildlife conflict, and channelised energy and time to ensure that.'

The interviews they print sound strangely stiff, replete with parenthetic clauses. The only resemblance to talk is the *Indlish* that the questions as well as the answers contain. An excerpt from the *Sunday Express*'s interview with Mulayam Singh Yadav in 2000:

> Q: Your party has been charged with weakening the Opposition in Parliament by lodging a *protest to* the adjournment motion moved by the Congress *on plight* of farmers. The strategy helped the BJP.
>
> A: The Samajwadi Party has *not lodged protest* against the adjournment motion but simply tried to put its viewpoint first. How can the Congress *which* itself is responsible for the mess *in which farmers are at present oppose* the anti-farmer policies. These policies were framed by the Congress and the BJP is only implementing them.

One could go on citing examples. The truth is, our English-language publications have never worked at handling dialogue. Having to translate from regional languages, and polishing up the English that is spoken, pose problems for their reporters and sub-editors. But that problem exists for all publications the world over. Here is how *Time* magazine (30 October 2000) handled dialogue in its report on the ravages of the Ebola virus in a Uganda village (American spelling retained):

> One of the first to die was Esther Owete. Sometime in early September, the 36-year-old from Kabedo-Opong, in northern Uganda, began complaining of a 'coldness in her body,' remembers her brother Richard Oyet, standing outside her mud-and-thatch hut. 'Then she said she had pains in the muscles in her legs.' Owete's chest began hurting. She became feverish and vomited blood. 'We thought it was malaria,' says a neighbor, Justin Okot. At a clinic in the nearby town of Gulu, Owete was injected with the antimalarial chloroquine and sent home. 'She didn't even last 24 hours,' says Okot. 'We didn't understand that someone could die that quickly. We began calling this thing *gemo*, which in [the local language] Luo is a type of ghost or evil spirit. No one knows about it, but it comes and takes you in the night.'
>
> Experts say they cannot pinpoint the first infection in this outbreak until the virus is contained. But if Esther Owete was the first case, then ground zero is her mud hut, now boarded up. There, minutes after her death, according to neighbors, Owete's distraught mother cried out for her grandson, Owete's one-year-old son Sam, to 'suck your mother's last milk so you too can die. There is no one here to look after you now.' He survived just four days.
>
> 'One died in that hut, my mother in there, one over there, the kid in there,' says brother Richard, 35, making his way around the tiny village, 'There is nothing left, no one to look after me. The pain is too difficult to tell.'

It's highly unlikely that people who live in mud-and-thatch huts in Uganda would speak flawless English. The dialogue in that report may have been obtained through an

interpreter, and was obviously touched up. But it retains the sound of talk because the sentences weren't tailored into complex-compound ones.

More than 50 years ago, Rudolph Flesch dealt with what eludes our English-language writers to this day. In the revised and enlarged edition of *The Art of Readable Writing* (Harper & Row, 1949), he said:

> Now of course you will say that you can't turn everything into dialogue. There must be a limit to this form of presentation. How much dialogue will factual writing stand?
>
> The answer to this question will surprise you. If you analyze a random collection of well-written, popular magazine articles, for instance, you will find that most of them are shot through and through with snatches of conversation and bits of direct quotation from what was *said*. The seasoned popular nonfiction writer knows that to interest his readers he must not only turn most of his material into narrative, but must then go one step further and turn a large part of that narrative into dialogue. All exposition needs some story: all needs some drama.
>
> * * *
>
> What really does make talk sound authentic? What are the things by which we immediately spot spoken English when we see it on paper?
>
> There are a number of answers. There are differences in grammar, in usage, and in idiomatic phrasing. But the main characteristics of spoken English seem to be two: loose sentence structure and a great deal of repetition.
>
> * * *
>
> The school teachers' taboo against sentence fragments and run-on sentences is even more of a superstition. Human speech teems with these constructions. In fact, on the average, it probably contains more sentence fragments and run-

on sentences than standard-brand 'grammatical' sentences. There would be more fragments and run-on sentences in writing too if we didn't disguise the true state of affairs by tricks of punctuation. Actually, the punctuation of anything that is freely spoken is purely an arbitrary convenience for the reader – as anyone can testify who has ever tried to punctuate the transcript of an ad-lib radio program. People just don't speak with commas and periods – they make themselves understood by forming words in sequence.

Those who work for English-language publications in India would do their readers a favour if they followed these simple rules:

- Don't enclose within quotation marks what wasn't uttered; it doesn't fool the reader.
- Don't translate into complex sentences what was uttered as fragments and broken sentences.
- Don't paraphrase all that's uttered; do let readers hear some dialogue.

61

Set the scene; get them talking

Our writers of English non-fiction have taken long to understand the importance of dialogue. In England, writers of fiction took long to realise that dialogue must sound like talk. Elizabethan dramatists were the first to use dialogue. But their stylised dialogue seldom sounded like talk. Each character delivered long chunks in blank verse, whether he was on the battlefield, or talking to friends. Shakespeare was perhaps the first to give some of his characters short, speech-like lines:

> CAESAR: The ides of March are come.
> SOOTHSAYER: Aye Caesar, but not gone.

But most of his characters delivered long compositions that are wonderful to read, though hardly credible as speech. For example:

> AJAX: Time hath, my lord, a wallet at his back,
> Wherein he puts alms for oblivion,
> A great-siz'd monster of ingratitudes.
> Those scraps are good deeds past
> Which are devour'd
> As fast as they are made, forgot as soon
> As done
> · · · · · · · · · ·
> For Time is like a fashionable host
> That slightly shakes his parting guest by th' hand

And with his arms outstretch'd, as he would fly,
Grasps in the comer. The welcome ever smiles
And farewell goes out sighing.

(Troilus and Cressida)

Prose drama followed that convention. Sheridan's characters (e.g. Mrs Malaprop in *The Rivals*) spewed 250-word chunks at a time.

When novels were first written, dialogue meant long, unbroken paragraphs that had to be deciphered carefully by following attribution such as 'cried he/returned she'. Not till the nineteenth century did novelists write realistic dialogue that was more easily readable: they began a new paragraph with each change of speaker (the convention in scripts for dramas). Writers like Emily Brontë used dialect in their dialogue. (Shakespeare had used this device in some of his dramas.)

A gradual shift to realism in fiction awakened writers to the importance of dialogue. There remained one big problem: since there is no way one can convey intonation through the written word, what could the writer do to get across the speaker's mood, or tone? The most common device was to add an explanatory note before or after each bit spoken: *She said with a smile . . ./. . . he explained/. . . he said admiringly/. . . he replied tersely/. . . she said consolingly.*

Dialogue weighted with such explanatory notes, and the adverbial tag (*-ly*) can become a drag through monotony and clutter. And yet, it is only natural that each writer is anxious to make up for the missing intonation. Skilled writers used those tags to advantage – by making them serve more than mere explanation. Some samples:

'As I was saying, that *seems* to be done right – though I haven't time to look it over thoroughly just now – and that shows that there are three hundred and sixty-four days when you might get un-birthday presents—.'

'Certainly,' said Alice.

'And only *one* for birthday presents you know. There's *glory* for you!'

'I don't know what you mean by 'glory', Alice said.

Humpty Dumpty *smiled contemptuously.* 'Of course you don't – till I tell you. I meant "there's a nice knock-down argument for you"!'

'But "glory" doesn't mean "a nice knock-down argument",' Alice *objected.*

'When *I* use a word,' Humpty Dumpty said, in rather *a scornful tone,* 'it means just what I choose it to mean – neither more nor less.'

The italicised bits in that excerpt from Lewis Carroll's classic (*Alice in Wonderland,* 1865) convey pictures ('smiled contemptuously'), as also tone ('scornful').

Bernard *tried to comfort me.* 'Prime Minister, I must say that I think you worry too much what the papers say.'

I smiled at him. How little he knows. 'Bernard,' I said *with a weary smile,* 'only a Civil Servant could make that remark. I *have* to worry about them, especially with the Party Conference looming. These rumours of a City scandal won't go away.'

But Humphrey *was unflappable.* 'Let's not worry about it until there's something more than a rumour. May I show you the Cabinet agenda?'

I *wasn't interested.* 'Please, Humphrey,' I said. 'The papers are far more important.'

'With respect, Prime Minister,' *replied* Humphrey *impertinently,* riled by my refusal to look at his silly agenda, 'they are not.'

(*Yes Prime Minister.* BBC Books, 1987)

The italicised bits there convey tone, but not pictures.

> I indicated the in-tray. 'When am I going to get through all this correspondence?' I *asked* Bernard *wearily*.
> Bernard said: 'You *do* realise, Minister, that you don't actually *have* to?'
> I had realised no such thing. This sounded good.
> Bernard *continued*: 'If you want, we can simply draft an official reply to any letter.'
> 'What's an official reply?' I *wanted to know*.
> 'It just says,' Bernard *explained*, ' "the Minister has asked me to thank you for your letter." Then *we* reply. Something like: "The matter is under consideration." Or even, if we feel so inclined, "under active consideration"!'
> . . . .
> So I *asked* Bernard: 'Then what is the Minister for?'
> 'To make policy decisions,' he *replied fluently*. 'When you have decided the policy, we can carry it out.'
> . . . .
> So I *asked* Bernard: 'How often are policy decisions needed?'
> Bernard *hesitated*. 'Well . . . from time to time, Minister,' he *replied in a kindly way*.
> <div align="center">(<i>The Complete Yes Minister</i>. BBC Books, 1981)</div>

The tags there are redundant: they convey neither visual images, nor tone (what does 'replied fluently' convey?)

Can we dispense with such aids? Parashuram (Rajshekhar Basu) is one writer who did. In stories where he dealt with a point of view or an idea, he set the scene with a minimum of narration, and the characters took over. A loose translation from '*Bawdon Choudhurir Shokesabha*' (Commemoration of Bawdon Choudhuri):

> Bawdon Choudhury is a recent entrant to Hell. Yamaraj was on his inspection round. As soon as he saw him, Bawdon

folded his palms, and prostrated himself at his feet.

Yama said, 'What is it you want?'

'Please, two hours leave.'

'When did you enter here?'

'I completed a month today.'

'And you want leave already? What'll you do with leave?'

'Please, I want to visit earth. At five this evening, they'll be commemorating me at the University Institute; I dearly want a peep.'

Chitragupta, the registrar of *Yamalaya*, stood at hand. Yama asked him, 'What had this spirit been up to?'

Chitragupta said, 'His name used to be Bawdon Chandra Choudhury; his occupation, advocacy, usury, and several other trades. For about ten years, he was a Corporation Councillor, and for five, an MLA. Been here a month; condemned to a thousand years in Hell for his many nefarious deeds. He's assigned to the C-section. He's been behaving himself well. A two-hour leave could be considered. He's naturally eager to hear what his friends and admirers say at his commemoration.

That format avoids the encumbrances of reporting dialogue. Parashuram relied on situation, choice of specific words, and a deceptively rough-and-ready manner. It's a technique our writers could emulate.

62

Dialogue in your daily

As we have seen:

- The sound of human voices enlivens fiction and non-fiction alike.
- To be convincing, dialogue must sound like talk.
- As with description, dialogue is most effective when the writer keeps himself out of it.

Readers who might still have doubts about dialogue as a tool for effective writing need only ask themselves whether Parashuram's *Bhim-Gita* (excerpts in 'The Power of Dialogue', pp. 360–5) would have been half as absorbing, or one-fifth as entertaining, had he set down those ideas in the essay format. Bhima's point of view might have been the subject of a discourse, and such discourses have been written as lengthy essays. The didactic and analytical essay became the fashion among Bengal's literati in the late nineteenth-century. They were inspired by the didacticism in Victorian-day writing.

The New Journalists showed as long as three decades ago how dialogue could make non-fiction absorbing. But journalists working for English-language publications in India feel such a device can never be used for daily reporting, or features in newspapers and magazines. The regional-language publications, especially the tabloids, have begun bold experiments that mainstream newspapers have never dared to try. (Two tabloids in Bangalore, for instance, have changed the way Kannada prose is written.)

Let's now see whether dialogue could be used to breathe life into such non-fiction as daily news, features, magazine articles, etc. Here are excerpts from a fairly brief report ('The General Goes Zapping Charlie Cong') the journalist Nicholas Tomalin wrote for *The Sunday Times*, London, during the Vietnam War. Tomalin accompanied an American general on his mission of killing Viet Cong guerrillas, and told his readers what he saw and heard:

> After a light lunch last Wednesday, General James F. Hollingsworth, of Big Red One, took off in his personal helicopter and killed more Vietnamese than all the troops he commanded.
>
> * * *
>
> 'Our mission today,' says the General, 'is to push those goddam VCs right off Routes 13 and 16. Now you see Routes 13 and 16 running north from Saigon toward the town of Phuoc Vinh, where we keep our artillery. When we got here first we prettied up those roads, and cleared Charlie Cong right out so we could run supplies up.
>
> 'I guess we've been hither and thither with all our operations since, an' the ol' VC he's reckoned he could creep back. He's been puttin' out propaganda he's goin' to interdict our right of passage along those routes. So this day we aim to zapp him, and zapp him, and zapp him again till we've zapped him right back where he came from. Yes, sir. Let's go.'
>
> * * *

The General sits at the helicopter's open door, knees apart, his shiny black toecaps jutting out into space, rolls a filtertip cigarette to-and-fro in his teeth and thinks.

'Put me down at Battalion HQ,' he calls to the pilot.

'There's sniper fire reported on choppers in that area, General.'

'Goddam the snipers, just put me down.'

Battalion HQ at the moment is a defoliated area of four acres packed with tents, personnel carriers, helicopters and milling GIs. We settle into the smell of crushed grass. The General leaps out and strides through his troops.

'Why General, excuse us, we didn't expect you here,' says a sweating major.

'You killed any 'Cong yet?'

'Well no General, I guess he's just too scared of us today. Down the road a piece we've hit trouble, a bulldozer's fallen through a bridge, and trucks coming through a village knocked the canopy off a Buddhist pagoda. Saigon radioed us to repair that temple before proceeding – in the way of civic action, General. That put us back an hour . . .'

'Yeah. Well Major, you spread out your perimeter here a bit, then get to killin' VCs will you?'

Back through the crushed grass to the helicopter.

'I don't know how you think about war. The way I see it, I'm just like any other company boss, gingering up the boys all the time, except I don't make money. I just kill people, and save lives.'

* * *

'Strike coming in, sir.'

Two F105 jets appear over the horizon in formation, split, then one passes over the smoke, dropping a trail of silver, fish-shaped canisters. After four seconds' silence, light orange fire explodes in patches along an area fifty yards wide by three-quarters of a mile long. Napalm.

The trees and bushes burn, potting dark oily smoke into the sky. The second plane dives and fire covers the entire strip of dense forest.

'Aaaaah,' cries the General. 'Nice. Nice. Very neat. Come in low, let's see who's left down there.'

'How do you know for sure the Viet Cong snipers were in that strip you burned?'

'We don't. The smoke position was a guess. That's why we zapp the whole forest.'

* * *

The pilot shouts: 'General, half right, two running for that bush.'

'I see them. Down, down, goddam you.'

* * *

Then a man runs from the tree, in each hand a bright red flag which he waves desperately above his head.

'Stop, stop, he's quit,' shouts the General, knocking the machine-gun so traces erupt into the sky.

* * *

'That's a Cong for sure,' cries the General in triumph and with one deft movement grabs the man's short black hair and yanks him off his feet, inboard . . . .

The red flags I spotted from the air are his hands, bathed solidly in blood. Further blood is pouring from under his shirt, over his trousers.

Readers will notice that Tomalin went about it in much the same way as Parashuram did: he briefly described each scene, and recorded the dialogue that belonged to that setting. The difference: Parashuram used his imagination and 'created' convincing dialogue; Tomalin used his tape-recorder and memory, and wrote it accurately.

Tom Wolfe, a leading exponent of New Journalism, wrote this foreword for Tomalin's report, which he included in his anthology:

> Newspaper editors are fond of arguing that the New
> Journalism cannot be adapted to daily journalism, either on
> the grounds that it works only with trivial ('Pop') subjects
> or breaks down under the demands of deadlines. In 1966
> Nicholas Tomalin was one of England's leading investiga-
> tive reporters, a 'hard news' journalist of great repute, when
> he used the techniques of the New Journalism to write this
> story. He went on the Zapping mission with the General and
> wrote the story in a single day. It had the most astonishing
> impact in England, creating for English readers the emotional
> reality of the war . . . and a somewhat horrified fascination
> in it. . . .
>
>   Not many newspaper writers have the talent or moxie of
> Tomalin and Breslin. But there is a worse problem: not many
> newspaper editors want to know that it can even be done.

Tom Wolfe wrote that in 1975, when his anthology (*The
New Journalism*, Picador) was first published in Great
Britain. A quarter of a century since, some newspaper editors
may hopefully have changed their minds.

63

The voice of the narrator

Defects in narrative writing are the very ones that make our talk uninteresting: monotony, dullness, preachiness, rambling accounts, irrelevancies – to name some of them. To avoid such defects, writers have used literary devices that are merely sophisticated ways of telling a story. If we left technical analysis aside, we'd see that there are three basic devices that narrative writers adopt:

1 The narrator directly addresses his readers and tells the story.
2 The narrator presents someone (other than himself) to tell the story.
3 The narrator does no more than introduce some characters, who act out the story.

The first is closest to the oral tradition; the second and third devices are inspired by the acting out of the narrative, which too was a part of our oral tradition. The singer of tales often embellished his narrative with gestures, posturing, change of tone and language effects to depict various characters – the tradition that Teejan Bai tries to keep alive, and with which Shaoli Mitra experimented successfully on stage. From such a tradition the drama evolved, and its success inspired the narrator to experiment with more sophisticated variants of the second and third devices.

Great stories have no doubt been told through the sole narrator's voice. But writers have always experimented with more subtle devices. They have tried to add more than only the narrator's voice, or tried to make us believe, ventriloquist-like, that the characters, not the narrator, are telling us the story.

Vyasa brought in Sanjaya, the first war reporter, to narrate to the blind Dhritarashtra what happened on the battlefield each day. That brought in a voice other than Vyasa's in the *Mahabharata*. The voices of characters other than Valmiki dominate the *Ramayana*. We hear Jatayu tell his story, Bali his, Ahalya hers . . .

Chaucer gave only brief introductions to each character he brought on stage. Each told a lively story; Chaucer stayed backstage. This device brought in a medley of voices in his *Canterbury Tales*. Daniel Defoe stayed in London and sent his readers off to a desert island, where they discovered a fascinating narrative in jottings by a marooned sailor named Robinson Crusoe.

Writers have sought to avoid the monotony of their voices by inventing such devices as diaries and letters that have told tales. In modern Bengali literature, writers such as Parashuram have stayed offstage and let their characters either tell or act out the narrative. They brought in powerful devices such as realistic dialogue that without fail absorbs the reader and helps the writer stay off-stage, and so helps make-believe.

Here's how Parashuram brings an eccentric on stage:

'Namashkaar. Will there be space for me?'
I was alone on a bench at the Dhakuria lake. It was near dusk and I was about to leave when the man asked me this.

'But of course,' I said, 'there's plenty of room on this bench.'

He was between 50 and 55; tall, lean and fair; had a neat parting in his salt-and-pepper hair, and wore Maulana Abul Kalam Azad's goatee and moustache. . . . He spread a big piece of paper in one corner of the bench, sat on it, and asked, 'May I know your name?'

I said, 'You certainly may; my name is Sushil Chandra Chandra.'

'Are you in a hurry to go? If you aren't, why not stay for a chat?'

What follows is the strangely credible narrative of Akrur Nandi, an incredible combination of pig-headed pragmatist, highly principled eccentric and fair-minded male chauvinist. Akrur tells and acts out his story; Parashuram only plays the *sutradhar* in *Akrur Sangbaad*.

In non-fiction, however, the sole narrator's voice has been the unvarying fare. Today, when non-fiction dominates what we read, the monotony of the sole narrator's voice through all our newspapers, magazines and periodicals has become a drag.

Let's take the average news story we read in our English-language papers each day. We are told that some Muslims in a 'Black Day' procession, protesting the demolition of Babri Masjid, are 'annoyed' at the sight of some shopkeepers doing business as usual. They throw stones at shops and vehicles. The reporter's narrative adds that the DGP said that there were no casualties, though some shops, two jeeps and a Matador van were damaged.

We have got so used to that kind of bland narrative that we no longer pay any attention to such items. Wouldn't a big difference have been made had the narrator (reporter) allowed some people in the procession to tell their story?

Assuming that the shopkeepers were non-Muslims, and that those in‚the procession were not outsiders, but were familiar with the shops: was familiarity the reason they had expected the shopkeepers to show some understanding of their hurt? Did the reporter penetrate their minds and find only 'annoyance' written there? Wouldn't it have been equally interesting had some of those shopkeepers told us their version? Did they intend to show indifference, or scorn? Or were they merely insensitive?

Our non-fiction writers have never been conscious of the monotony of their voice. No wonder they see nothing amiss in relying on no more than a single source for the information they serve. (Many reporters in our English-language papers act as mere stenos of police officers and bureaucrats.) Let's hear what journalists who experimented with alternatives to the sole narrator's voice have to say. This is Tom Wolfe, the pioneer of the New Journalism wave:

> The voice of the narrator, in fact, was one of the great problems in non-fiction writing. Most non-fiction writers, without knowing it, wrote in a century-old British tradition in which it was understood that the narrator shall assume a calm, cultivated and, in fact, genteel voice. The idea was that the narrator's own voice should be like the off-white or putty-coloured walls that Syrie Maugham popularised in interior decoration . . . a 'neutral background' against which bits of colour would stand out. *Understatement* was the thing. You can't imagine what a positive word 'understatement' was among both journalists and literati ten years ago. There is something to be said for the notion, of course, but the trouble was that by the early 1960s understatement had become an absolute pall. Readers were bored to tears without understanding why. When they came upon that pale beige

tone, it began to signal to them, unconsciously, that a well-known bore was here again, 'the journalist' a pedestrian mind, a phlegmatic spirit, a faded personality, and there was no way to get rid of the pallid little troll, short of ceasing to read. This had nothing to do with objectivity and subjectivity or taking a stand or 'commitment' – it was a matter of personality, energy, drive, bravura . . . style in a word. . . . The standard non-fiction writer's voice was like the standard announcer's voice . . . a drag, a droning. . . .

('Like a Novel', *The New Journalism*, edited by Tom Wolfe
and E W Johnson, Great Britain: Picador, 1975)

For the writer of non-fiction, that carries an important message: don't limit your narrative to the monologue; let other voices in.

Index

Index

Index